CW00420682

150 GOLDEN YEARS

This book is dedicated to all past and present conductors and members of Black Dyke (Mills) Band

150 GOLDEN YEARS

The history of the Black Dyke Band

Roy Newsome

First published in the United Kingdom in 2005
by
World of Brass Publications,
Salvationist Publishing and Supplies Ltd
1 Tiverton Street, London SE1 6NT

British Library Cataloguing in Publication Data
A CIP catalogue record for this book is available from the British Library.

ISBN 0 85412 741 0

Typeset by Print and Design Unit, THQ
Printed in England by Page Bros (Norwich) Ltd

CONTENTS

FOREWORD

I CONGRATULATE Roy Newsome on this excellent book. A lot of time and energy must have gone into researching and compiling all this material.

Apart from a book of anecdotes compiled by Frank Dean some 30 years ago, very little has been written about Black Dyke (Mills) Band. Most of the history of this famous band has been passed down through the ages by word of mouth. Roy Newsome has produced a very concise history of the band from its Peter Wharton roots to the present day.

As a small boy I met some of the men from the Bower period, including Tom Bottomley, Harry Waddington and Fred Bower. They were old men but they were informative and very interesting to listen to.

The Arthur O. Pearce era is very, very accurate and I was in the band during his last two years. When I joined, some of the older players had been with 'Pop' Pearce (our nickname for him) for most of his time at Black Dyke and the history of the band was passed down from these men to new members.

Harry Mortimer's first two years as Black Dyke's professional conductor were the last two years of Arthur O. Pearce's reign and this was an exhilarating time for us younger members, but we all learned so much from Harry's brother, Alex, later.

I enjoyed all of my time at Black Dyke and reading this book has brought back so many happy memories, particularly the Maurice Murphy, George Willcocks period.

Good luck with this book Roy and again, Well Done!

Geoffrey Whitham

John Foster 1798-1878

The Founder

PREFACE AND ACKNOWLEDGEMENTS

WHY do people climb Everest? Legend has it that they do so 'because it is there'. Black Dyke Band is the brass band equivalent of Everest and for many years I've had a secret wish to trace its progress from the early beginnings up to the present time. Of course, it reached the peak long ago and has remained there, weathering the storms but revelling in the glory of being on top of the world.

I was heavily involved with the band as one of its conductors for over a decade and my son, Martin, had five glorious years as its bass trombone player during the 1980s. I have, therefore, what might be called a vested interest in what I still think of as Black Dyke Mills Band. When, some time ago, Nick Childs asked if I might be interested in compiling a history to coincide with the forthcoming 150th anniversary I could hardly wait to get started.

I've always been a compulsive hoarder and still have many of the programmes and much of the correspondence from my time at Black Dyke between 1966 and 1977. In addition to this I now have access to copies of *British Bandsman* going back 60 years, to the old monthly magazine *Brass Band News* from its first edition in 1881, and also to many of the various other brass band publications which have appeared from time to time.

Of course, not all of Black Dyke's activities are recorded in these magazines. Come to think of it, if they were, there would be no room for anything else! It is also true that many of the reports are somewhat coloured by the enthusiasm (or otherwise) of the contributors. Nevertheless, by painstakingly searching through all of these various sources it has been possible to put together what I hope will be seen as an honest and definitive account of the history of what is now called the Black Dyke Band.

It is often said that contesting is the life-blood of the brass band movement. Whilst I don't totally agree with this, there is more than a grain of truth in it. Black Dyke has always taken its contesting seriously, has been eminently successful in it, but has viewed it as a means to an end rather than as the end itself. It has enjoyed the publicity and the accolades which have come through success on the contest platform, but more importantly, it has seen contest preparation as a means of keeping its standard of music-making on the concert platform at the highest possible level.

Black Dyke's real strength in the contest arena has been its consistency. It does not win every contest it attends, nor would it be healthy if it did. In fact, in most eras there has been at least one band that could claim a better record than Black Dyke at the time. In the late nineteenth century Meltham Mills, Wyke Temperance and Kingston Mills each offered a strong challenge and for many years Besses o'th' Barn shared the laurels with Black Dyke as the most successful band. Early in the twentieth century bands such as Wingates Temperance and Irwell Springs were at the top of their form, then came St Hilda Colliery, Foden's Motor Works and Brighouse & Rastrick; in later times there was powerful opposition from Fairey Aviation, Munn & Felton's and CWS (Manchester). All of these and others have been and in some cases still are great bands and all have offered strong challenges. However, these challenges have been for relatively short periods of time. Black Dyke has been amongst the greats almost continuously for an incredible 150 years. It is the pacemaker of the brass band movement and continues to be the band that other bands most want to beat.

* * * * *

Many people have helped me prepare this book. In particular Geoffrey Whitham, who has done me the honour of writing the Foreword and who is the principal subject of Chapter 6, has helped a great deal. He is a living encyclopaedia where Black Dyke is concerned; his knowledge and his incredible memory never cease to amaze me. His willingness to share these has contributed enormously to the book.

Geoffrey Whiteley, the band's administrator, has also been most helpful, with advice on the text, allowing me access to copies of *Black Dyke Bugle* and supplying many of the photographs which will, I hope, help bring the text of the book to life. I have attempted to use photographs from the particular periods under discussion. Some of these are of a poor quality, but I feel that this is preferable to using more modern photographs.

I have been unable to trace the copyright owners of several of the photographs used in this book, but have included the words 'With Acknowledgement' in their captions. I hope that the owners will accept that this has been done in good faith, and I offer them my thanks in retrospect for the use of their photographs.

I am most grateful to Major David Dalziel of The Salvation Army for reading through my scripts and making many helpful suggestions.

I must also thank the University of Salford for allowing me access to the magazines in its archive and in the Adelphi Library.

Last, but not least, I say thank you to my dear wife, Muriel, for all her patience and tolerance, for reading and re-reading the text and ensuring that my comments were within the bounds of respectability.

To anyone else who has, in any way at all helped me scale this Brass Band Everest, I say please accept my thanks for your help and advice. It has all played its part in the writing of this book.

Roy Newsome
Bury, Lancashire
June 2005

INTRODUCTION

How it all began

by Geoffrey Whiteley, Administrator, Black Dyke Band

A 'PONDASHER' is an avid supporter of Black Dyke Band, so the man who founded it all, John Foster, must surely be the first. Many articles, features, historical reports and much compiled technical data have been written over the years about the Foster family, the mill and the band. In this introduction I will endeavour to give a clear and true account of the man and the mill which provided the finance to support the band.

John Foster – The First Pondasher
John Foster was born on 20 January 1798, son of Jonas Foster (1774-1830) and the grandson of Jonathan Foster (1730-1818) who lived in the nearby village of Denholme. Jonas came to live at Black Carr Farm, Moor Royd Gate, near Thornton where, in addition to farming, he owned two coal mines. There is no record of which these were, but an ordnance survey map of 1854 shows that there were ten coal pits in various states within a radius of about one mile from the farmhouse at Moor Royd Gate. In the Queenshead area – part of what was later to become known as Queensbury – there were many coal and clay mines. These were small drift mines set in the hillside, into which the miners would walk, not at all like the deep mines in major coalfields.

In the early 1800s, when John Foster was sent to Thornton Grammar School, the Foster family could not be regarded as poor; neither could they be counted among the very wealthy. On leaving the grammar school John worked for his father as book-keeper for the collieries for a time before returning to school, this time to Brookhouse School in nearby Ovenden.

On 16 May 1819, at the age of 21, John Foster married Ruth Briggs at Halifax Parish Church. Ruth was the daughter of Abram Briggs who owned land in Queenshead, including Black Dike Farm. John and Ruth set up their home at Low Fold, where their first three sons – William, Samuel Briggs and Johnstone Jonas were born.

This was also the year in which John started a business as an employer of handloom weavers working in their own homes. The earliest records of his business activities are lost, and therefore, details are available only from 1828 onwards. The sources of the capital which enabled him to become a worsted manufacturer remain a matter for conjecture – was it a loan or a gift from his father, or had Miss Briggs had a substantial dowry?

Whatever the source, John Foster must have been a very astute businessman, for in the textile industry, the years between 1819 and 1827 were unstable. The year 1818 had been a good one but it was followed by two years of depression. Recovering from this in 1821, the business continued successfully until 1825. In that year a combers' and weavers' strike paralysed the industry, already affected by a further depression. A revival came in 1827, by which time Foster was sufficiently prosperous to build Prospect House on land which had been part of his father-in-law's Black Dike Farm.

It was here that the other three sons were born – Abraham Briggs, John and Alfred. There were also five daughters, Sarah, Mary Ann, Ruth, Hannah and Jane. The eldest son, William (1821-1884), was educated at a private school, joining the business at the age of 13. At the age of 21 he was taken into partnership with his father, the business title becoming 'John Foster and Son Ltd.'

By the year 1830 John Foster employed 700 or more handloom weavers, who received payment in kind from his shop and coal mines, rather than all in cash. The 'Truck Act', outlawing payment in kind, was passed on 15 October 1831, although Foster's shop was still in existence in 1842. There is, however, no evidence to suggest that as a shopkeeper and major employer he abused his position.

This must have been the busiest and most productive part of John Foster's life. He had earlier been an amateur French horn player in Peter Wharton's band in his spare time, and in addition to running his business was largely responsible for the building of Queensbury Parish Church, begun in 1843 and completed in 1845. Obviously a man of vision, on a painting of the mill completed in 1842, there is a touch of Victorian artist's licence, with a faint outline of the church

Black Dike Mills c. 1842 – from an early painting

on the horizon, although construction had not even started. (On 12 May 1995, Black Dyke Band gave a concert in the church to celebrate its 150th anniversary).

In 1861 John Foster bought Hornby Castle, near Lancaster, for the sum of £205,000. The *Manchester Guardian* reporting the sale tells the following story:

> He [John Foster] was a man who paid little attention to personal appearance and when, at the close of the sale of the estate, a rough-looking individual walked into the best room of the local inn the landlord frowned. He was chatting with some of the 'better end' of those who had attended the auction proceedings, and tramp-like strangers were not for such select company. "T' bar for you," he said with a jerked thumb. The stranger retired. Later the landlord joined him in the bar and found him willing to listen to the tale of the day's doings; a tale that was a lament. "They do say," said the landlord, "that one of them wool chaps from Bradford way has bowt it. I've a new landlord". The stranger nodded; his reply was devastating, "Aye, I'm him".

Hornby served as a retreat for Foster, but though he became less active at the mill, his affections for Queensbury still held strong and he visited Prospect House regularly until 1877, when he gave Hornby

Castle to his eldest son, William. John then returned to Queensbury, where he died on 6 March 1878. He was buried in Queensbury Parish churchyard in a family vault. Among his bequests was a sum of £4,000 for the poor of the parish. Ruth survived him by four years, dying on 15 November 1882 and being buried in the same vault.

So here was a man who, when he married, was described as the son of a small farmer, with only rudimentary literacy. His wife, Ruth, could not even sign her name on the marriage certificate, but made her mark instead. Yet, after a relatively short period of time in business, they had somewhere in the region of 2,000 employees. They both contributed greatly to the benefit of their family as well as to the well-being of the people of Queensbury and Hornby.

For many years John and Ruth Foster and their family had strong links with Queensbury and their influence outside the business was of great benefit to young and old alike. At the beginning of the 19th century Queensbury had less than 100 houses, with around 470 inhabitants. Following the founding of the mill, the Fosters built and owned over 400 houses, to be occupied by their workers. At that time the Fosters paid half the total rate of the village. They kept in close contact with the spending of local revenue, as there was a Foster on the Local Board, or District Council, for 41 of its 72 year existence and in the years when they were not represented, they had appointees elected.

John Foster was very much involved with the petition and subscription to build the parish church. His son William built the National School in 1850, and they both also gave support to the many chapels in the village. In 1863 the Fosters erected the Albert Memorial, the most northerly tribute in the country to the late Prince Consort. It was more than just an ornamental edifice, as it was also a functional

The Albert Memorial

fountain for which the people of Queensbury were grateful when drought dried up the wells. The Victoria Hall was another memorial to royalty and was built at the firm's expense by its own workforce, to be a social and cultural centre for the inhabitants. Although it was built to celebrate Queen Victoria's Jubilee of 1887, it was not opened until 17 January 1891. Without question, all the buildings that the Fosters were involved with were the best of their type.

In 1856 or 1857 John Foster of Queensbury was granted armorial bearings. The family motto is *Justum perficito nihil timeto*, which translates to 'Act justly and fear nothing'. Black Dyke Band is proud to have the privilege of the Stag's Head from the full coat of arms and the quotation as their insignia.

Some later Fosters

As a measure of his success John Foster would see his son Jonas buy Cliff Hall Estate, Halifax for £15,600 and Moor Park Estate, Ludlow for £128,000, the former in 1867 and the latter in 1873. In 1869 John Jnr. bought Egton Manor Estate, Whitby for £155,100, while in 1872 Abraham purchased Canwell Hall in Staffordshire, for £191,000. William, who was as responsible for the success of the mill as his father, apart from owning Hornby Castle, bought an estate near Liverpool for £150,000 in 1869 and built Harrowins House at Queenshead in 1856. In addition to his directorship of the mill he was a director in many railway enterprises and was largely responsible for the change of name of the village to 'Queensbury' in 1863. The Foster family eventually had residences all over Great Britain.

The fourth son of William, Colonel Herbert Anderton Foster, was born in 1853 and was probably the best-known locally of all the family. He lived the whole of his life in Queensbury and was involved with its many activities. In 1890 he built Littlemoor Castle in the village, where he brought his bride, Edith, daughter of Lord Brudenell Bruce in 1907. Among the many guests entertained at the Castle were Lord Roberts and Sir Edward Elgar. Colonel Foster also had a love of the sea; he had a yacht of 371 tons which was 160 feet long and 22 feet broad. He was one of the last members of the Foster family to live in Queensbury.

The Mill

At the time that it was proposed to build a mill on land at Black Dike Farm, the village of Queenshead had as many as ten stage coaches passing through daily, on their way to Bradford, Leeds, Halifax and Manchester. Across the moors at Haworth, the Rev. Patrick Bronte was bringing up his family, whose first novels were to be published in 1847; and Sir Charles Barry was about to rebuild the Houses of Parliament. George Stephenson's Stockton and Darlington Railway had been established as the world's first steam-hauled passenger service, 27 miles long; ten years later Britain had 338 miles of railway track and, by 1850, 6,600. On a hillside north of Malton (North Yorkshire), Sir George Caley was about to make the first flight by converting a kite into what has been called the first true aeroplane. Caley's coachman became the first person to leave the ground in free flight, soaring across a valley on Caley's Yorkshire estate for 500 yards. When the excited spectators reached him the coachman called out "Please, Sir George, I wish to give my notice, I was hired to drive not to fly".

Adolphe Sax was working on the new valved instruments, Chopin was settling in Paris where he met Liszt, Mendelssohn, Berlioz and Bellini, and Beethoven had just died while sketching out his 10th symphony. This certainly was a time when things were happening.

Work started on the foundations for the first part of the mill in January 1835. The labourers who did the digging were employed by John Foster, who also purchased 'Spades, Shovels and a Wheel-barrow', and provided 'Delver Ale' at a total cost of five shillings and sixpence. Stone for the walls, stone for flagging the floors, the mill yard and the roof, all came from local quarries. He made bricks at his own brickworks, located across the road from the mill, always making full use of the indigenous materials. There is a note for payment by John Foster of 'Duty on bricks, 42,000 at five shillings and ten pence'. Clay from his drift mines was one of the commodities in which he traded and which he was sending all over the North of England.

Although Foster appears to have employed labourers and supplied materials, the skilled work of building the mill was done on contract by various firms and craftsmen. The work proceeded swiftly. The mill chimney was begun in February and the masons were paid £2 3s. 1d.[1] for 'feighing for chimney'. On 18 April the boiler arrived

---

[1] The old English system of denoting money was in pounds, shillings and pence (£ s. d.). There were 12 pennies (pence) in the shilling and 20 shillings in the pound.

from Bowling Iron Works (5 miles away, near Bradford). By September the mill was nearing completion and on the 28th there was a celebration, noted as: 'Finishing chimney, Ale £1 0s. 0d'.

Just over a week later, on 6 October 1835, an entry was made in the account book by William Foster (aged 14) stating that the engine had started and that the first plumes of smoke from the new chimney had announced to the district that Black Dike Mills were in running order. In ten months from the first sod being cut, the spindles began to turn in the new mill. Little had been lost in production during this period; a rented spinning mill at nearby Great Horton (Cannon Mills) continued to supply the yarn.

The handloom weavers who were buying yarn from Foster and producing cloth in their own homes could see the rapid progress being made when they visited the warehouse adjoining Prospect House. Here they sold their finished product, safe for the moment in the knowledge that the new mill was intended for spinning, but not without apprehensions of its future development.

The first range of buildings to be known as Black Dike Mills included not only the spinning mill, its chimney and boiler house, but also the new warehouse in the mill yard, built between April 1836 and March 1837, and the new counting house which flanked and, in its upper storey, extended over the gateway to the main yard. Modifications to the mill were doubtless necessary when the first power looms were installed in 1836. The accounts relating to this first range of buildings continue until February 1838, by which time the outlay, which had risen since January 1834 when the first step towards expansion was taken, now amounted to £5,924 4s. 2d, accounted for as follows:

Engine, shafting, cast iron pillars	£1,678	6	2
Land	£168	5	0
Stone	£585	0	7
Timber	£721	9	1
Sand & lime	£54	2	10
Lead, spoutings, etc.	£80	12	11
Expenses in brick making	£47	0	0
Masons	£626	13	1
Joinering	£90	3	5
Glazing	£84	11	2
Roofing & flooring	£86	6	2
Plastering	£50	1	8

Plumbing & blacksmith	£28	12	6
Painting	£17	8	0
Architect	£10	0	0
Miscellaneous	£338	15	5
Total expenses involved in building Black Dike Mill	**£4,685**	**8**	**0**
Machinery paid for at Cannon Mill 1834	£848	0	2
Rent paid at Cannon Mill	£370	16	0
	£5,904	**4**	**2**

At this point in the history of Black Dike Mills we see another redeeming feature of its founder John Foster, who, it must be said, was already becoming a wealthy man and, perhaps it could be argued, taking advantage of others less fortunate. However, I think not, for two reasons. He was well established in Prospect House with the warehouse adjoining, where the handloom weavers came to sell their products. To this day, on the outside of the boundary wall, set at regular intervals, are deep round holes in the stone work. These were known as 'Whoozing holes'. Into them was inserted the end of a rod to which was attached a creel containing the warp, still wet from sizing. The rod was rotated and the warp thus spun round rapidly in the creel, which is the principle employed in the latest domestic clothes driers. So here was a man who was rapidly developing a mill on one side of the road with the latest technology and who, on the other side, had his own house and warehouse where he bought, from the handloom weavers, their home production.

Prospect House – also showing the warehouse

It would have been quite easy for him to have adopted a take it or leave it attitude – 'either come to the new mill and work for me, or try selling your product elsewhere'. In fact, his method of giving the weavers four different options showed his astute approach to business. People could either continue to weave in their cottages, sell their loom to him and work for him, take their loom to the mill and rent space, or go and work in the mill doing another job. Whichever option they chose, Foster ended up with both the product, and with employees for his new venture.

In 1855, when John Foster formed the Black Dike Mills Band, the balance sheet of his company makes interesting reading. The total assets were over £300,000. The Balance Sheet showed the following:

£68,557	Machinery and buildings
£197,764	Stock
£10,831	Investments
£2,154	Money in bank
£70,271	Cash in hand at the Mill

The Gas Works

Plans for John Foster's own gas works were passed on 1 September 1868. The mill then became the supplier of gas for street lighting and nearby houses, as well as for the mill itself. The Local Board (Council) paid for the street lights. This went quite satisfactorily until, on 19 December 1881, a special meeting was called to oppose a Halifax Corporation Bill, then before Parliament, to supply Queensbury with gas. It was pointed out that Foster's workmen had laid the mains, erected, repaired and maintained all the street lamps and that gas was being supplied at the same cost to consumers as that proposed by Halifax Corporation.

On 3 October 1882 a letter was received by the local Council from the Gulcher Electric Light & Power Co, saying that they were applying for power to supply the district of Queensbury with light by electricity. The Clerk of the Council was instructed to reply that the Board was satisfied with the present lights and would oppose the application.

On 24 September 1900 the Council decided to buy all the street lamps owned by Foster's. The offer to take over the lighting, repairing and cleaning was subject to the price of gas being reduced by 4 pence per 1,000 cubic feet. It is not known whether this reduction was made, but, in November 1901, the Local Board agreed to a price of 35 shillings each for the 55 gas lamps and pillars owned by the mill. (Electric street lights did not arrive in Queensbury until September, 1929).

In 1933 the Council considered taking over the gas works from Messrs John Foster & Son, but were advised against it by the Board of Trade. Foster's continued to supply the gas, but discontinued its

Black Dike Mills c. 1900

manufacture, buying in bulk from Bradford, until the Nationalisation Act of 1947.

Financial matters

When one considers that in 1875 Foster's had 962 power looms, it gives some idea of the volume of production. The expansion of the machinery and mill buildings which took place after 1852 and the resultant increased need to carry larger stocks presented no financial problems to a firm which could carry in excess of £100,000 of its assets as cash in hand. The firm now turned its attention to opportunities for further profits afforded by the stock exchange, the value of money invested rising from £4,860 in 1853 to £349,736 in 1862. By 1867, when the balance sheets came to an end, £697,176 was invested in stocks and bonds of all kinds, ranging from annuities and foreign government stocks and bonds all over the world and railway stock in India, Portugal, Russia, to investments in the Alton, Aylesford and Winchester lines. In London, G. H. Cozens, who had acted as Fosters' agent in the purchasing of mohair, was able to represent them in dealing with city brokers, while in New York the firm of Butterfield & Co, who had handled Foster's cloth exports to the United States, found themselves being asked not to send remittances for the sales of cloth which they had undertaken, but to invest the money on Foster's behalf.

In addition to these increasingly important investments in stocks and bonds, as detailed earlier, the partners of the firm were always on the lookout for landed estates which might prove a profitable investment. For example, they turned down a suggestion for an investment made to them by their accountant, having decided 'upon waiting until some eligible land investment offers itself', the first of these being Hornby Castle.

None of the properties which the Fosters bought appeared on the balance sheet as an asset. Hornby was debited against John Foster's capital account over the two years 1860 to 1861; the others were all dealt with in the same manner. Therefore any items appearing on the balance sheet after 1859 were purely business items and did not include the value of these landed estates, which, though purchased out of the resources of the firm, were debited against individual partners and treated as their own personal assets.

By 1867 the firm, although still primarily a textile manufacturing company, was as much interested in the fortunes of the London money market and Stock Exchange dealings as in the fluctuations in the price of wool. Indeed, they were willing to invest their money in far more risky ventures. In 1862, for example, they subscribed £1,500 towards a venture being organised by a Manchester firm of merchants to break the Federal blockade of supplies for the Confederate forces. These supplies were valued at some £60,000. In the event, the venture failed. The ship chartered, the *Princess Royal*, was attacked off Charleston during the night of 28 January 1863. It was run aground, abandoned and then re-floated by a Federal crew and was thus captured.

Industrial relations

It is worth noting for both present and future generations that John Foster's approach to business and the community played a large part in the success of the company. Here is an extract from *Fortunes Made in Business*, published in 1887:

> '1836 ... at Queensbury, John Foster had seven hundred employees of the old fashioned type, handloom weavers, who naturally looked upon the power loom with dire misgiving. He managed them with much address and with keen appreciation of their ideas and foibles. Those who cared to do so were put to work on the machinery which he determinedly introduced, but those who preferred the old methods were allowed without demur to work their time out on the familiar hand-loom.'

Inside a weaving shed

Also, while the mill was under construction in the period 1834-1848, there was considerable unrest elsewhere in the textile industry and on one occasion there was fear of trouble from Chartists passing through the village on their way to a mass demonstration in Bradford. John Foster's workers united to defend the mill against possible attack by the mob. Queensbury certainly had its Chartists but their activities do not seem to have been directed against Messrs Fosters.

In fact, however, on 21 April 1848, ten days after the famous Chartists meeting on Kennington Common, Messrs Fosters were presented by their employees with a clock, which was located over what at that time was the main gateway to the mill. The inscription reads

> This clock was presented to Messrs. John Foster & Son on Good Friday 21 April 1848, by their workmen in gratitude for the Regular Employment their business talents have procured for all employed at Black Dike Mills of late years and particularly during the panic of 1847.

Messrs John Foster & Son were also regarded as good employers by the Royal Commission on Labour, 1893. There are many instances of benefaction towards the community by John Foster and his family, too numerous to detail here. These two press reports give an indication of their interests. The *Manchester Guardian* of 28 March 1854 carried a three-column report of a 'Soirée at Black Dike Mills, Queenshead'. The following extract and comments are taken from it.

> While providing for the physical exigencies of the poor around them the proprietors of Black Dike Mills have recognised the inalienable duty of providing also for the intellectual aspirations and development of those beneath them. For this purpose they have purchased a library, which is henceforth to be at the service of all the mill-hands on payment of a quarterly subscription of 1/6d each. The number of volumes now accessible to these plebeian students is 511, which are classified thus:- Mathematics, Natural Philosophy, Mechanical Arts, Natural History, Biography, History, Chronology, Antiquities, Geography, Topography, Voyages and Travel, Poetry and Drama, Novels Tales and Anecdotes, and General Literature.

There was also some entertainment during the 'Soirée', and *Messiah* was performed.

A horse-drawn fire engine

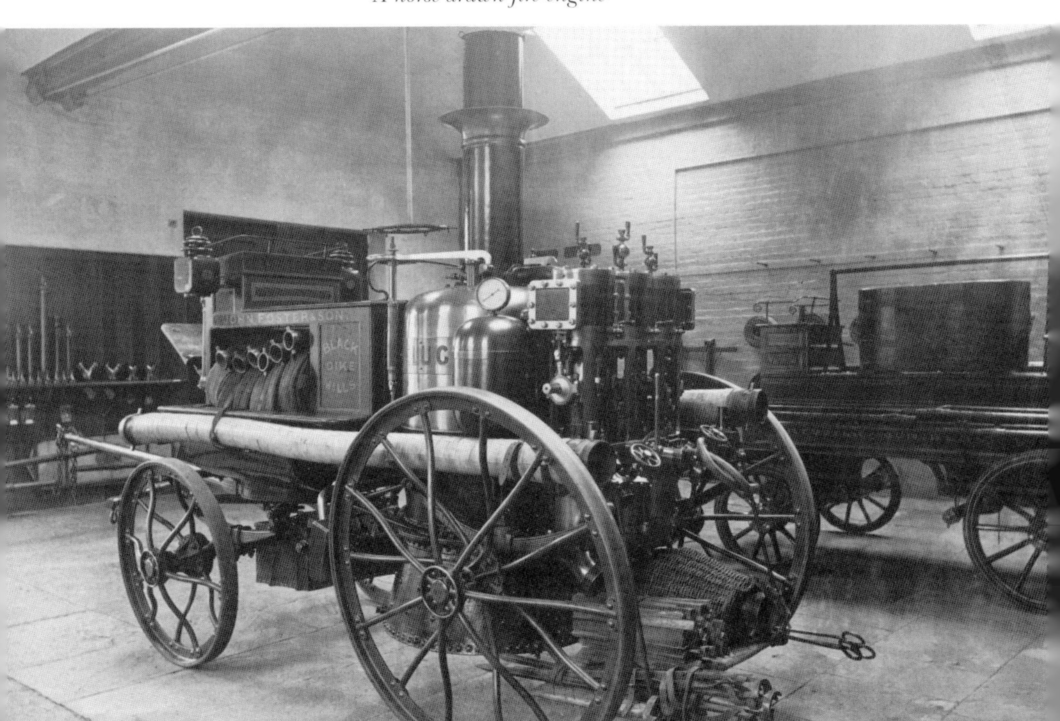

A year later the company of John Foster & Son Ltd took the momentous step of rejuvenating the ailing Queenshead Band and, as will be seen in subsequent chapters, Black Dyke Mills Band was born.

Geoffrey Whiteley, with acknowledgement: *Black Dyke Mills, A History*, Eric M. Sigsworth and Frank Barrett.

Geoffrey Whiteley, with the band's 'silverware'

CHAPTER 1

The background: Peter Wharton's and the Queenshead Bands

THOUGH this book celebrates the founding of Black Dyke Mills Band in 1855, the band has roots going back to earlier times. According to an article written in 1906:

> In 1816 there appear to have been bands organised in the village of Queensbury, and Peter Wharton's Reed Band took first position, the late Mr. John Foster being a member, and playing the French horn.[1]

How much of this is fact and how much hearsay we may never know for certain. However, there definitely was both a Peter Wharton and a John Foster, and many bands were formed at this time. It is also a fact that the particular French horn was still in existence at the time the article was written.

Despite many theories that village bands descended from the Waits and from church bands, modern research suggests that the military band was by far the biggest influence in their development. There were full-time bands attached to regiments of the regular army and also part-time bands, associated with the militia and the Volunteers. They were at their height during the later years of the Napoleonic Wars. After Napoleon's defeat at Waterloo in 1815 many army musicians became redundant and as they returned to civilian life they helped form village bands. Instruments, particularly brass instruments, were quite primitive at the time, as the valve had not yet been invented.

Queensbury is in an area whose history goes back beyond the 18th century. From 1702, what was still a hamlet became known as Queenshead, which took its name from a local hostelry – The

---

[1] USA/Canada tour souvenir booklet, page 36.

Queen's Head. This was a coaching house, where stagecoaches regularly called *en route* from Bradford to Manchester or from Leeds to Liverpool. Queenshead was one of several small villages that would eventually form Queensbury. Stone quarrying and farming were the principal occupations in what was a very rugged area, 1,100 feet above sea level. By 1816 there were two turnpike roads passing through the village and the principal forms of livelihood were farming and hand loom weaving.

Peter Wharton (1790-1843) was the son of Richard Wharton, landlord of an inn at Clayton Heights called The Old Dolphin. Peter married Susannah Scott in 1809, shortly after which he moved to another village in the district, called Ford. Here he opened The New Dolphin, of which he was landlord from about 1818 to 1830. He was also a farmer, played the clarinet and was his band's leader. In earlier times such groups were referred to as 'Bands of Musick' but it was now common for bands to take their name from the leader. It is not known whether or not there were any military connections nor how many players there were in the band, but it is unlikely that there would be more than ten. The band rehearsed in the inn and a year after its formation Peter Wharton is said to have travelled to Manchester to purchase some music from a military bandmaster. It was customary, however, for leaders to write out all the band parts for their members, as there was no standardization of instrumentation, no standard size of band and no published music.

As we saw in the Introduction, John Foster was born in 1798 and would therefore be a young man of 18 at the time of the Peter Wharton band's formation. At the age of 21, John founded his own business and also married Ruth Briggs, daughter of a landowner who lived at Black Dike Farm.[2]

In 1827 Prospect House was built on the very road where the mill was later to be built. This was John Foster's home until he retired from the business in 1870. Some future generations of the Fosters allowed the band to rehearse on the lawn during the summer months.

Foster was the largest of several merchants operating in the area. It has been estimated that the population of the district was 25 times

[2] During most of the 19th century the spelling 'Dike' is generally found, but from around 1890 the spelling 'Dyke' is also found. The change was gradual but for the sake of consistency I have used 'Dike' up to and including the 1906 tour and thereafter have adopted 'Dyke'.

greater in 1860 than it had been in 1800. This reflected a general growth in the population of Britain and also the mass migration of people from the country to industrial towns during this period.

Having built up good connections through the domestic system Foster, seeing the success of mills in Bradford and Halifax, decided to build a factory in the hill-top region between the two. The mill was concerned primarily with spinning, previously done in Bradford, providing yarn for the weavers. It was built on land acquired from Foster's father-in-law.

In 1842 the first weaving shed was erected and John Foster's son, William, became a partner in the company. By now, the collection of buildings was known as Black Dike Mills. Further extensions took place and by the year 1868 there was another weaving shed, a combing shed and a spinning mill.

* * * * *

Meanwhile, another band appeared in the village, called the Queenshead Brass and Reed Band. In the book *The Brass Band Movement* it is stated that 'Wharton's Band was disbanded through the loss of members by removal but a new reed band arose in 1833...'[3] This suggests that perhaps there was not such a huge gap in time between the demise of one and the founding of the other. Perhaps Wharton's band survived until he moved from The New Dolphin in 1830. The only known history of the new band appeared in a local newspaper in 1855:

> In the year 1853 (this should, obviously, be 1833 - RN), a number of young men, residents at Queenshead, and the greater part of whom, if not all, could play on various musical instruments, agreed to form themselves into a band, to be called the 'Queenshead Band'. This band soon acquired for itself, and for a long period retained, a deservedly wide-spread fame, being in its zenith from 1838 to 1843, at which time it consisted of 18 musicians. In a few years afterwards the band lost, by deaths, removals, and other causes, a considerable number of old players, whose places could not be filled up in the neighborhood by equally talented performers, although great efforts were made to do so, and it consequently sank in public estimation. When this state of things had continued for some time, it was

[3] Russell and Elliot, page 66.

> changed into a brass band, but that did not produce any material improvement.[4]

Eighteen players, though above average, was not unusual. Instruments would still be primitive, with clarinets, maybe a piccolo or flute, keyed bugles, natural trumpets and horns (with no valves), trombones, and ophicleides or serpents. At the time of the change to all-brass, in the early fifties, cornets, saxhorns[5] euphoniums and tubas would be available, as well as trombones.

A significant change had occurred in the type of person who became a bandsman. This was very much the era of the class system, but whereas in the 1816 band members would be mainly from the middle classes, by 1833 bandsmen were, almost without exception, from the working class. The newspaper report of 1855 continued:

> Messrs. John Foster and Son, of Queenshead, having lately become acquainted with the depressed position of the band, determined to make an effort themselves to raise it up again. Accordingly they have purchased from the eminent maker, Mr. Joseph Higham, Victoria Bridge, Manchester, a new set of instruments, which have this week been delivered to the band, that in future is to be denominated the 'Black Dike Mills Band'.

This is all typical of the times. Many industrialists were becoming involved with their local bands. It is often suggested that they had ulterior motives in doing so. That was sometimes true but was certainly not the case with the Fosters, who were well aware that they were helping maintain some kind of quality of life both for the bandsmen and for the villagers by breathing new life into the band. It is also worth noting that Higham was the chief supplier of instruments in the North of England at the time.

As a former brass player himself, John Foster was well aware that if the band was to succeed he would need to provide musical tuition for its members. He did this by appointing a bandmaster to look after routine musical matters and a professional conductor who would train the band for contests. The first bandmaster was a local man, James Galloway – possibly the Queenshead bandmaster. The first professional conductor, Samuel Longbottom, came from

---

[4] *Halifax Courier and Guardian*, 15 September 1855.

[5] Saxhorns had been developed in France by Adolphe Sax – see Chapter 2.

James Galloway, the first bandmaster

Mixenden, a village on the outskirts of Halifax. He must have been quite an experienced musician as he played the organ and the violin, and was particularly interested in oratorio. In keeping with the title 'professional conductor', he would be seen as middle class.

With new instruments, tuition and the provision of uniform and rehearsal facilities, the new band was set fair and thus the Black Dike Mills Band was formed – in September 1855.

During the remainder of the century not only were the mills to become the employment centre of the district, but a healthy bond was established between the Fosters and the community.

CHAPTER 2

The first decade of Black Dike Mills Band

THE *Halifax Courier* article quoted in the previous chapter stated that there were 19 members in the new band. The band's entry form for the 1860 Crystal Palace contest (to be discussed later) has been preserved in the band's archive. This gives the names of all the players at that time, along with their instruments and their jobs in the mills. A photograph of the form is reproduced on page 28.

It is worth noting that, though the credit for forming the band has often been given exclusively to John Foster, a 1902 report states: 'the Queenshead Band [was] taken over by the late Mr John Foster, Senr, the late Mr William Foster, the late Mr Jonas Foster, Mr A. B. Foster and Mr John Foster, Junr.' This would seem to establish that the band was well and truly a company concern. These five were the elder John Foster and his four surviving sons. All became partners in the firm but William was the driving force, even more dominant than his father once he had been made a partner. His importance in the firm was reflected by the fact that the name 'John Foster & Son Ltd', established in 1842 was never changed, despite the later partnerships of the other sons.

The band was almost immediately called upon to enter contests. The directors probably felt that there would be a certain amount of reflected glory for the company if the band were to be successful. Little would they realise at the time just how successful the band was to be. It must be said, however, that because of the band's name most of the glory was credited to Black Dike Mills rather than to John Foster & Son Ltd.

In July 1856, just 10 months after the new instruments were delivered, the band entered its first contest. This was in Hull and the band were runners-up to one of the most successful bands of the time, Smith's Leeds, conducted by Richard Smith, a famous cornet player and a leading brass band conductor.

Richard Smith, an early influence

There were two further prizes in 1857 – a 1st prize of £10 in Halifax and a 2nd of £6 at Batley. The band had entered the Hull contest again but did not attend, probably because of a rule stating that any band that had won a prize of £10 or more would not be allowed to compete.

1858 brought success at three more contests – one in Dewsbury, another in Cleckheaton and the third in Bradford. The following year saw a repeat of the 2nd prize in Hull and a win at a contest that was part of York's Annual Flower Show. This win attracted by far the biggest prize to date – £30, a substantial amount by the standards of the time.

Contests were often quite important social occasions for the towns in which they were staged. The 1856 Hull contest is a case in point. It was held in the local Zoological Gardens and attracted a crowd estimated at 14,000. The success was in part due to the collaboration between the organiser, Enderby Jackson (who will be discussed later) and the railway companies. In fact, the growth of the railways was an important element in the development of brass band contests. Following the opening of the Stockton & Darlington line in 1825, by 1837 there were some 2,400 kilometres of track in Britain. The so-called 'Railway Mania' of 1843-49 attracted a great deal of investment and by 1851 all major British towns and cities were linked by rail. Excursions, with cheap return fares, helped promote rail travel.

Hull, with its docks and its importance as a fishing port, would be well served by the railways. On the day of the contest, excursion trains were run to Hull from several towns in Yorkshire and Lincolnshire, with cheap fares for bands and their supporters. Part of the deal, to add to the event's publicity, was that the competing bands must parade through the streets in their respective home towns. On arriving in Hull for the contest they were required to march to the Gardens playing 'lively airs'. Though 21 bands entered, only 12 actually played. Their sizes varied from 12 to 17. They were required to play two test pieces – *Yorkshire Waltzes*, composed by Jackson especially for the contest and another piece of their own choice. The contest provided a day's entertainment for a large number of people and an incentive to competing bands to play to their highest potential. The bands also benefited from the publicity surrounding the event.

* * * * *

Manchester was another important railway centre and was chosen as the location for what was to become the most important annual brass band contest in Britain for the remainder of the 19th century. This was in the Zoological Gardens known as Belle Vue. It was a couple of miles away from the city centre but there was a local railway station adjacent to it, known as Longsight. Visitors regularly poured into Belle Vue by the thousands through this station. The first brass band contest to be held there took place in 1853. Though there were only eight bands (some reports say even fewer), there were 16,000 people in the grounds. Black Dike first entered the Belle Vue contest in 1856. Seven bands played but Black Dike, led by Frank Galloway, was unsuccessful.

This is all rather confusing. Why did Samuel Longbottom not conduct the band? And what had happened to James Galloway, the first bandmaster? It was quite common for bands to play without a conductor at these early contests. Frank Galloway was never officially named as bandmaster or conductor but from 1860 he had been the band's soprano cornet player. The most likely answer is that whilst Longbottom and possibly James Galloway would be involved in coaching the band for the contest, on the day it played under the direction of the 'leader', in this case Frank Galloway, who would both play soprano cornet and direct the performance. According to the 1851 census and other reports there were lots of Galloways living in the district. Whether or not the two involved with Black Dike were related to each other is unclear. In fact, there is no record of a Frank Galloway, but there are a number of references to Francis Galloway, who I have assumed must have become known as Frank.

Black Dike did not enter another Belle Vue contest until 1859 when, owing to the fact that only three bands had applied, the contest was cancelled. They now stayed away until 1862 when, again under the leadership of Frank Galloway they won the 1st prize of £30, plus a silver plated cornet valued at 13 guineas.[6] The following year saw a further win, again with a prize of £30 but this time the 'special' prize was a euphonium. An innovation this year was that bands were required to use B flat cornets rather than those pitched in A flat, as in previous years. Black Dike were accused of playing on cornets in A but denied this. The judges concluded that the band had played according to the regulations, but that the instruments were slightly flat.[7]

It was quite normal for the adjudicators to ask to hear certain bands a second time in order to confirm their results. In 1863 they asked Black Dike and Bacup Old (otherwise known as the 4th Lancashire Rifle Volunteers) to play again. Bacup had been placed first on the set test piece and Black Dike first in the own choice section. Following the play-off Black Dike were declared winners. Bacup were unhappy about this, feeling that as they had given the better performance of the set test they should have been declared winners without resorting to a play-off. Our heroes were, understandably, quite happy with the outcome.

William Rusworth, bandmaster 1863-1870

From 1863 Black Dike had a new bandmaster, William Rushworth. Like Samuel Longbottom, he was a native of Mixenden and was born around 1830. He became a noted cornet player and in the late 1850s was a member of Belle Vue's professional band. Black Dike had

---

[6] In pre-decimalization currency, a guinea was 21 shillings, or £1 1s.

[7] *Huddersfield Examiner*, 6 September 1862.

entered the 1860 Crystal Palace contest but a difference of opinion had arisen between the band and its solo cornet player who left, believing that the band would be unable to attend the contest without him. Two members were sent to Belle Vue to interview and engage Rushworth. He came, not only helping win the contest, but staying with Black Dike for a number of years. Frank Galloway remained as leader and on his retirement in 1862 William Rushworth became bandmaster. Having been a great player, he now proved also to be an excellent conductor and is credited with having laid the foundations of Black Dike's greatness.[8]

There is continuing confusion about the roles of these early leaders/bandmasters and even of that of Samuel Longbottom. Records, such as they are, suggest that James Galloway was the first official bandmaster but that Frank Galloway, perhaps as leader, helped the band to its Belle Vue win in 1862, though it was, apparently, conducted by Longbottom. Rushworth is credited with having led the band's 5th prize-winning performance in 1864.

Samuel Longbottom conducted at the 1865 contest but again there was controversy. The weather was outstandingly good and some 30,000 people arrived at Belle Vue. Even the streets of Manchester were said to be crowded. Twelve bands had entered but only eight competed. Published results indicate that Black Dike was disqualified but that they had won a cornet valued at seven guineas. On seeking out contemporary reports I discovered that in fact two bands were disqualified – Black Dike and Denton Original. It seems that a certain cornet player, a Mr J. Salkeld, had illegally played with both bands. This led to the disqualifications, meaning that neither band could be considered for a major prize. However, in addition to the usual prize money, on this occasion Highams had offered two cornets, to be awarded to the two best cornet players. Both were awarded to the bands that were disqualified – Black Dike and Denton Original. This seems to me to have been 'stranger than fiction', as the person who caused the disqualification actually won two cornets for the disqualified bands!

* * * * *

[8] This information comes from an article by 'Pondasher' in *Brass Band News* of March 1916, written at the time of Rushworth's death at the age of around 86. He had retired to Harrogate, where he died, but he was buried at Illingworth church. The original 1860 solo cornet player, who was not named, was said to have been back in the band by 1871, as the repiano cornet player.

Most brass band enthusiasts are aware of the Crystal Palace contests that were founded in 1900 – the forerunners of the present National Brass Band Championships held in the Royal Albert Hall. However, many may not be aware that there was an earlier series that ran from 1860-63. The principal organiser of these was Enderby Jackson, mentioned above in connection with the 1856 Hull contest.

Enderby Jackson (1827-1903) was born in Hull. As a boy he played trumpet in a local band but on leaving school he became a professional flautist, playing in the orchestra of a touring opera company. He was present at a band contest held on the estate of Burton Constable, near Hull, in 1845. The 18-year-old was so impressed by the enthusiasm of the participating bands and their supporters that he took it upon himself in later life to write music for bands with which he came in contact on his travels, and also to organise more contests. The 1856 Hull contest was one of these and there were several others, in places as diverse as Newcastle and Bristol. In his unpublished autobiography, written many years later, Jackson claimed to have been a key figure in the setting up of the 1853 Belle Vue contest. Some historians, however, have questioned the validity of the claim. What is not in doubt is that he organised the Crystal Palace contests in the 1860s. The huge glass edifice, erected in Hyde Park for the Great Industrial Exhibition of 1851 had been dismantled and moved to Sydenham in South East London, where it continued to be used for exhibitions and concerts.

The first contest in the series took place on Tuesday and Wednesday, 10 and 11 July 1860, and was extensively reported in a number of national newspapers, including *The Times* and *Daily Telegraph*. Said to have been the first band contest ever held in London, it was massively publicised and, as in the case of other contests already discussed, owed much of its success to the railways. Amazingly, Jackson had struck a deal with the railway companies that enabled bands to travel to London from their nearest railway station free of charge.

Black Dike was one of the 44 bands that took part in the Tuesday event, dubbed 'The Great National Contest'. Bands were divided into six groups for a preliminary round, playing on platforms erected in various parts of the grounds. Three adjudicators were assigned to each platform and they selected the best two bands to proceed to the final round, for which all 18 adjudicators officiated. The outright winner was Black Dike, playing the so-called *Gloria from Mozart's 12th Mass,* and selections from Bellini's *La Sonnambula* and Weber's *Preciosa.* Described in the official programme as 'a subscription band supported by the wealthy proprietor of the Mills', the band collected a prize of £40 and a silver cup. In addition, the ophicleide player was awarded a circular bass, valued at 35 guineas.

Following the competition the members of all the bands assembled in what was called the Handel Orchestra, to perform a short concert under the baton of Enderby Jackson. The whole process was repeated on the following day in a competition called 'The Sydenham Contest'. A massive 70 bands participated. Many of them had also competed on the previous day, though the bands that had won 1st and 2nd prizes were barred. The sound that the 1200 players must have made under the large dome doesn't bear thinking about!

The event was an outstanding success. Some 29,000 people attended over the two days, and though the remaining three Crystal Palace contests became progressively less spectacular, the first had established Black Dike Mills Band in the forefront of amateur brass bands.

Black Dike returned to Crystal Palace in 1862. This year there were only 26 bands in total, divided into four groups. Black Dike qualified for the final round and won the 2nd prize of £30 and some music.

* * * * *

In addition to the Belle Vue and Crystal Palace contests in 1862, Black Dike also attended a contest in Birmingham during August, winning the 2nd prize of £15 and a silver cup. Covering long distances was becoming more viable as the railway system developed, though when travelling by train the band had to get itself either to Halifax or Bradford, by horse-drawn waggonette. The railway station in Queensbury did not open until around 1880 and even then it was located about a mile away from the bandroom.

Perhaps because of the change of bandmaster (to William Rushworth) and possibly some changes in personnel, contesting activities were now somewhat curtailed. In 1863 the band apparently competed only at Belle Vue where, as has been seen, it won 1st prize for the second year in succession. Three contests appear in the records for 1864 – producing a win at Skipton and 3rd prize at Batley, along with a modest 5th at Belle Vue.

The following year saw an escalation in contesting activities. In addition to the disqualification at Belle Vue, referred to above and which, incidentally, denied the band a 4th prize, the band competed at contests in Accrington, Haslingden, Nottingham, Kirkstall (Leeds), Skipton, Drighlington, Keighley and Matlock. These produced two wins (Nottingham and Drighlington) five 2nd prizes and a 4th. This was quite a profitable year, with prize money totalling over £90. Four instruments were also won, in addition to the Belle Vue cornet. These successes suggest that the band was still in good form and also reflect an escalation in the number of contests.

* * * * *

The 1860 entry form gives a list of the members of Black Dike Mills Band who competed at Crystal Palace in 1860. It is interesting to note that a clarinet is included. A number of otherwise all-brass bands included one of these in their instrumentation until well into the 1860s. They were generally made of brass so, despite the fact that they were reed instruments they were acceptable, and were certainly capable of adding extra colour and weight to the band's upper register.

Cornets were now well established and the saxhorn was very much in vogue. This designation stemmed from the name of Adolphe Sax (1814-94), a Belgian-born instrument maker who spent much of his life working in Paris. As well as being the inventor of the saxophone he made improvements to the valved brass instruments which had come into use in the 1840s. He created a matched set of instruments at various pitches, all using the three-valve system and called 'saxhorns'. The alto saxhorn was at the same pitch as the cornet but had a more mellow sound. It was later superseded by the flugel horn. The so-called 'Fugle' would, in fact, be an early flugel horn. Descending from the bugle, it was often called the fugle. The tenor saxhorn was what would now be called simply the tenor horn and the baritone was the equivalent of the modern baritone, though it was usually referred to at the time as the bass saxhorn.

The tenor trombone was probably a valve trombone. These were common in brass bands until the early 1870s, when the slide tenor trombone outlawed them. The bass trombone would certainly have

CRYSTAL PALACE, SYDENHAM.

TABLE OF PARTICULARS to be Filled-up by each Band intending to compete in the Brass Band Contests to be held at the above Palace on Tuesday and Wednesday, July 10th and 11th, 1860.

Name of Band .... (John Foster & Son) Black Dike Mills, Queenshead near Halifax

Name of Contests entered for .... Tuesday July 10th 1860

Title of Music, Composer's name, &c., selected to play on Tuesday, July 10th, 1860 .... Selection, La Sonnambula – Bellini

Title of Music, Composer's name, &c., selected to play on Wednesday, July 11th, 1860 .... ——

Name of Companies Railway, also the Railway Station you wish to start from, and the distance from nearest large Town .... Great Northern Railway, Halifax.

Particulars of Prizes won during the years 1858 and 1859 .... Particulars enclosed

Have you portable Music Stand you can bring to Sydenham if required? If so, please describe it; also please state if you can appear in Uniform. .... Not any Music Stands (would prefer a circular stand) Shall appear in Uniform.

Names of Performers.	Profession or Trade.	Instruments played upon.	Key the Instruments stand in.
Galloway Frank (Decd 1885) ×	Warehouseman	Soprano Cornet	Eb
…gger Jonas	Warp-Dresser	Bass Clarionet	„
Rushworth William × (3rd Conductor)	Woolsorter	Solo Cornet	Bb
Rothera Jubal	— do —	Re Piano — do —	„
Rushworth John	Machine Wool Comber	Second Cornet	„
Gregson Joe	Warp Twister	— do —	„
Rushworth Robert	Warp-Dresser	Alto Sax	Bb
Fawcett Jonas × (2nd Conductor)	Wheelwright	French Horn	Bb
Halliday Abram	Cordwainer	Tenor Sax	„
Smith John	Woolsorter	Bugle Horn	„
Firth Greenwood	Warp Dresser	Tenor Trombone	C
Oldfield Abram	Machine Wool-Comber	Bass — do —	„
Firth William	Wool-Washer	Bombardon	Eb
Halliday Samuel	Cordwainer	— do —	„
Taylor John	Warp Dresser	Euphonium	Bb
Holdroyd John	Woolsorter	Bariton	„
Greenwood James	Warehouseman	Ophicleide	C
Longbottom Samuel	Manufacturer	Conductor	

Bands necessitated by sickness or other causes to make any alteration from the particulars here given must obtain the Referee's sanction before any deviation can be permitted.

N.B.—Any Band not returning this Form properly filled-up to the Managing Secretary, Mr. Enderby Jackson, 21, Prospect-Street, Hull, on or before Thursday, the 21st day of June, 1860, will be considered as declining to compete, and their Entrance-Fee, or Fees, in consequence, be forfeited.

John Howe, Printer and Bookbinder, Old Corn Exchange Printing Rooms, 50, Market-Place, Hull.

The 1860 Crystal Palace entry form

a slide. It would probably be the G trombone, famous for the handle that allows the player to control the slide when fully extended. The euphonium would be much the same as it is today, but with a smaller bore and no fourth valve. Bombardons would be of the circular type, known as helicons. The ophicleide is a bass instrument that looks something like a bassoon but which is played through a mouthpiece similar to that used on a euphonium. It was the successor to the serpent and predecessor of the euphonium and the tuba. There would certainly be at least one drummer in the band, but as he was not allowed to play at the contest he is not listed.

A photograph thought to have been taken in about 1865, possibly celebrating the wins of 1862-3, shows a slightly smaller band, with no ophicleide and no French horn. There is also only either an alto saxhorn or a fugle – not both. Two drummers are shown – one with a bass drum and the other with a military-style marching drum.

It has been suggested that the uniforms worn in this photograph indicate that the band had joined the Volunteers. This was a militia-type part-time army, mustered in 1859 in readiness for a threatened invasion by the French that never took place. Many bands enlisted and, as it is known that at least one member of the Foster family

Black Dike Mills Band c. 1865 – the earliest known photograph

joined the Volunteers in Bradford it is quite possible that Black Dike also 'joined up'.

* * * * *

There is little or no evidence regarding the kind of engagements the band undertook at this time, but there is a collection of what must be the first pieces of music played by Black Dike Mills Band. These are contained in a number of music books that have survived. The contents of the books are shown in Appendix A, and though these provide possibly more questions than answers, they do indicate the type of music played by the band in its early years.

The books carry the name John Foster & Son and bear the title 'Black Dike Mills Military Brass Band', another pointer to the possibility of a connection with the Volunteers. Eight books have survived, for the following instruments:

Clarinet, Solo cornet, Cornet secondo
Fugle, Alto saxhorn, Tenor trombone
Ophicleide, Bass drum

I would guess that originally there were also books for soprano and repiano cornets, tenor saxhorn, baritone (bass saxhorn), bass trombone and bombardon.

When were they written? All the parts were written by hand, probably by Frank Galloway, though his name appears only once, as the arranger of the quadrilles, *Bonnie Dundee.* Piece number 17, *Yorkshire Waltzes* is the piece played by Black Dike at the 1856 Hull contest, indicating that at least the first 17 items in the books were written within a few months of the band's founding. Some may even be copies of pieces played by the Queenshead Band. The excerpts from *Il Trovatore* and *La Traviata* (items 37 and 40) could, of course, have been written later than the dates of the respective first London performances of the operas (1855 and 1856), though it is interesting to note that a selection from Verdi's *Il Trovatore* was the set test piece for the 1857 Belle Vue contest. Black Dike did not attend, but they could well have been playing their version of the selection at the same time. Two of the items – numbers 29 and 43 – were composed by Louis Antoine Jullien (1812-1860), a somewhat eccentric showman who conducted orchestras in London, Paris and New York, and who toured the North of England with a large professional wind band in 1858. Jullien's lighter pieces were quite popular in the late 1850s.

With five polkas, six waltzes (in addition to the *Yorkshire Waltzes*) and five sets of quadrilles,[4] it seems obvious that the band was regularly called upon to provide the music for dancing within the community of Queenshead, at local fêtes, and at some of the functions of churches and chapels in the district.

Three items, numbers 5, 18 and 27 in the book indicate a link with oratorio and the church, but the books are also littered with extracts from the operas of the Italian composers Bellini, Donizetti and Verdi – very much in the popular taste of the time, whilst the overtures by Mozart and Rossini were quite forward-looking for a brass band. The term 'Cavatina' generally refers to a single operatic aria, those in the Black Dike books are mainly short selections.

The band would not, in these early days, give concerts as such, but the operatic and oratorio excerpts would make useful showpieces, interspersed between the dances. These would also impress any members of the upper classes who happened to hear them – including members of the Foster family. They would be seen as 'improving' the minds of the members of the lower classes. Though I believe that the books would be completed by 1860 at the latest, they were probably used by the band at local functions well beyond that date.

For marching engagements the players would require smaller, single copies of the music. I have seen no evidence of the survival of any pieces in this category, but the part books would certainly not be of any use.

* * * * *

Thus, through contesting and other activities between 1855 and 1865, Black Dike Mills Band had established itself as one of the leading bands of the time. It was well to the fore in its instrumentation, had a settled personnel and good backing from a major textile company. It had reasonable access to main line railway

---

[9] The quadrilles were a set of five sequence dances, generally danced by four couples. They were the forerunners of the Lancers, still popular in 'old time' dancing.

stations and so was able to move around the country. It also seems to have been developing good relations in the community, continuing where its predecessor the Queenshead Band had left off.

During the period following the establishment of the band the village of Queenshead developed rapidly. In 1863 the area took its new name of 'Queensbury'.

CHAPTER 3

The Phineas Bower era

OF THE MANY legendary players who have been members of Black Dike Mills Band, Phineas Bower was one of the most outstanding. He was the principal euphonium player from 1867-74, at which point he also became bandmaster, holding this position until his retirement in 1895.

Phineas Bower, bandmaster 1874-1895

Phineas was born on 12 September 1846. His father, Isaac, was a violin maker and cellist, so it was not surprising that from the age of 12 Phineas took up the violin and at 16 was having lessons with a Bradford violin teacher.

In 1866, by which time he was 20, Phineas was advised by Greenwood Firth, Black Dike's solo trombonist, to take up a brass instrument. He obtained a tenor horn, had lessons from the then solo horn player, Jonas Smith and subsequently joined the band himself. Almost immediately, the solo euphonium player, John Taylor, fell ill.

It is interesting to note that both Greenwood Firth and John Taylor were in the band that played at Crystal Palace in 1860. Another member of this band, its solo cornet player William Rushworth, mentioned in Chapter 2, was now bandmaster and offered the euphonium position to Phineas. Abram Fawthrop, another member of the band, gave him free lessons.

His first public appearance on the euphonium was at a Leeds Labour Demonstration in 1867 and his first contest was at Hull in the following July. There were four more contests that year (1868), with wins at Todmorden and Blackpool, a 2nd prize at Skipton and a 3rd at Belle Vue. The Blackpool prize of £50 was the largest won so far. Jonas Smith, who had taught Phineas, won a Horn Solo contest held in conjunction with the Todmorden event. Even more significantly and, indeed, quite remarkably, Phineas won the special prize of a euphonium, valued at over £23, at Belle Vue. He presented it to Abram Fawthrop as a sign of his gratitude. This was the first of six instruments to be won by Phineas (some reports say five).

Another young man, Joe Naylor, who later became Black Dike's solo horn player, also had lessons with Fawthrop. It is difficult to get a clear picture of the type of person who became a member of Black Dike at this time and it was very useful to find a 'tribute' to Joe Naylor.[10] The article described him as 'the best tenor sax horn player in the world'. He was born in 1855 in Northowram, adjacent to Queenshead. When he was four years old the family moved into Queenshead and by the time he was eight Joe was working half-time at Black Dike Mills. As a boy and as a young man he sang in a chapel choir, from the age of 10 he played the concertina and later joined a local drum and fife band. He was, therefore, something of a musical enthusiast when, at the age of 14, he took up the tenor horn and joined Black Dike Juniors. In 1872 he succeeded Jonas Smith as Black Dike's solo horn player.

There was now an escalation in brass band contests and in 1869 Black Dike entered no less than 13. These brought the band three more 1st prizes, three 2nds, two 3rds and a 4th. But also, reflecting the quality of the band's soloists, William Jasper, 'a soprano player of great reputation', won three special prizes and Phineas Bower won his second euphonium.

Jasper succeeded Rushworth as bandmaster in 1870. He had played with a number of bands including, significantly, Leeds Model – conducted by Richard Smith, mentioned in Chapter 2 as conductor of the winning band in the 1856 Hull contest. Smith also dominated the Belle Vue contests from 1854 to 1857. However, Jasper had vacated the position within the year and there was no bandmaster at Black Dike for a time. Nevertheless, in 1871, the band

---

[10] This was in *Brass Band News*, September 1895.

attended three local contests before going to Belle Vue and recording its third victory there. The test piece was an arrangement by William Winterbottom, bandmaster of the Life Guards, of a selection from Rossini's opera, *The Barber of Seville.* The general consensus was that the piece was too easy for many of the bands and this was born out by the fact that five of them were recalled to the platform to play again. The 1st prize went ultimately to Black Dike, conducted by Samuel Longbottom. The band also won a B flat bass and Phineas won his third euphonium.

Jasper returned as bandmaster in 1872, remaining until 1874, when Phineas succeeded him. Inevitably this was a quiet period and no contests were undertaken in 1872. However, contesting was resumed in 1873, with five of them, including yet another controversial day at Belle Vue. The test piece this year was a selection from Meyerbeer's *Dinorah,* in the second of what were to be many arrangements by Lieutenant Charles Godfrey (Jnr), bandmaster of the Royal Horse Guards. Conducted again by Longbottom, Black Dike was awarded 3rd prize. There was also a gold medal for the band, a soprano cornet for Jasper and both a trombone and a euphonium for Phineas Bower. This caused a storm. Having played his own solo, Phineas put down his euphonium, picked up a valve trombone and played the trombone solo, earning the prizes for the best performances of both solos. The contest management requested that he give back one of them but, dour Yorkshireman that he was, he refused.

William Jasper, twice bandmaster

No one quite knew how this had been possible. Checks were constantly made as bandsmen mounted the platform to ensure that no-one had more than one instrument. How, then, could Phineas have had both a euphonium and a trombone? It was suggested several years later that one of the cornet players had hidden his own instrument in an overcoat pocket and carried on the valve trombone, which he then passed to Phineas. Sharp practice maybe, but they got away with it – on that occasion at least.

However, when the rules for the following year were published it was noted that the use of valve trombones was forbidden and that a band would be disqualified if any player performed on more than one instrument. Be that as it may, Phineas had now won four euphoniums and a valve trombone!

Incidentally, in this same year (1873), the size of the contesting band was increased. Hitherto, 19 had been the maximum number of players allowed. From now on, up to 24 could play, a figure that applied until the end of the Second World War.

In 1874, at the age of 28, Phineas Bower was asked by the members of the band to become bandmaster. The early seventies had been an unsettled period and stability was required, especially as the band's father figure and founding professional conductor, Samuel Longbottom, was nearing the end of his career. Phineas not only accepted the challenge, he agreed to become corresponding secretary and also continued as solo euphonium player when the professional conductor was around. Six contests were entered this year, but not Belle Vue. However, Phineas won euphonium number five at a contest in Pomona Gardens, Manchester – a rival of Belle Vue's.

Belle Vue was the only contest attended during 1875, but there was no prize, and this proved to be Samuel Longbottom's swan song with Black Dike. He had served as professional conductor for 19 years, during which time the band had won prizes to the value of £1,220, with a win at the 1860 Crystal Palace contest and three at the Belle Vue 'September'. He would be a difficult act to follow.

No contests were entered in 1876 – probably a year in which various people were considered for the post of professional conductor. In the following year the decision was taken and it was announced that Black Dike's new supremo was to be Joseph Fawcett.

* * * * *

Joseph Fawcett was a member of a well-known Yorkshire musical family. His father, Thomas, was a cottage weaver in the village of Horsforth. He played the cello and was also a singer and a conductor. Thomas had six sons, three of whom – including Joseph

– became trombonists. There were then 12 grandchildren – all of whom became talented instrumentalists.

Joseph was the second son of Thomas and as well as playing trombone he was conductor of the Little Horton Glee Union. As a trombonist he played with a number of local bands before joining the then celebrated Saltaire Band, which was funded by Sir Titus Salt in much the same way that Black Dike was funded by the Fosters. Richard Smith, whose influence has already been noted, conducted this band. Saltaire was placed second to Black Dike in the 1860 Crystal Palace contest, returning in 1861 to win. As a member of this band, therefore, Joseph Fawcett had experience of high-class band playing. Richard Smith who, incidentally, in 1857 founded the first ever brass band music publishing company, in Hull[11], must have inspired his development as a musician.

Though remaining at Black Dike for only a little over two years, Fawcett had quite an impact. He took the band to Belle Vue three times, picking up 2nd prize and Phineas's sixth euphonium in 1877; no major prize – but the trombone 'special' in 1878, and in the following year, winning 1st prize. During his term Black Dike attended 15 contests in addition to those at Belle Vue. These were rewarded with 13 prizes, including three firsts.

An innovation during this period was the introduction of a separate march contest at some events. The format was that all the bands played their march and then, after a short break, they all played the main test piece. Under Fawcett, in addition to the main prizes, Black Dike also won a 1st prize and three seconds in these march contests.

It will be recalled that, following the incident in 1873, valve trombones were not allowed at Belle Vue. Black Dike, like many other bands, had therefore to make changes in their trombone section. Furthermore, with the enlarged band, there were now generally three trombones – two tenors and one bass – all slide instruments. Phineas's son, Fred, had joined the band at around the same time as Phineas became bandmaster. He was to serve the band for many years, eventually becoming its solo trombone player.

For reasons now lost in the mists of time Joseph Fawcett resigned from the post of professional conductor of Black Dike in 1879. He

---

[11] This still operates as a leading publisher of band music, trading as R. Smith & Co. and based in Aylesbury.

was replaced by one of the most illustrious band conductors of all time, Alexander Owen.

* * * * *

Most leaders of the earliest wave of brass bands had their first experiences in music either through a military establishment or through touring – with an opera company, a travelling circus or a menagerie. Enderby Jackson toured with an opera company whilst Richard Smith had probably played in circus bands. By the 1870s there was a new generation of band trainers and conductors who had acquired much of their musical experience through brass bands. Fawcett was one such conductor; Owen was another.

Alexander the Great

Alexander Owen (1851-1920) was brought up in an orphanage[12] where he played in the school band. On leaving he was apprenticed, worked for a time at the Earl of Ellesmere's collieries at Worsley, and played in the Duke of Lancaster's Own Yeomanry Band. The bandmaster here was John Ellwood, a leading exponent of the slide trumpet. Though born in Lancaster, Ellwood worked professionally for a time in Leeds before settling in Manchester where he played in various orchestras, including the Hallé. He was bandmaster of a number of bands and also adjudicated at the Belle Vue contests of 1853 and 1854. He was, therefore, widely experienced in both orchestral and band music and must have had a considerable effect on the young Owen.

At the age of 16, Alexander (Alec) became the solo cornet player of Stalybridge Band before moving to Meltham Mills Band, near

[12] It was, in fact, the Manchester Union, Moral and Industrial Training School, known as the Swinton Industrial Schools. Many of the boys from this school became army band boys whilst others, including Alec Owen, joined local bands.

Huddersfield. Playing solo cornet here, he helped Meltham become the first band ever to perform the hat-trick[13] at Belle Vue. On completion of this the band was barred, by rule, from competing at Belle Vue for the next two years. A number of players now left Meltham and Owen, who had already been gaining conducting experience with a local band, would have had little hesitation in moving to Black Dike when offered the post of professional conductor there in 1880.

We are now into the era of 'The Great Triumvirate'. This was the group name of a trio of leading brass band conductors – John Gladney, Edwin Swift and Alexander Owen. Between them they directed most of the elite bands – as well as many others. In 1880, for example, of the eight bands that competed in the Belle Vue September contest, three were conducted by Gladney, three by Owen and the other two by Swift. In 1884 Gladney conducted Honley (placed 1st), Linthwaite (placed 4th) and Kingston Mills; Owen conducted Oldham Rifles (placed 2nd), Black Dike (placed 3rd), Besses o' th' Barn (placed 6th), and Trawden, Mossley and Bury, while Swift took Littleborough Public (placed 5th) and Todmorden Old. Three years later Gladney conducted five bands, Owen two and Swift three, again picking up all six prizes between them. This left seven other unplaced bands for the rest of the world's conductors!

The figures are typical of the times and indicate that these three (and others) really were professional brass band conductors. They made a comfortable living travelling from one band to another and further supplemented their earnings by adjudicating and by making special arrangements of contest pieces for their bands, generally full of difficult solo passages for the star players.

Looking specifically at Owen's Belle Vue connections: prior to his appointment at Black Dike he had played solo cornet with Meltham during their most successful period. He had also conducted Boarshurst Band in the 1879 contest – having to obtain special dispensation to play with one band and conduct another.

Black Dike, it will be recalled, had won the 'September' in 1879 under Fawcett, so were obviously in good form for their new professional conductor. Owen took full advantage of this by leading

---

[13] This term is used to denote that a band has won a particular contest three years in succession.

them to two further victories – in 1880 and 1881, thus giving them the coveted Belle Vue hat-trick. Of course, this also meant that they incurred the statutory two-year 'ban'.

However, Owen, having now won the contest twice with the mighty Black Dike proceeded, in 1882, to win with the un-fancied Clayton-le-Moors Band, located near Accrington. He thus completed a personal hat-trick and also proved that he could do well with one of the non-crack bands.

In 1884 Black Dike returned to Belle Vue to take third place. The contest this year was declared to be the most successful ever, with a crowd estimated at 100,000 in Belle Vue's grounds.

However, by 1885 the contest had reached breaking point. There was another 100,000 crowd, but there were also many more bands. In the previous year 42 bands had entered but only 19 actually played; this year 45 entered and a massive 32 competed. The contest lasted from 11 in the morning till 9.30 in the evening, and the later bands were said to be 'accompanied by noises from the fireworks display' – a regular late evening attraction at Belle Vue. The contest was held in a room 'crowded to suffocation' all day, with many bandsmen fainting.

Kingston Mills were the winners, conducted by John Gladney. Black Dike were unplaced. They were, of course, conducted by Alec Owen, who also conducted seven other bands, collecting the 3rd prize with Besses and the 4th with Oldham Rifles.

Shortly after the contest Owen wrote a letter to *Brass Band News*, criticizing the Belle Vue authorities on a number of counts. He was dissatisfied that Charles Godfrey was an adjudicator every year and that he had arranged all of the test pieces since 1872. Owen also said that the ventilation in the hall was totally inadequate and that far too many entries had been accepted, making the contest too long. He was so incensed that he vowed never again to conduct a band in the Belle Vue contest. There was a mixed reaction in the correspondence columns of the magazine, some writers agreeing whole-heartedly with Owen but others pointing out that he had not complained when his bands had won.

The authorities obviously took note of the criticisms. Though they remained steadfast regarding Godfrey's involvement they overhauled the ventilation system and, most significantly, took steps to limit the number of participating bands. From 1886 not more than 20 entries were to be accepted for the 'September'. To cater for the remainder, a new event was instigated – the 'July' contest, open only to bands that had not won any prize at Belle Vue during the previous four years. Thus, the forerunner of the present-day 'Grand Shield' contest first took place at Belle Vue in July 1886. Nineteen bands played and improvements to the hall's ventilation were noted. However, true to his word on this occasion, neither Owen nor his bands appeared in the following September.

In 1887 he relented and returned to Belle Vue, but with just two bands – Black Dike who won 2nd prize and a 5-valved euphonium, and Besses, placed third. The winners were Kingston Mills, completing their hat-trick under Gladney. An acceptable 17 bands competed this year, so Owen's tirade had had a marked effect.

This was, in fact, Owen's last Belle Vue with Black Dike. It will have been noticed that amongst his other successful bands the name Besses o' th' Barn keeps cropping up. This is the name of a village located just south of the town of Bury that is the home of the band. It has generally been known simply as 'Besses'. Owen became its professional conductor in 1884. Nothing unusual was read into this at the time but when, in July 1988, he resigned from Black Dike but remained with Besses, a certain bitterness developed between the two bands.

Owen's departure from Black Dike in July 1888 seems to have been quite sudden. He took the band to five contests during June and July, winning two of them. The rift appears to have begun at a contest in Boston (Lincolnshire). Owen was conducting both bands and would normally have played solo cornet with both. However, on this occasion there was a rule that meant that though he could conduct both bands, he could play with only one. This led to Owen playing solo cornet with neither, a fall-out between the two bands and his resignation from Black Dike. There were three contests in August – at which Black Dike was conducted by John Gladney. I have found no formal announcement of the changeover, just the following statement in *Brass Band News*:

> Our readers will notice in reading the reports of the Leeds Forge, Newcastle, and Kidsgrove contests that Mr. A. Owen has resigned his appointment as conductor of the famous Black Dyke[14] Mills Band, and has been succeeded by Mr. J. Gladney. What is the reason for this severance of a long and brilliantly successful companionship we do

[14] The new spelling now appears in some reports.

> not know nor care to inquire. We simply mention the fact as an item of news.[15]

This 'item of news' was not headlined and would have been easy to miss by any casual reader. Owen continued his work at Besses, remaining there until his death in 1920. Ironically, on one of the first meetings of the two bands under Gladney and Owen – in a contest at Barrow-in-Furness on 10 August 1888 – they tied for first place.

Of course, there were numerous contest appearances by Black Dike other than those at Belle Vue and I have assumed that Owen conducted at them all. Attendances at 84 have been identified during his seven and a half years in office. A number of them had an extra 'wing' – a march contest or a glee contest.[16] In the main events – usually selection contests – 33 first prizes were won, whilst 10 wins were recorded in march contests.

The 1882 commemorative jug

In 1882 a commemorative jug was issued. A number of these have been preserved and on them, painted by hand, is a full list of prizes won by Black Dike between 1856 and 1882. Why the jug was issued is not clear, but the total value of prizes won at the time was £2,011 9s. 0d. Perhaps it was to recognize that the total had passed the £2,000 mark.

The band travelled far and wide for its contest appearances – as far south as Clapham and as far north as Edinburgh, as far west as Liverpool and as far east as Lincoln. Top prize money varied between £25 and £40 – and this should be viewed

[15] *Brass Band News*, 1 August 1888, p. 3.

[16] A glee is a vocal composition in several sections. Unlike the madrigal, which was largely contrapuntal, the glee was of a more simple construction and generally harmonic in style.

in the context that an average weekly wage for most bandsmen was around £1.

The Belle Vue contest carried the true benchmark of achievement, but two other contests call for a mention. The first took place as part of the Edinburgh International Exhibition of 1886. Several high profile brass bands had played during the summer on the Exhibition's bandstand – including Black Dike, but the contest was not held until 23 October. It was hailed as 'The Championship of Great Britain'. Besses were the winners, Black Dike being placed second, both conducted by Alec Owen. The highly informative programme stated that Black Dike had won 13 prizes in glee contests for six instrumentalists.

The band's instrumentation at this time included three flugel horns – a preference of Owen, and the bass section comprised two bombardons (E flat basses), a B flat bombardon (the single bass) and a BB flat bass (the so-called 'double B'). These larger basses were only just filtering into brass bands. The solo players were listed as J. Riley (soprano cornet), A. Owen and W. Sharp (cornet), J. Naylor (tenor horn), J. Sykes (baritone), P. Bower (euphonium) and Sam Radcliffe (trombone). Phineas Bower was obviously still playing. There is a list of 70 pieces from the band's repertoire but few of the titles would be recognised by bandsmen of today.

A second high profile contest took place in 1887 as part of the Newcastle Exhibition. The Edinburgh results of the previous year were repeated.

* * * * *

John Gladney (1839-1911), Owen's successor at Black Dike and the 'elder statesman' of the brass band world at this time, was born in Belfast, son of a military bandmaster – also called John. Young John became proficient on the violin and piano and was competent on most instruments found in a military band. He eventually concentrated on the clarinet and in 1860, at the age of 21, joined the Hallé Orchestra, remaining there for 30 years.

He made his debut as a conductor at Belle Vue in 1871 with Burnley Volunteers, who picked up 5th prize under his direction. Shortly after this he was offered the position of 'professional bandmaster' at Meltham. It was here that he exploited his experience in the wider world of music, making Meltham into the

John Gladney, 'Father of the Brass Band'

finest band of the era and leading them in Belle Vue's first hat-trick (1876-77-78). Whilst at Meltham he established the instrumentation of the band, almost as it has remained to this day, earning for himself the title 'father of the brass band'.

Following the Meltham hat-trick Gladney became professional conductor of Besses (1879-83). In 1884 he led Honley[17] into first place at Belle Vue and by now was the professional conductor of Kingston Mills Band, based in Hyde, Cheshire. He completed a hat-trick with them in 1885-86-87 and thus came to Black Dike in 1888 literally 'at the top of the tree', with a brass band pedigree second to none

True to Belle Vue form, the 1888 'September' created more mayhem. Sixteen bands competed and as usual there were huge crowds in the Gardens. The contest was held in a large ballroom, said to be filled to capacity throughout the day, as bandsmen 'doffed hats and jackets to play'. The test piece was a selection from Wagner's *Flying Dutchman* arranged, as usual, by Charles Godfrey who was also one of the four adjudicators. The view was expressed that the playing was not up to the usual standard, 'because of a lack of understanding of Wagner'.

The top four prizes went to Yorkshire bands – the first to Wyke Temperance (Swift), the second to Black Dike (Gladney), the third to Todmorden (Swift) and the fourth to Wyke Old (Gladney). This did not please the largely Lancastrian crowd; their hero, Alec Owen,

---

[17] Honley is adjacent to Meltham and after Meltham's hat-trick several of its members joined Honley, contributing to the 1884 success. Honley's hey day was short-lived, however, its only later successes at Belle Vue being two 4th prizes and a 5th.

though taking five bands, secured only 5th and 6th prizes. According to the *Manchester Guardian*:

> That Besses-o'-th'-Barn Band was not awarded the first prize was a surprise to many – ourselves included; but that it should not even have been placed amongst the first six was inexplicable.

Another report stated that 'the judges were subjected to some hustling as they left the room'. Prior to that they were hissed and booed to the extent that Godfrey vowed never to judge in future contests where Yorkshire and Lancashire bands were involved. The Wars of the Roses were not yet over!

In 1889 it was the turn of Black Dike to be left out of the prizes. In fact, it was a poor year for Gladney, none of his four bands making a mark. The crowd was a massive 110,000 but there were no reports of trouble. Godfrey had arranged the test piece but was not on the panel of adjudicators. In fact, he did not judge again at Belle Vue for many years. In this year G. F. Birkinshaw was appointed principal cornet player of Black Dike to fill part of the gap left by the departure of Owen. Though the band went home from Belle Vue empty handed, Birkinshaw won the cornet 'special'.

The following year also seems to have passed off without major incident. Gladney had three bands, winning with Batley Old,[18] taking 4th prize with Black Dike and 6th with Kingston Mills.

However, 1891 was to be Black Dike's year once again, with its first win under John Gladney. They won in fine style, with a cash prize of £30, a euphonium, a cornet and a soprano cornet.[19] The band's 'secret weapon' this year was a newly acquired solo cornet player, the 17-year-old John Paley.

Black Dike did not score in 1892. This year saw rivals, Besses, achieving their first win under Alexander Owen.

1893 was Gladney's year but not Black Dike's. He directed Kingston Mills's winning performance but Black Dike had to be

---

[18] The Batley win created a new record for both band and conductor. Together they had also won the 1890 July contest. Batley Old now became the first band ever to win both the 'July' and the 'September' in the same year. The feat has been repeated only once, when Black Dyke's neighbours, Brighouse & Rastrick, achieved this particular 'double' in 1929.

[12] There was also an instrument called a 'doubleophone' – probably a two-belled euphonium.

satisfied with seventh place. No doubt they took comfort from the fact that Besses were placed eighth! However, Besses picked up their second Belle Vue win in 1894. Kingston Mills were second under Gladney, with Black Dike placed third. In 1895, the last year of Phineas Bower's bandmastership, Black Dike again won the September contest, Edwin Swift claiming 2nd prize with Wyke Temperance, whilst Alexander Owen took 3rd with Besses.

Away from Belle Vue, as has already been seen, Gladney led the band through the later contests of 1888. In these he and the band picked up three 1st prizes and a 2nd. The band now went through a relatively lean period in contests. Possibly there were a number of changes in personnel. It is even likely that Gladney himself wished to make changes. Whatever the reason, there now seems to have been a period of re-building. The tally of prizes won in 1889 was a mere three 2nds, a 4th and a 5th. The following year was even worse, with only one 2nd prize and two 3rds – one of which was at the Edinburgh Exhibition contest. In 1891 the band attended only Belle Vue, but with spectacular results, as was seen earlier. 1892 was a somewhat fallow year, with no reward at Belle Vue and only one other contest attended, with 2nd prizes won for both the selection and the march.

There was something of an upturn in 1893, both in terms of the number of contests entered and results. Nine contests were attended, earning four 1st prizes, two ties for first and second place, two 2nd prizes and a 4th. There were also two instrumental prizes and two 2nd prizes in march contests. At the Blackpool contest, in September, the 1st prize of £75 was the largest prize offered to date. At this event professionals were not allowed to play so Harry Bower (brother of Phineas) occupied the 'hot seat' and helped Black Dike secure the big prize.

In 1894 the band was again very active contest-wise, with 10 contests attended in addition to Belle Vue. The results were quite spectacular, with six 1st prizes, a tie for 1st, 2nd and 3rd, two 2nd prizes and a 3rd. There was also a 1st and a 2nd prize in March contests. Over £400 in cash was won this year, along with a large number of 'specials'. In the last full year during which Phineas Bower was bandmaster, in addition to winning Belle Vue, which also attracted a special prize of a euphonium, the band won three other 1st prizes, a 3rd and two 4ths.

* * * * *

Little has been written about Black Dike's early engagements but by 1880 concerts formed an integral part of the band's work, and successes on the contest platform led to an increased demand for concert work.

A number of events were reported which took place during the Owen-Gladney years. The first was a concert given in Queensbury celebrating the Belle Vue hat-trick. It took place in the local school hall in December 1881 and was the band's first public appearance wearing the gold medals presented for this achievement. Included in the programme was a solo played by Owen, described as 'remarkable for brilliant execution and clearness of tone'. Two of the Belle Vue test pieces from the hat-trick years were also played and, according to *Brass Band News*, 'the performance of these selections left nothing to be desired'.[20]

The year 1886 heralded the band's first appearances in extended engagements, up to a week in length. These took place in Edinburgh, Newcastle and Manchester. Performing at the Edinburgh International Exhibition (see above for details of the contest) it was claimed that the band performed 91 different pieces of music. It received magnificent ovations and at the end of one performance Alec Owen was 'chaired' to the park gates where Phineas was waiting with a cab. This was said to have been the first time a brass band had played in Edinburgh.

It was Silver Jubilee year in 1887. This proved to be a busy year, with 104 engagements including appearances at Exhibitions in Newcastle, Manchester and Saltaire. Then, in 1888, the band appeared for a week at the Glasgow Exhibition.

Things seem to have cooled off after these hectic years. Nevertheless, a typical year could be quite busy, and with the appearance of more indoor events the 'season' was lengthening. Certain engagements were subject to weather conditions and many took place mid-week. It is also good to note that, as still happens, the band was frequently helping to raise funds for various good causes. One local engagement was taking part in the opening of the Victoria Hall in Queensbury on 17 January. The official Programme of the opening ceremony states that:

> The Black Dike Mills Band will perform a selection of music in front of the Hall from 10.30 to 11.0 o' clock, at which hour the main door

[20] *Brass Band News*, January 1882.

> will be formally unlocked by Mr A. B. Foster, with a Silver Gilt Key, which will be handed to him by Miss Mary Foster. The party will then proceed to the platform of the Concert Hall.

Then followed a short religious ceremony with an address by the Bishop of Wakefield and choruses sung by a local choir. There was also the presentation of marble busts of the first John Foster and his eldest son, William, offered by the workpeople. The Hall was erected by the members of the Foster family 'as a place of assembly, instruction and recreation for the people of Queensbury'. There was a public hall – suitable for concerts and plays, a reading room and a library on the ground floor, with recreation rooms and a lecture room on the first floor. A separate entrance gave access to the swimming baths. The whole building is still intact, forming a kind of community centre for the residents of Queensbury.

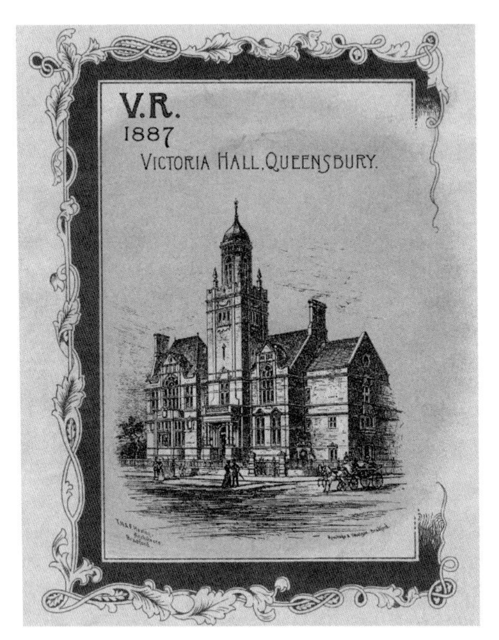

A rather special occasion occurred during January 1892. Not really an engagement, it was a celebration of the band's Belle Vue win the previous September. Following a parade through the streets of Queensbury the band assembled in the Stag's Head Inn for a dinner, provided by the Fosters. For the speeches and presentations that followed Colonel Foster, High Sheriff of Lancashire presided; other members of the Foster family supported him. Following the various speeches, Phineas Bower presented the instruments that had been won at Belle Vue to Colonel Foster. He, in turn, handed them back to the band for future use. It was stated that Black Dike had fulfilled over 60 engagements in the previous year and that there was every promise of a successful 1892 season.

Visits by the famous band could be quite colourful affairs, as may be seen from the following report:

> BLACK DYKE MILLS BAND – On Saturday afternoon, February 6th, the local bands at Hull paraded at the Corporation Pier to receive the above band, who were to give a series of concerts on behalf of the medical charities. Thousands of people assembled to hear the famous musicians, who were escorted to the Circus by the Railway Servants' Band, the Waterloo Band, and bands of the Holborn Street and Oxford Street Missions, the whole comprising 120 performers. ... On Sunday afternoon and evening free concerts were given, with a collection, and the building was packed on each occasion.[21]

Though the band remained busy throughout the succeeding years, it seems that much of the band's work was being undertaken locally. It continued to help with fund-raising for charity and for the benefit of other bands, and maintained its high status in all its music making.

One particularly interesting engagement during Phineas Bower's last year took place in Birmingham, in March. A report gives an outline of the programme – quite a heavy one, with selections from Berlioz's *Faust*, Spohr's *Last Judgement*, Wagner's *Lohengrin* and Rossini's *William Tell*. There were also Bellini and Schubert selections and Weber's overture, *Oberon*. The soloists were John Paley (cornet), Charles Jeffrey (trombone) and John Bailey (euphonium). There were two 'extravaganzas' – *A Hunting Scene* and *Derby Day*. These received a bad press as being unworthy choices for such a concert. Also in the concert were a piano soloist and a vocal quartet from Lichfield Cathedral. The band played to a large audience, many of whom had travelled on excursion trains.

Some high profile band members

The first in the line of illustrious solo cornet players at Black Dike was G. F. (Fred) Birkinshaw, first appointed in 1879. A native of Barnsley, George Frederick Birkinshaw was born in 1852 and commenced playing at the age of six. In 1862 the family moved to Leeds where Fred, still only 10, was playing professionally in theatre orchestras. After a short spell as bandmaster of a local band he joined Black Dike. When Alexander Owen moved from Meltham to Black Dike in 1880 Birkinshaw moved to Meltham to become their new solo cornet player. He remained there until 1883 after which he was engaged as solo cornet/conductor at Besses. This proved to be

[21] *Orchestral Times and Bandsman*, March 1892.

Black Dike Mills Band c. 1893; John Paley is in the middle of the back row

for one season only. He then conducted a number of local bands but returned to Black Dike periodically on short-term contracts.

The next star cornet soloist was Alexander Owen himself. He was with Black Dike from 1880 when, effectively, he changed places with Birkinshaw. As has been seen, he was at Black Dike until 1888, after which Birkinshaw returned for a time. Birkinshaw's career came to an abrupt end in 1896, however, when he contracted a brain disease and died, at the early age of 43.[22]

In 1891, as has already been seen, a 17-year-old young man became the band's new solo cornet player. His name – John Paley. He was born in 1874, son of Joseph Paley, bandmaster of Saltaire Band. Joseph, naturally enough, encouraged the boy and it is said that he could already play scales at the age of four – on a cornet mouthpiece! John's first public appearance came when he was six, playing *Home Sweet Home*. By the time he was 12 he was taking part in performances of *Messiah*, playing *The Trumpet Shall Sound*, and was also winning solo competitions. His initial stay at Black Dike was short-lived, as in February 1892, against his father's wishes, he sailed to America to join the world-famous band of Patrick Gilmore.

---

[22] Birkinshaw's death was reported in *Brass Band News* of March 1896. It was to his memory that William Rimmer composed the march, *Viva Birkinshaw*.

Tragically, Gilmore died in the September. Paley then returned to England and in 1893 rejoined Black Dike.

For most of the period covered in this chapter, Phineas Bower was Black Dike's solo euphonium player. His achievements in that capacity have already been seen. John Taylor had played solo euphonium from 1860 (possibly earlier) until 1866 and Phineas succeeded him in 1867. He remained as solo euphonium player until he was succeeded by John Bailey, who came to Black Dike from Leeds Forge in 1893, moving to South Wales four years later.[23]

Black Dike's first tenor trombone player was Greenwood Firth. He joined the band on its formation in 1855. If, as is likely, he initially played on a valve trombone, it is certain that from 1874 he would have learned to play the slide version. He remained a prominent member of Black Dike until 1879 when he was succeeded by Edwin Stead, one of three brothers who had formed the backbone of the Meltham Mills hat-trick band.[24] He came to Queensbury soon after the completion of Meltham's hat-trick and then participated in Black Dike's hat-trick – becoming the only person ever to be in the winning band at Belle Vue on six consecutive occasions – 1876-77-78-79-80 and 81.

It is not clear how long Stead remained with Black Dike, but Sam Radcliffe was named as solo trombone in 1886 and Charles Jeffrey took over the position in 1891. Jeffrey had a most interesting career. He was born in nearby Calverley in November 1856. His father was a violinist and young Charles took violin lessons from the age of seven. However, when he was nine he joined Calverley Band, playing soprano cornet. By the time he was 13 he was playing solo cornet with Bramley Band, but five years later moved to Saltaire, becoming 'second man' to Joseph Paley. Charles then moved to Keighley, where he conducted Marriner's Band.[25] After two years he returned to Saltaire to play baritone. He then took a 24-week professional engagement in Morecambe, playing the euphonium. Returning to Saltaire, he took up the trombone and became one of the finest exponents in the district. In 1891 he was invited to become Black Dike's solo trombone player – at the somewhat late age of 37.

---

[23] John Bailey was to become the highly respected conductor of the Cory Band in 1901.

[24] The other two were Wright Stead, soprano cornet and Richard Stead, solo euphonium, who later became a noted adjudicator.

[25] This was another quite famous band, though it never quite reached the top flight.

Black Dike was being well served by its solo cornet, euphonium and trombone players. These, traditionally, were known as the 'primary soloists'. The 'secondary soloists', on soprano cornet, flugel horn, solo tenor horn and 1st baritone also played an important part in the band's successes, and were frequently amongst the awards of medals and instruments.

Rivalry with Besses

Amongst the District Correspondents in *Brass Band News* – all writing under pseudonyms – the one for the Bolton District, writing as 'Trotter', was one of the most controversial and at the same time one of the most entertaining. Some of his comments were written in normal English but he often broke into a broad Lancashire dialect, adding to the fun. He was an avid Besses supporter, constantly extolling their virtues and highlighting their successes. He had many a dig at his opposite number, corresponding as 'Pondash',[26] who wrote for the Queensbury District. The digs and the responses were generally good-natured at first. For example, in May 1890 Trotter wrote:

> The Besses-o'-th'-Barn have done nothing special this month, in fact, there is no chance for them at contests, all being for young bands, such as the Dike (Down, Yorkshireman). However, they are waiting patiently until their turn comes.

Trotter's topic in August was more general, prodding about the advantages of sponsorship enjoyed by such bands as Black Dike, and the consequent disadvantages which bands such as Besses had to endure. A month later the topic was Alexander Owen *versus* John Gladney, Trotter maintaining that Owen's track record was better than that of Gladney and that Gladney had learned a great deal from Owen. In fact, both men had the greatest respect for each other but it was fashionable in the columns of *Brass Band News* to try to boost the reputation of a favourite personality. Thus, things were getting gradually more heated. In the September issue, Pondash gave his views on some of the points raised by Trotter, also commenting on

---

[26] According to Geoffrey Whiteley in *The Black Dyke Bugle* Issue 13, 'Pondash' was a former member of the band called Joe Wood (not to be confused with Joe Willie Wood of a later era). It seems that the term 'Pondasher' – taken to mean a fan of Black Dyke's – stems from this *nom de plume* (see page 1).

the poor manners shown by some Besses players after winning the Edinburgh contest. However, he tried to cool things, concluding:

> Hoping 'Trotter' will now draw the line, and shake hands, as I intend in the future to only write about my own district bands – hoping he will do the same and oblige a well-wisher of every bandsman, both in an out of the district of PONDASH.

This seems to have put an end to what would be seen today only as 'winding each other up'. However, the rivalry between the two bands themselves continued for some years, with challenges from the bands via their respective secretaries and also through various soloists. One letter from Phineas ended, 'You will get the biggest licking you ever had Trotter, and you've had a few'. Though the challenges never came to anything the wrangling went on and marred many of the reports about what were undoubtedly the two great bands of the era.[27]

* * * * *

After 29 years of devoted service Phineas Bower retired in February 1895, at the age of 54. He was presented with an inscribed gold watch and chain valued at £40, a further £40 in cash and various other items, during a concert given by the band. Two members of the Foster family were involved in the presentations. According to *Brass Band News* of March 1897, Phineas resigned from the band because he had been offered a more responsible job in the Mills. However, he undertook to continue his banding and for the next 11 years conducted Black Dike Juniors.

In a short speech Phineas revealed that during his time at Black Dike there had been a total of 125 different players in the band, which had attended 187 contests – winning 75 of them. There had been six 1st prizes and three 2nds at Belle Vue, and at the contest in Hawes, North Yorkshire, which the band attended first in 1881, out of nine contests the band had won seven. Phineas had dealt with all correspondence for the last 21 years, estimating that he handled

---

[27] Trotter continued his ramblings in *Brass Band News* for many years, always praising Besses and decrying other bands. He became something of a laughing stock for other district correspondents but I still see his comments as 'wind-ups' rather than malicious insults.

around 1,000 letters per year. In the article about Joe Naylor, referred to earlier, it was claimed that during his 23 years with the band it had undertaken 945 engagements, including four appearances before royalty. This reflects an incredibly busy time, during which, let it not be forgotten, the bandsmen had also to hold down their jobs in the mill.

Remarkably, during the Phineas Bower period, Black Dike won 50 instruments as special prizes, which included 15 cornets, 14 euphoniums, 10 trombones, five soprano cornets and two baritones – quite a haul. Phineas could look back with pride on 29 years in which his band had appeared in the top three at Belle Vue on 13 occasions, with five wins, four 2nds and four 3rd prizes.

* * * * *

Phineas Bower died on the morning of 1 May 1922, aged 75. Sadly, this was the day of his 50th Wedding Anniversary.

CHAPTER 4

The Harry Bower era

HARRY BOWER was a younger brother of Phineas. Both were natives of Queensbury and Harry commenced his playing career at the age of 10 as soprano cornet player in Black Dike Juniors. Abram Fawthrop, who had taught Phineas (see Chapter 3), was now bandmaster of the Juniors and he soon moved Harry on to the cornet, where he quickly progressed to the solo cornet position.

Harry Bower, bandmaster 1896-1911

He moved into the senior band in 1881 as the 3rd cornet player. A year later he had moved up to repiano and subsequently played assistant to both Birkinshaw and Paley. At a contest held in Blackpool in 1893, mentioned in Chapter 2, no professionals were allowed to play. Harry took over as the solo cornet player and helped the band to its lucrative 1st prize of £75.

On the retirement of Phineas Bower at the end of 1895, Harry became bandmaster. John Gladney was still the professional conductor. William Rimmer was the next professional, serving through the years 1908 and 1909. He was followed by Joseph Weston Nicholl, who was in office until 1911, the year of Harry Bower's retirement from the band.

* * * * *

The remaining years of the 1890s saw two more Belle Vue wins for Black Dike under Gladney, in 1896 and 1899.

In 1900 a new name appeared amongst the major prize-winning conductors, that of William Rimmer, who conducted Kingston Mills which came second to Black Dike. 1897 was potentially a hat-trick year for Black Dike but they were not in the prizes. Rimmer was there again, however, with a 2nd prize and a joint 4th. The 'September' results that year were highly controversial, with neither Black Dike nor Besses in the top six. Both bands refused to compete in 1898.

During the closing years of the century there was less co-operation from the railway companies and the crowds at Belle Vue were diminishing. In 1899 there was an estimated crowd of 60,000. Not bad, you might think, but it was well below the 100,000 mark, achieved and even exceeded in earlier years. This was a good year for Gladney, who led Black Dike into first place and Hucknall Temperance into second. Rimmer picked up only a 4th prize on this occasion, but by conducting four bands in the contest he was joining the 'big guns' in the popularity stakes.

Success in other contests continued to come Black Dike's way in a period when there were regularly over 200 contests per year in England, Scotland and Wales. In addition to the Belle Vue 1st prize in 1896 the band won seven other 1st prizes and tied for a joint 1st – out of eight contests – virtually a 100% success rate. The six contests of 1897 brought five 1st prizes and a 2nd. The 2nd prize was won at a much publicized but not very successful event called the 'Victorian Era Exhibition Contest', held at Earl's Court, London. This ended a remarkable sequence: from 20 contests attended between 5 August 1895 and 28 August 1897, including those at Belle Vue, the band had won 19 – including 16 in successive contests, though in two of the wins they shared 1st and 2nd prizes. 1898 was a quiet year, the band attending only three contests.

'Normal service' was resumed in 1899, however, with a 1st prize and two cornets won at the New Brighton Tower contest, a field day at Belle Vue, with a cornet, a trombone and a B flat bass in addition to the 1st prize. There was then a 3rd prize and a cornet at Leicester. The New Brighton contest, held during the Whitsuntide weekend, was to become an important event in the brass band calendar. Its Musical Director was Granville (later Sir Granville) Bantock, a composer who in future years had a major influence on brass band repertoire.

* * * * *

Reports of concert engagements were quite spasmodic but it was reported that in June 1896 there were 23, with a further 28 in July. There were 12 engagements between 2 and 18 August. On completing an engagement at Elland Flower Show on the 18th the bandsmen boarded a midnight train to London *en route* to a contest in Bournemouth. After winning the 1st prize of £50 they were engaged to give an evening concert. They arrived back home on the 20th and completed six more engagements before the end of the month. The band was now travelling further afield and engagements included visits to Derby, Leeds, Ripon and West Bromwich, as well as the Bournemouth trip. Later in the year an advertisement read:

> Black Dyke Prize Band (The Champion Band of England) will play two hours' concert programme, Albert Hall, Sheffield, Saturday, November 7, commence at eight. Cheap trains from all parts.

Concerts such as this were obviously big events, drawing audiences from far and wide.

1897 was Queen Victoria's Diamond Jubilee year and proved to be a very busy year for the band, with no fewer than 135 days on which it was playing – including Christmas Eve and Christmas Day. Appendix B gives a list of engagements. The disposition of the dates suggests that time off work for band engagements was no problem. The most substantial engagements were: Liverpool – a full week being spent at Aintree as part of the Diamond Jubilee celebrations, and Glasgow – with two concerts per day for a week. There was also a five-day engagement in Bridlington and three days at a Leicester Exhibition. There were a number of additional overnight engagements, for example, 20 March in Bedford and 21 in Luton, then 22 November in Liverpool and 23 in Birkenhead. One of the more interesting 'single' engagements was that in Halifax on 17 June, when Black Dike 'opened' a new bandstand in People's Park before an estimated audience of 10,000.

In Chapter 3 there was comment about the writings of one 'Pondash'. This pseudonym spawned a small group of writers who periodically informed *Brass Band News* about the band's activities. The official correspondent for Queensbury District continued to appear for some time as 'Pondash', but articles also appeared by 'Pondasher', 'An Old Pondasher' and even one by 'Junior Pondasher'. Nevertheless, news appeared only spasmodically and it is impossible to gain a clear picture of what the band was up to, despite occasional mentions in 'Hebden Bridge', 'Bradford' and 'West Riding' notes.

Amongst the 1898 'dates' there was a day at Birmingham Town Hall, with two large audiences and with the hall for the evening concert 'full to the brim'. In September there were a few more days in Bridlington. Here, praise was very high, with the noted soloists being John Paley and Charles Jeffrey. November saw Black Dyke in Bristol where they were met at the station by three bands and paraded to the Drill Hall. Reports told of marvellous playing but only moderate audiences. The band gave two concerts on Saturday, two on Sunday and one on Monday.

In the November *Brass Band News* it was claimed that Black Dike had completed a staggering 150 engagements during 1898 – even breaking the record of the Diamond Jubilee year. With this level of activity contests were inevitably taking a back seat. A comment in *Brass Band News* of March 1899 seems to underline this: 'This famous band is still running its prosperous course, and as a concert band becomes more and more popular'.

New uniforms were provided for the band this year. It was noted that the Fosters were commanding officers and 'liberal supporters' of the 2nd West Yorkshire Volunteer Artillery. The new uniforms were in the style of the Artillery Regiment and the bandmaster was given a military-style frock coat.

* * * * *

Moving into the 20th century, a new major contest was now instituted – The National Brass Band Championships. This was organised by the Bristol-born businessman, John Henry Iles (1871-1951). He had been present at the 1898 Belle Vue September contest. Even with the absence of the two banding giants (Black Dike and Besses) he was very impressed with what he saw and heard, just as Enderby Jackson had been at Burton Constable in 1845. In a similar manner, Iles threw himself wholeheartedly into fighting the cause of these working class musicians. He became the proprietor of *British Bandsman* and made himself Editor-in-Chief. He also took over the music-publishing firm of R. Smith & Co, and became president of the London and Home Counties Brass Band Association. He then organized a concert in the Royal Albert Hall (The 'Absent-minded Beggar Concert', to be discussed later), with the support of the highly influential Sir Arthur Sullivan, Britain's most successul composer of the time. This was the catalyst that led to the founding of the 'Nationals', the first of which took place in 1900 at the Crystal Palace in South East London.

The Nationals took a little while to settle down but after one or two changes they took their place alongside the Belle Vue September contest, both of them attracting high profile bands. One of the principal attractions of the Crystal Palace contest was the trophy – said to be worth 1,000 guineas – which went with the 1st prize. There were three sections in 1900, with 15 bands in the highest, including Black Dike and Besses. The test piece was a shrewdly chosen selection called *Beauties of Sullivan* - arranged specially for the occasion. One of Alec Owen's lesser bands, Denton Original, were the winners, with Black Dike in second place. This result was not well received by the crowd, but Black Dike were said to have accepted it gracefully. The Nationals were held in July and history almost repeated itself in September at Belle Vue. Here, however, John Gladney took the first two places, winning with Lindley Band, from Huddersfield, with Black Dike again in the runner-up position.

Though the number of contests held reached 250 per year during the early part of the new century, in 1900 Black Dike entered only one other contest, that at New Brighton.

The only contests entered in 1901 were at New Brighton and Knaresboro, where the prizes gained were a 3rd and a 2nd. Black

Crystal Palace – the first home of the National Championships

Dike did not compete at Crystal Palace this year due to an engagement at the Glasgow International Exhibition.

There was now to be a change of solo cornet player. John Paley, who had served the band well since his return from America in 1893, severed his connection towards the end of 1901 in order to concentrate on conducting. His successor, Ceres Jackson joined the band fairly soon after this, winning a cornet prize in May 1902.

Ceres Jackson with a Bach trumpet

Little is known about Ceres, but as well as being a fine cornet player he was in demand as an orchestral trumpet player, especially for his performances of *The Trumpet Shall Sound* (from Handel's *Messiah*). He was formerly a member of Bramley Old Band and it is thought that when he left Black Dyke – around 1909, he moved to London.[28]

1902 saw another upturn in the band's fortunes, with a win at Nottingham in May – including medals for three soloists: Ceres Jackson, Harry Charnock (tenor horn) and Fred Bower. He was the son of Phineas and was now playing solo trombone after the departure of Charles Jeffrey at about the same time as Paley – and for the same reason. Black Dike then made history by winning both the September and the Nationals – the first such 'double'. Amongst the special prizes won this year were a solid silver cornet, presented at Belle Vue and valued at £63 and a gold-plated cornet, won at Crystal Palace. Awarding the maximum 140 points here, the adjudicators wrote, 'Criticism is out of the question'. The band won £40 and the right to hold the 1,000 Guinea Trophy for a year. 80,000 people were said to have attended the contest. The only other competition entered this year was the one known as the Preston Guild Contest, which took place the day following the Belle Vue

[28] There are some quite humorous anecdotes about Ceres Jackson in Arthur Taylor's book *Labour and Love. Brass Band News* of March 1931 reported that he had died in Leeds Infirmary following an accident in which he was knocked down by a motor car.

Double Champions, 1902. Ceres is to the left of the trophy and John Gladney is on the back row wearing a top hat

September contest. It was held only once every 20 years, to coincide with a local festival. Here, a 1st prize of £40 was added to the 'double'.[29]

It was again noted in *Brass Band News* that whereas leading bands used to play at contests almost every Saturday in the 'season', most were now content to attend just two or three per year.

In 1903 only the two major contests were entered, resulting in a 2nd prize in Manchester and a 3rd in London. The years 1904 and 1905 saw Black Dyke winning and then coming second at the Belle Vue contests but coming out of London with just one 6th prize (in 1904). Neither contest was entered in 1906 because the band was touring Canada and North America.

However, 1905 was the year in which William Rimmer began his remarkable feat of five successive personal doubles. In this year he led Irwell Springs to victory in both contests, repeating this in both 1906 and 1907 with Wingates Temperance – through which they became the first band to achieve a 'double-double'. In 1908 Rimmer directed Black Dyke's winning performance in the Nationals and Irwell Springs' at Belle Vue. A year later he did the same again – with Foden's and Shaw.

---

[29] 1902 was the Jubilee year of Belle Vue itself, so extra prizes were awarded.

'Mr. Rimmer' a highly respected gentleman

Meanwhile, in 1907 John Gladney conducted Black Dyke for the last time. There was no prize at London, but at Belle Vue it was placed second to Wingates, under Rimmer.

To no-one's surprise Rimmer was appointed as Gladney's successor at Black Dyke. William Rimmer (1861-1936) was one of the most versatile of all brass band conductors and was part of a great 'banding' family. His father, Thomas, conducted Southport Rifles for over 20 years. William had a brother, Robert, who became a noted brass band personality and Robert's son, Drake Rimmer, also became a well-known conductor, adjudicator, composer and arranger. William began taking piano lessons when he was nine, but his introduction to bands came some years later, when he became a drummer in his father's band. He then took up the cornet, playing under his father and also under Henry Round, co-founder of Wright & Round – an early pioneer of the brass band. Amongst bands with which he played later were Kingston Mills and Besses, becoming solo cornet player with the latter for a short time. He became musical editor of the *Cornet Band Journal* (published by F. Richardson) in 1897, followed several years later by similar positions with R. Smith & Co and then Wright & Round. An article about him, written in 1899, described him as 'a prolific composer, conductor, editor, judge, and, above all, a teacher of rare ability'.[30] He came to the fore as conductor of Wingates Temperance Band, which he conducted for some 20 years.

Concert engagements from 1900

The year 1900 signalled a new era for brass bands, not only with the founding of the National Championships, but with a series of high

[30] *British Bandsman*, 1 September, 1899.

profile concerts and concert tours, including reciprocal overseas visits, some organised through the influence of J. H. Iles.

The first major event was a concert in the Royal Albert Hall, London, featuring 10 brass bands from many parts of Britain and including Black Dike. The Boer War was at its height and there were many casualties on both sides. Amongst the charities set up to alleviate the sufferings of British soldiers and their dependants was the *Daily Mail* Kipling Fund. Iles associated himself with this by organising the Albert Hall concert. Sir Arthur Sullivan had composed a song called *The Absent-Minded Beggar*, using words by Rudyard Kipling. The proceeds of the song were donated to the Kipling Fund and Iles approached Sir Arthur, persuading him to allow a march to be written using the *Absent-Minded Beggar* tune. The march would be performed by the massed bands in the Albert Hall concert – conducted by Sullivan himself. The concert became known as 'The Absent-Minded Beggar Concert' and Sullivan's involvement virtually guaranteed its success. It also brought brass bands to the attention of many people who had not previously associated them with what they saw as the real world of music. The concert and the participating bands also benefited from a massive advertising campaign, paving the way for Iles to institute the National Championships later in the year.

The concert was a huge success. Each band contributed an item – Black Dike playing Gladney's selection from Mendelssohn's *Elijah*. The 10 bands combined under Sullivan's baton to play *The Absent-Minded Beggar March*, Sullivan's most famous Hymn *Onward Christian Soldiers* and an arrangement of *God Save the Queen*, incorporating *Rule Britannia*.

The concert received substantial press coverage. There was a huge audience – estimated at 10,000 by the *Daily Mail* (but at 6,000 by other newspapers). The soloists included a rather young Clara Butt and the concert raised between two and three thousand pounds for the charity. Even more important historically, it brought Britain's brass bands to the capital and placed them in a concert situation such as no one had previously envisaged.

Iles's next project was to re-create what he had seen and heard in Manchester in 1898. Having got Sullivan on his side, he enlisted his support in the founding of the Championships – not least in obtaining permission to use the 1,000 Guinea Trophy – at the time lying dormant in the Crystal Palace vaults after having previously been used in a male voice choir contest. Sir Arthur was a director of the Crystal Palace Company so his assistance was crucial.[31] Though Black Dike were less successful in the London contests than at those held in Manchester, they were regularly in the prizes and also often appeared in the evening massed band concert which followed the Championships.

Following the Absent-Minded Beggar Concert in January, 1900 appears to have been another busy year for Black Dyke, with full week engagements in Morecambe and Birmingham and almost every day filled to the end of August.

1901 saw the death and funeral of Queen Victoria and Black Dike spending a week at the Glasgow International Exhibition. The following year was Coronation Year, creating extra engagements for all bands. It was also noted that:

> When Black Dyke were winning 1st prizes all over the country from 1876 onward, they had very few engagements. But at present they are practically engaged every day in June, July and August.[32]

Amongst Black Dike's 1903 engagements was a tour of South Wales and the West Country and another week in Birmingham. There were also many more routine engagements. Also during this year, Black Dike Mills Band made its first gramophone records, amongst the earliest known by a brass band. Five were issued on single-sided 7-inch discs and a remarkable 20 on single-sided 12-inch discs. These appear to have been recorded between 6 and 8 August. There were also 15 Edison Bell wax cylinders. It is not clear when these were recorded but they were issued in 1905. No further recordings were made until 1923.[33]

Tragedy struck early in 1904. There was a weekend in Lancashire, with a Saturday concert in Accrington and two Sunday concerts in Preston. Following the Preston evening concert the bandsmen boarded a train for Glasgow, where a week's engagement was booked. Inexplicably, one fell from the train and was killed instantly. He was a cornet player, Hartley Scott, who had been in the band for 25 years.

---

[31] The timing of Iles was impeccable, as Sullivan died on 22 November 1900.

[32] *Brass Band News* July 1902, page 5.

[33] For details see *Brass Band Cylinder & Non-microgroove Disc Recordings* by Frank Andrews.

There were several changes in personnel at this time. A comment in the October *Brass Band News* reported that Black Dike was now a 'young band – with several new faces'. It was claimed that 11 of the members had been trained by Phineas Bower in the Junior Band.

The routine continued throughout 1905 and into 1906, but then came news of the band's first overseas tour.

The tour of Canada and America

The information given below comes mainly from two of the bandsmen's diaries, now held in the band's archive.

In 1906 Black Dike Mills Band undertook what was its most adventurous project up to that time. They left Bradford on the 11.10am train on Friday, 29 June, arriving back there at 11.50am on 24 November, having travelled over 12,500 miles at a time when exceeding 30 miles per hour was almost the equivalent of breaking the sound barrier these days! Foster's provided new uniforms and the band gave over 200 concerts.

Travelling from Bradford to Liverpool, the bandsmen embarked on the 'Empress of Ireland', making her maiden voyage. Crossing the Atlantic took eight days, during which time the bandsmen experienced much bad weather – thick fog and heavy swells on the sea, with waves 'like mountains'. Arriving in Quebec at 5am on 7 July the band played a few tunes before bidding farewell to the captain and officers of the ship. They had also played before leaving Queensbury, again outside the railway station in Bradford, and had given concerts on board ship, raising money for the Liverpool Seamen's Orphanage.

They disembarked at 9am and by late evening had given two concerts to audiences consisting mainly of French-Canadians. Playing their Selection from *Faust* by the French composer Berlioz evoked great enthusiasm from the audience, but when the band played *La Marseillaise* their listeners went wild. They were also given a banquet by the local Yorkshire Society, at which everyone spoke in a broad Yorkshire dialect.

The next city was Montreal, where the band was based for a week. Following two concerts on the final Saturday they travelled all night, by train, to Toronto – a distance of 340 miles. There were two concerts per day here and an extract from the Toronto *Mail and Empire* gives an idea of the response to the band:

> The band is well balanced and the tone is excellent. The most meritorious part of the band was the bass section, the tone being full and smooth and pleasing. The cornet players are worthy of high commendation. ... The audience showed a distinct appreciation of the classical nature of the programme.

Leaving Toronto, they visited the town of Galt, remaining there for three days. The following are extracts from a local newspaper report:

> A reception and hearing, enthusiastic in the highest degree, was given by the people of Galt to the famous Black Dike Band in Dickson Park last night. ... The playing was a revelation to the great majority of the people. It is undoubtedly one of the best bands which has favoured Galt with a visit, if not the best. ... When occasion desired the band could play with extreme softness and delicacy of tone, but in the stronger passages they were not found wanting. The band is not addicted to rag time music.

There now followed several days during which the bandsmen were literally living out of their suitcases, performing what would today be called one-night stands.

They had a number of interesting experiences on this first leg of the tour. They had, for example, made contact with a number of Yorkshire Societies and had seen, for the first time, a crematorium. Whilst in Montreal they discovered that there were no burials during the winter as the ground was too hard to dig. There was a 'dead house', with shelves able to hold 1,000 coffins.[34]

In Toronto, concerts were given on an island on the lake, with audiences of up to 20,000 people, most of whom had crossed to the island on large ferryboats. During one of the concerts a heavy storm blew up, with thunder and lightning. Through an electrical fault a fire broke out in one of the stands. Mr Gladney kept the band playing and this had a calming effect on the crowd, helping avert what could have been a disaster.

The band left Canada at Midnight on Saturday 28 July, bound for Detroit in USA for the second leg of the tour. The train crossed the border in the middle of the night and they were now in the state of Indiana, arriving in Muncie at 7.15 the following evening. They were very tired after a long and tedious journey of nearly 300 miles.

---

[34] This still applies in these northerly regions.

There were plenty of coloured people here and all the staff in the hotel where the band stayed were negroes. In some of the towns coloured people were not allowed to go to the band concerts. The impression given by the diarists is that they felt less comfortable here than in Canada which was, of course, one of the Dominions, and where a large part of the population were recent British immigrants. It was also now much hotter and the bandsmen wore white coats for their concerts.

Moving further south, the next state visited was Kentucky. In some towns here there was tension between whites and blacks, it being less than 50 years since the abolition of slavery. Public hangings still took place and though the bandsmen didn't actually see one they saw the gallows. Policemen were armed with revolvers. In one town a registrar came to the hotel where the band was staying, to perform a marriage. The ceremony lasted less than two minutes and there was no wedding ring. The bandsmen were not impressed.

Concerts continued as the band moved around Kentucky and Indiana. Most places were visited for only one or two days and it was luxury to have five days in Evansville, reached by boat on the River Ohio. The band also stayed for five days in Toledo.

Travelling north, they arrived in Buffalo (New York). On the following day the bandsmen were back in Canada for the third leg of

The bandsmen in oilskins at Niagara Falls

the tour. Crossing the border once again, they had their first sight of the Niagara Falls. Many of the bandsmen had the unforgettable experience of donning oilskins and going under the Falls. They now arrived in Hamilton, on the shores of Lake Ontario and known as the 'Birmingham of Canada'.

There were several more one-night stands before they arrived in Ottawa, Canada's capital. Here they encountered the first of several quirks in the drinking laws. All the saloon bars were closed from 7pm on Saturday until Monday morning. However, it was possible to cross the river into Quebec and drink all day and all night – if you so desired.

Three days were spent in Ottawa before the band moved back into America, passing through the states of Vermont and Massachusetts, and visiting Rhode Island. The next main centre was Boston – then the third largest city in America. There was an overhead railway round the city and some of the bandsmen commented on a resemblance with Liverpool – except for an absence of public houses! There was also a fairly strong Salvation Army presence, which has survived to this day.

There were now more one-night stands. As the 'fall' was approaching, there were beautiful colours on the trees. In the town of Lawrence there was a British Club which offered hospitality to the band in the form of a 'good Yorkshire dinner'. Other places visited included Gloucester, an old fishing town known as 'the Grimsby of America'. It was the closest point to England and was the place where the first Trans-Atlantic cable was laid. In Lewiston, Maine, an illegal barrel of beer was provided for the bandsmen, labelled 'Apples'. In Augusta, the capital, they saw a house being moved – fully furnished. Tree branches and even telephone lines were cut to facilitate the removal. A concert in nearby Marlboro was advertised as follows:

JOHN FOSTER & SON, Ltd
World Renowned Black Dike Mills Band
From Queensbury, North Bradford, Yorkshire, England
First American and Canadian Tour
Conductor - John Gladney
Asst. Conductor - Harry Bower
Absolutely the Finest Brass Band in the World
Winners of the Great National Challenge Trophy and over $60,000 in prizes

Holders of 23 Challenge Cups, 100 First Prizes
And 400 Other Prizes Including 500 Gold Medals
'Simply Magnificent. They Excel any Band I Ever Heard' - Sir Arthur Sullivan
Endorsed by John Philip Sousa, Creatore, Sir Alexander Mackenzie.

The band moved back into Massachusetts now, where the winter was setting in. There was much interest in the town of Worcester where a man who had served his apprenticeship at Black Dike owned the Queensbury Mills.[35] The following is taken from a local report on the Worcester concert:

> The audience was exceedingly enthusiastic and every selection was greeted by long continuous applause. ... The work of Ceres Jackson, the cornetist, deserves more than a passing mention. A selection by Damare gave him ample opportunity to display his ability in bringing out the clear, sweetened tone of this instrument.

Crossing the border into Canada for the last time the band now faced a 16-hour journey covering 560 miles. Back in Toronto some of the bandsmen saw a show given by the famous American escapologist Houdini, then at the height of his fame. Six days were spent here and after two further days in Montreal the band returned to Quebec, where there was deep snow and the streets were filled with sleighs.

Friday, 16 November was the band's final day in Canada. The bandsmen embarked at 11.30am and because not many passengers were travelling they enjoyed the luxury of first class cabins.

The return journey also took eight days. Again there was bad weather but as on the outward voyage there were concerts on board. Concerts on the two journeys raised over £52 for the Seamen's Orphanage. On 24 November the ship was tugged up the River Mersey as daylight was breaking. Black Dike Mills Band was back in England.

There seem to be no records regarding the financing of the tour except for part of a contract which has survived. This was an agreement between John Foster & Son Ltd and one of the band members, Thomas Scatliff,[36] a soprano cornet player. His

---

[35] The Queensbury Mills were established in 1900. They produced mohair and worsted yarns – like their counterparts in Yorkshire, and employed over 500 operatives.

[36] Thomas Scatliff died in 1944.

remuneration was to be £2 per week, paid by the Company. Fifteen shillings would be paid to the player and the balance paid directly to his wife. Presumably similar contracts had been agreed with other band members; by this method of payment the Company was ensuring the well-being of families whilst their menfolk were on tour.

Scatliff was required to pay £25 to the Company 'as security for the observance by him of his duties and obligations ...' There was also a clause in the agreement stipulating that a bonus would be paid in the event of a profit being made on the tour. If it resulted in a loss, however, a proportion of the £25 would be retained. The cost of the tour must have been enormous but one assumes that concert fees and collections would be returned to the Company in return for payment of the men's wages. Whether the tour made a profit or a loss we shall probably never know.

* * * * *

Back from the tour, Black Dyke was quickly into its round of concerts. Included amongst those in the latter part of 1907 were two in St George's Hall, Bradford. There were also two in Halifax, given 'as a complimentary benefit' for the tour manager, a Mr Henry Drake.

Through an interview with Harry Bower it was learned that there had been an offer of a lucrative 12-week return tour in the USA but this was turned down because of engagements already booked for 1908. These included numerous local 'dates', plus engagements in Birmingham, Coventry and Goole, and a tour in the West and South of England between 5 and 24 August. This looked like being the busiest season ever. Following much speculation, Black Dyke attended a contest in Bradford and for the second year running won the Lord Masham Cup. After claiming 2nd prize at Belle Vue there was an English tour lasting from 1 October to 6 November.

* * * * *

In January 1908 the Halifax District correspondent of *Brass Band News* casually announced that John Gladney had 'severed his connection with Black Dyke after 19 years'.[37] This was even more

[37] John Gladney died three years later.

low-key than the announcement of Alec Owen's departure in 1888, with no mention of it editorially. There were rumours that William Rimmer was likely to be his successor and in fact, by mid-January he was already taking rehearsals. The Halifax correspondent added:

> Mr Rimmer's easy way of explaining away all the difficulties has been a revelation to Black Dyke. I do not wish to speak at all disparagingly of Mr Rimmer's predecessor, as he has been a good man for Dyke, but, of course, it takes young ones to beat old ones.

In fact, Gladney was now 67 years old and Rimmer 46 – really in his prime and the first of the new generation that was to take over from the Triumvirate.

There was also now a change of policy as Black Dyke resolved to attend as many contests as its engagement schedule would permit. This may well have been a condition of Rimmer's appointment. Nevertheless, the 1908 diary included a fortnight in Edinburgh, a week in London and a further two-week tour in an unspecified area.

The band's concert repertoire was also undergoing a revision, with some of Rimmer's latest arrangements being used. These included a selection of music by *Tchaikovsky* and Rimmer's classic arrangement of Liszt's *Hungarian Rhapsody No. 2*.

There was much speculation about Black Dyke attending the New Brighton contest, with challenges thrown out by the band's supporters to its major rivals, including Besses and Wyke Temperance. In the event, Irwell Springs were the winners, with Black Dyke second – both bands conducted by Rimmer. By August, however, four other contests had been attended and duly won. Most of August this year was spent in Scotland – 10-23 in Edinburgh and then visiting other Scottish towns until the 31st.

Belle Vue was revenge day, with a win for Black Dyke and 6th prize for Irwell Springs. However, 'Springs' had the last laugh. The Crystal Palace contest was a triumph for Rimmer, who took 1st prize with Irwell Springs, 3rd with Wingates, 4th with Shaw but a lowly 5th with Black Dyke.

By the end of 1908 Harry Bower claimed to have conducted Black Dyke on 1,000 engagements and also in four contests, on each occasion winning 1st prize. He was also now accepting adjudicating appointments, was a tenor singer and was at one time choirmaster at the Old Dolphin Chapel.

The contest policy was to continue in 1909, with as many as possible entered in the next season subject, of course, to availability. A minor bombshell was dropped when, in November, Louis Allison,[38] who had played second man to Ceres Jackson since the start of the Tour, announced that Jackson had now left Black Dyke and that he, Louis Allison, was to take his place. However, in January 1910 the Hebden Bridge correspondent revealed that Allison had signed up for a year with Lee Mount band.

The band world was rocked even more at the beginning of 1910 with the news that William Rimmer was to retire from contest conducting. This was in order that he could take up a full time conducting appointment with the Southport Municipal Band. He would be available to coach bands 'out of season' but that was of little use to major bands such as Black Dyke.

Weston Nicholl, a fine musician

It was announced in March that Joseph Weston Nicholl (1876-1925) was to take over. Weston Nicholl, as he is generally referred to, was unknown in the brass band world but was a first class organist and also an orchestral conductor. He hailed from Halifax but had studied the organ in Europe with two leading 19th century organists - Rheinberger in Munich and Guilmant in Paris.

There were other changes in personnel at this time, with the loss of a euphonium player and a member of the horn section. Louis Allison had gone but Ceres Jackson returned, whilst Willie Wood moved from flugel to become Jackson's assistant.

Several contests were entered in 1910, with Weston Nicholl conducting. The only win, however, was in Hull, with no prizes at either Belle Vue or Crystal Palace. Black Dyke's rivals now included

---

[38] Allison had played soprano cornet with Kingston Mills at the tender age of 13 and had then played cornet with Wingates for some years.

the up-and-coming Foden's, as well as the established Wingates Temperance and Irwell Springs. Engagements continued to come the band's way, and were generally conducted by Harry Bower.

1911 was Coronation year. Black Dyke were undoubtedly at a low ebb at the start of the year but by February all the empty places had been filled and with three rehearsals per week there was optimism that the worst was over. New Weston Nicholl transcriptions were finding their way into the band's programmes.

In an excellent article about brass bands,[39] Professor Dave Russell compares three programmes played in Huddersfield's Greenhead Park. The first was played by Black Dyke in June 1901, the second by the same band in June 1911 and the third by Linthwaite in August 1911. These are reproduced in Appendix C, from which it will easily be seen that the June 1911 programme played by Black Dyke has far more musical interest than the other two. This was, of course, due to the influence of Weston Nicholl.

There was no denying, however, that in terms of popularity and contest successes, the band had slipped well down the proverbial greasy pole. Following a win at Belle Vue in 1908 along with a 5th at Crystal Palace, a 2nd prize at Belle Vue in 1909 – all under Rimmer, there was no prize at either event in 1910, the first year of Weston Nicholl's term of office. In 1911 the band did not compete at Belle Vue, and went on to win nothing at Crystal Palace. There were also a number of poor results in local contests. These had a demoralising effect on the band and were affecting its demand for concert engagements. The following article appeared in December 1911:

> It has generally been known for some little time that matters were not running smoothly with regard to the Black Dyke Band; then it got abroad that Mr. Harry Bower was retiring from the bandmastership. All sorts of rumours as to the cause got about and inquiries on the matter have been very numerous, so in order to clear the matter up I made it my business to see Mr. Bower himself. It is true that Mr. Bower sent in his resignation and will terminate his appointment on New Year's Day. Mr. Bower gives as his reason that he has had a long connection with Black Dyke Band, and he feels that he ought now to launch out for himself as a band teacher and adjudicator.[40]

---

[39] In *Popular Music in England 1840-1914.*

[40] Yorkshire Notes in *British Bandsman*, 23 December 1911.

The start of 1912, therefore, as the Halifax District correspondent put it,[41] 'saw the band at an absolutely low-water mark'. The directors were determined to put things right and made several changes. Willie Wood became the new solo cornet player. His assistant was the young Harold Pinches from Sheffield, a future distinguished Black Dyke solo cornet player. Ives Fieldsend came in on soprano cornet, W. J. Beckwith moved from solo cornet in the Juniors to flugel horn in the Seniors, while Ernest Ambler took over on solo horn. Harry Waddington, who had previously played both horn and solo euphonium took over the 1st baritone chair, whilst Fred Bower remained on solo trombone and Harry Sutcliffe on solo euphonium.

J. A. Greenwood became the new professional conductor in succession to Weston Nicholl, and Harry Bower was replaced as bandmaster by Arthur O. Pearce. Thus ended another era for Black Dyke Mills Band.

---

[41] *Brass Band News*, March 1912.

CHAPTER 5

The Arthur O. Pearce era

THE NEXT period to be discussed lasted from the beginning of 1912 until the end of 1948. It covered two World Wars and, like the previous era, attracted three professional conductors to Black Dyke – J. A. Greenwood, William Halliwell and Harry Mortimer. The bandmaster during the whole of this time was the legendary Arthur O. Pearce.

Arthur O. Pearce, The Prime Minister of Brass Bands

Arthur Oakes Pearce (1871-1951) was born in Halifax. From the age of 13 he played the side drum, first with the quaintly-named Bethel New Connexion Band in Ovenden and then with the brass band of the Halifax Band of Hope. After some time he moved to the baritone and then to solo horn. He remained with this band until he was 20 and during his last year played soprano cornet. Moving to Copley Mills Band, he played solo cornet, later becoming the band's conductor. Despite being self-taught he was very successful and was soon acting as band trainer to a number of local bands.

Due to illness, he was out of banding for a time but on his recovery he joined the Volunteers and for three years was in the Duke of Wellington's regimental band, rising to the rank of band sergeant and deputy bandmaster. During this period he conducted Brighouse & Rastrick Temperance Band periodically, prior to resigning from the Volunteers and taking Brighouse on a regular basis. He was there for three years but in 1909 became bandmaster of King Cross Band, a noted combination on the outskirts of Halifax, whose professional conductor was William Rimmer. This was the year that Rimmer gave up contest conducting (see Chapter 4) and though he conducted both Shaw and Foden's at Crystal Palace, he withdrew his services from King Cross, having insufficient rehearsals booked and being unavailable for any extras. Consequently, Arthur Pearce conducted at the contest and the band came away with 6th prize. In 1911, on the eve of the Coronation of King George V, he had the honour of conducting the band at Buckingham Palace. A year later he became bandmaster of Black Dyke. At the same time J. A. Greenwood replaced Weston Nicholl as professional conductor.

1912-1921 – the J. A. Greenwood years

Arthur O. Pearce was a teetotaller; he was also a first-class organiser and a strict but fair disciplinarian. Along with his considerable musical experience he was, therefore, well placed to help Black Dyke out of the doldrums. As has been seen, the band was passing through one of its less impressive periods. In the April *Brass Band News* of 1912 the Halifax District correspondent expressed the following opinion:

> It was very unfortunate that Mr. Pearce should have to commence his duties when the band was at a low-water mark, but his appointment has proved beyond doubt to be the right thing. Where chaos formerly existed, order is now the thing. ... The bandsmen, having realised that Mr. Pearce will stand no nonsense, are now settled down.

There were now fewer engagements, though playing standards appear to have been maintained, despite what are referred to as 'scurrilous reports' in a contemporary paper.

There were now several changes in personnel. Willie Wood had joined Black Dyke after the Canadian Tour as a flugel horn player, remaining on that instrument for two years before moving to cornet as assistant to Ceres Jackson. He deputised for Ceres on a number of occasions and became the principal solo cornet player for a time after Jackson's departure. Willie retired from Black Dyke in 1912 to become a professional musician.[42] Louis Allison then returned but was soon to be replaced by the 19-year-old Harold Pinches.

Harry Sutcliffe was the solo euphonium player and Fred Bower was still on solo trombone. By the end of 1912 George Keeton had replaced Sutcliffe, Harold Pinches had left and there was also a vacancy for a soprano cornet player. In fact, there were seven player changes during 1912 in addition to the bandmaster and professional conductor. In the December issue of *Brass Band News*, Arthur Pearce wrote:

> We have gone through a very trying season, and having to reorganise in the middle of the season is a very difficult situation to be in, but we mean to do better next season.

Meanwhile, during J. A. Greenwood's first year as professional conductor, Black Dyke gained 2nd prizes at Bradford and New Brighton, and 4ths at Belle Vue and Crystal Palace. It also had its first taste of the famous Whit Friday march contests, winning two 1st prizes. So, despite the changes, things were now moving in the right direction.

There were further changes in personnel during 1913; Hubert Hepworth from Slaithwaite was appointed soprano player.[43] The solo horn player was now George Downs, and Herbert Abrahams moved from solo horn at King Cross to 1st horn at Black Dyke. In the middle of the year Harold Pinches returned as principal solo cornet player and Ernest Shaw of Halifax took over on solo euphonium,[44] George Keeton moving to second.

In August, the Halifax correspondent of *Brass Band News* reported that Black Dyke was now in better shape than it had been since Rimmer's departure, with more prizes coming the band's way in local contests. Winning the Bradford contest for the third time in succession meant that the Lord Masham Cup had been won

---

[42] Willie Wood, after a number of years playing professionally, returned to brass bands as a conductor. He had some successes with Horwich R.M.I., Brighouse & Rastrick and Wingates, and later with Crossley's Carpet Works bands. However, his name will always be associated with Besses. He died in 1981 at the age of 94.

[43] Hubert Hepworth remained with Black Dyke until 1920, though he had some time out for military service. He was then the conductor of Black Dyke Juniors for about 25 years. He died in March, 1961.

[44] Shaw was from a well known banding family. More of him later.

outright. However, there was no prize this year at Belle Vue but there was a 3rd at Crystal Palace.

Engagements were becoming more plentiful and early in 1914 it became apparent that another busy season lay ahead. An Easter tour was said to have been a big success, with large crowds attending and many people turned away.

This was also a better season for contests, spearheaded by a win at New Brighton – a win which had eluded Black Dyke for some years. On this occasion they took 1st prize under Greenwood, beating Halliwell and Foden's into second place. There was also a welcome win at Belle Vue – the first since 1908. However, Britain was by now at war with Germany and several events were cancelled, including the Crystal Palace contest.

* * * * *

Despite the air of optimism that had pervaded the band press during the years leading up to the war, banding, like many other forms of entertainment, was facing competition from the growth in the popularity of jazz. Things as diverse as ballroom dancing and sport were also gaining support, eroding the dedication of bandsmen and diminishing the enthusiasm of their audiences. Nor did it help that many bands had made little change to their repertoire since the 1890s. A general decline in religion also had an adverse effect on brass bands.

The war did nothing to stem this tide, which was nibbling away at the edges of the world of brass bands. Nevertheless, contests continued, engagements were undertaken and brass band music publishers continued releasing their endless stream of marches, dance music and selections.

The Great War, lasting from 4 August 1914 to 11 November 1918 bore little resemblance to its counterpart of 1939-45. It was obviously as horrendous, but in different ways. Despite the horrors of the trenches and gas warfare, it never became the 'People's War'; there were no mass bombing raids on major cities such as were experienced in the 1940s. A casual reader of *Brass Band News* during the years 1914-18 could be forgiven for thinking that nothing serious was happening in the world. Granted, there were fewer contests and fewer bands entering them. There was an awareness that bandsmen were going off 'to serve King and Country' – but by and large they were being replaced by the many youngsters coming into banding. The size of *Brass Band News* remained at 12 pages until 1917, when it was reduced to 10, with a further reduction to eight in February 1918, and fewer copies being printed.

The realities of the war were, however, extremely serious. Within three days of its declaration Lord Kitchener was calling for 100,000 volunteers to join the army and by 22 August the British Expeditionary Force was in France. Volunteers came forward in their thousands and conscription was not introduced until 1916.

At first no one expected the war to last more than a few months and neither did anyone envisage the loss of life that would be incurred. The eventual death toll for members of the armed forces was in excess of ten million, around three quarters of a million of them from the United Kingdom. At the end of the war *British Bandsman* estimated that 25,500 bandsmen had served in the forces and that over 3,000 were killed, wounded or missing. More than 120 medals were awarded to bandsmen for gallantry, including five Victoria Crosses.

* * * * *

Belle Vue contests remained at the forefront of banding. The July contest, which had been expanded to two sections in 1912 continued in that format before reverting to a single section contest in 1915. The 'September' continued and, as the Crystal Palace contests were abandoned in 1913 and not restarted until 1920, it was the only wartime contest at national level. From 1915, for a few years, it was held on a Saturday rather than on the first Monday in September. There were now fewer competing bands and not all were in the top flight. Not surprisingly, cheap rail fares were withdrawn.

Looking specifically at Black Dyke during the war years, there were obviously more frequent changes of personnel – with regular call-up as well as the departure of older players and removals to other districts. By September 1918 the band had lost 32 members during the war years, many being replaced by members of Black Dyke Juniors. However, there were times when the bandsmen were working from 6am to 8pm, meaning that rehearsals began later, usually three times per week. There was a steady flow of engagements but time off work was a rarity.

Both Greenwood and Pearce remained in office throughout the war and they maintained steady progress in terms of repertoire, making use of new music from the pens of Weston Nicholl, Rimmer and Greenwood himself.

Harold Pinches played solo cornet until mid-1917, when he was called up. John Paley stood in for him for a time. It was expected that Harold would be given leave to play at the 1917 Belle Vue contest but within a few days of the contest this was cancelled and William Rushworth,[45] still only a boy, helped out. J. C. Dyson[46] of Brighouse then took over and, following his resignation in the summer of 1918, the 16-year-old Owen Bottomley became the band's principal solo cornet player. Owen had been doing well in solo contests and his father, Thomas, had been a member of Black Dyke's cornet section since the 1890s.

Harold Pinches, a great cornet player

Having obtained 1st prizes at Belle Vue and New Brighton in 1914, the band now took quite a dive in its contest results, showing no signs of recovery until 1920. The grand total of its wartime prizes was a 2nd at New Brighton in 1915, 3rd at Belle Vue in 1916 and 2nd there in the following year. No prizes were won in 1918 and the 1919 records show just a 4th prize at Belle Vue.

The war was now out of the way and things were looking rather better by 1920, with a 1st prize at the Newcastle Exhibition – including medals for cornet, flugel, euphonium and bass trombone

[45] William (Billy) Rushworth came from King Cross Band to Black Dyke. He then played for Brighouse for a time but spent most of his brass band career as the distinguished solo cornet player of Besses before becoming a professional trumpet player, joining the Sadler's Wells orchestra.

[46] J. C. Dyson later became a successful conductor and adjudicator.

– a 2nd prize in Glasgow and a 1st at Fallowfield (Manchester). 1921 also brought 1st prizes in Glasgow and Newcastle. The Glasgow event was quite a big affair – part of an International Exhibition. Seventeen bands competed in the top section for a Gold Shield worth £1,500 and substantial monetary prizes.

Black Dyke also now had a quartet – two cornets, tenor horn and euphonium. Between 1918 and 1920 they had attended 12 contests, winning seven and being unplaced only once. The early members of the quartet were Harold Pinches, Fred Haigh, Herbert Abrahams and Ernest Shaw.

However, by now another band was making its presence felt at the top level, St Hilda Colliery from South Shields. From 1906 this band had made steady progress under J. A. Greenwood, but in 1910 William Halliwell was appointed professional conductor. Two years later, under his guidance, they took 2nd prize at Belle Vue and became the Champion Band of Great Britain by winning the Nationals at Crystal Palace. They followed this up with a 2nd prize in the following year, after which the Crystal Palace contests were suspended.

St Hilda's made a spectacular return after the war, winning at Crystal Palace in both 1920 and 1921. During these two years Black Dyke's tally of prizes in the two major events was merely a 5th prize at Belle Vue in 1920, and 3rd at Belle Vue and 4th at Crystal Palace in 1921. These results sounded the death knell for Greenwood at Black Dyke. Following what was described as 'a poor show' on the test piece *Life Divine* in 1921, the appointment of William Halliwell as his successor was announced.

1922-1934 – William Halliwell takes over

Britain was now in a perilous state. Following the euphoria of 'winning' the war, the reality of paying for it – in a period of high unemployment – became a bitter pill to swallow. Many people were on the breadline, facing dole queues, the means test and a life-style almost unimaginable today, though others were benefiting from profits made out of the war and a reduction in the cost of living. Bands were also facing a 'two-tier' system, the poor ones becoming poorer and in many cases folding, and the better ones taking on prestigious and lucrative engagements.

Black Dyke had consolidated its personnel. Harold Pinches was back on solo cornet and Hubert Hepworth had been replaced on soprano cornet by Gershom Collison.[47] Fred Bower moved down to 2nd trombone to make way for the up-and-coming Elijah Boam.

By 1922, despite the enormous social problems, Black Dyke Mills Band, along with other élite English brass bands, was getting back into its stride. The personnel was now settled, with Arthur Pearce firmly established in his tenth year as bandmaster and William Halliwell becoming the professional conductor.

William Halliwell (1864-1946) was born at Roby Mill near Wigan. As a boy he played the organ and at 16 took up the cornet. He also played trumpet in an amateur orchestra and was soon conducting local bands. He followed William Rimmer as professional conductor of Foden's, leading them immediately to the double in 1910. He subsequently completed four more personal doubles. By now he had succeeded Rimmer as the leading brass band conductor and even before coming to Black Dyke was enjoying successes with several top bands, including Foden's, Irwell Springs, St Hilda's and Wingates Temperance. Though not particularly successful at Black Dyke, by the time he retired from contesting in 1939 he had directed 17 winning performances with various bands at Belle Vue, and 11 at Crystal Palace – an all-time record.

William Halliwell, winner of 28 major titles

Amongst Black Dyke's engagements in 1922 was a week in Pittencrieff Park, Dunfermline, one of many engagements it was to enjoy north of the border. On the contest front, the Glasgow contest,

[47] Gershom Collison hailed from Wisbech in Cambridgeshire. He played in a local band and also with a theatre orchestra. He played in an army band during the War, after which he joined a Nottingham brass band, playing soprano cornet. After two years there he moved to Black Dyke, in 1920. He left in 1934 to become bandmaster of the Canal Iron Works Band, later taking a similar appointment with Hammonds Sauce Works Band. He died in 1971.

which had been won in 1921, was won again. In addition to retaining the shield and winning £100, twenty-five gold medals were presented to the band for winning two years in succession. There was also a win at a contest in Sheffield – another £100 plus a trombone, and a further 2nd prize at Newcastle. Most importantly, Black Dyke won 2nd prize at Belle Vue, its best result there for some time.

1923 was an eventful year. Amongst the band's summer engagements was a 14-day stint in Southport and 15 days in Glasgow. The band also paid its first visit to Belfast, spending five days there during July. In August, whilst the band was on tour, Gershom Collison underwent a surgical operation on his mouth, resulting in Black Dyke's withdrawal from the Belle Vue contest. Nevertheless, the band attended three other contests during the year, winning at Hawes and taking 2nd prizes at both Crystal Palace and Halifax.

The Halifax contest was organized by Black Dyke's former professional conductor, Weston Nicholl, who also composed the test piece, a Tone Picture: *The Viking*. This 'Empire Brass Band Contest' was held at Thrum Hall, home of the Halifax Rugby Club and attracted an audience estimated at 20,000. The 1st prize of £150 – the highest prize money ever paid out at that time – was won by Foden's, with Black Dyke in second place. Black Dyke also took 2nd prize at Crystal Palace – won this year by Luton Red Cross Band, the only southern band ever to win the Nationals.

Amongst the visitors to Queensbury during 1923 was HRH the Prince of Wales (later famous as the king who abdicated). The band, resplendent in new uniforms, gave a short concert and the prince complimented Colonel Foster on its playing.

Engagements for 1924 poured in and despite having declared its intention to attend all 'first class' contests, again the band competed at only three, winning 3rd prize at Blackpool and once more coming 2nd at Crystal Palace. It again withdrew from Belle Vue – this time owing to pressure of engagements – and was unsuccessful at the second Halifax contest. For this, Weston Nicholl made a transcription of the incredibly difficult organ sonata, *The Ninety-fourth Psalm*, by the German composer Julius Reubke. The contest was won by Newcastle Steel Works Band from Australia, touring Britain at the time. This band went on to win at Belle Vue and took 3rd prize at Crystal Palace.

Black Dyke's visitors this year included the well-known composer Professor (later Sir) Granville Bantock, brought to a rehearsal by

Weston Nicholl. Bantock 'expressed himself as highly pleased with the splendid playing of the band, which he heard at its very best'.

An unusual event took place at the Manchester Hippodrome on Good Friday when Black Dyke combined with its old rival, Besses, in two highly-acclaimed concerts. There were also extended engagements in Southport, Liverpool and Blackpool, as well as the now almost obligatory Scottish tour. Nor were these types of engagement confined to the summer months. During October Black Dyke played at the first British Empire Exhibition, held at Wembley,[48] and then was in York from 16-18 December and Edinburgh for the New Year – playing there from 27 December to 4 January.

Black Dyke were booked for 10 weeks' performances during 1925. There was a sad occasion this year, with the death of Joseph Weston Nicholl. The respect accorded to him was marked by a concert in People's Park, Halifax, given by the combined bands of Black Dyke and St Hilda, conducted by William Halliwell. Included in the programme was *The Viking*, composed for the 1923 Halifax contest. The audience for the evening concert was estimated at 10,000 and, as reported in *The Bandmaster* of 15 June:

> As the last notes of *The Viking* died away in the evening the bandsmen and the vast crowd stood bowed in an impressive silence, the men uncovering, in tribute to the memory of a great musician.

By now Black Dyke was becoming involved in what today is called 'The Media'. Its early gramophone recordings were mentioned in Chapter 4. No more were made until 1923, when an abridged version of the Crystal Palace test piece *Oliver Cromwell* was recorded on a 10-inch Regal disc. Black Dyke had won 2nd prize playing this. In 1924 the band recorded *The Viking* on two 10-inch discs, and two marches. *On the Cornish Coast* was recorded in 1924 – again a 2nd prize piece for the band at Crystal Palace. 1925 saw the release of three Black Dyke recordings – two light pieces on one, the 1925 Crystal Palace test piece *Joan of Arc* on the second and a selection, *W. H. Squire's Songs*[49] on the third.

---

[48] Wembley Stadium was one of several buildings erected for this exhibition, staged in 1924 and 1925.

[49] William Henry Squire was a composer and a professional cellist. Amongst his compositions were a number of drawing-room ballads. The selection recorded by Black Dyke became very popular with bands and remained in programmes until the late thirties.

There was now another important development. The BBC had been set up in 1922 and by May 1925 articles in *Brass Band News* were commenting on 'wireless concerts reaching unseen millions'. Black Dyke gave its first broadcast from the second Wembley Exhibition. It went out 'over the air' from 4.15pm to 5.15pm on Monday, 5 October 1925. The following programme was played:

March	*Tannhäuser*	Wagner
Suite	*Three Dale Dances*	Arthur Wood
Overture	*Joan of Arc*	Denis Wright
Cornet solo	*Shylock*	Thomas Lear
Selection	*W. H. Squire's Songs*	arr. J Ord Hume

Yet again, owing to pressure of engagements, Black Dyke did not attend Belle Vue. It did compete at Crystal Palace, however, but was unsuccessful.

* * * * *

The depressed state of the working classes was mentioned earlier. Despite the prosperity enjoyed by Black Dyke Mills Band, conditions were deteriorating in the rest of the brass band world and, indeed, in the nation as a whole. Unemployment and short time were rife, soup kitchens were common, and members of many bands were reduced to busking on street corners, hoping to make a few coppers to add to their meagre incomes.

Things came to something of a head in 1926 when a general strike was called. This was precipitated by colliery owners imposing reductions on miners' pay in order to compete with cheap coal – some of which was imported from Germany! The miners used the slogan 'not a minute on the day, not a penny off the pay'. Other workers supported them but the main strike lasted only from 3-12 May. After this the others returned to work whilst the miners remained on strike. The employers held out, however, and the miners eventually had to return to work, faced with the choice of that or starvation for their families.

Yet, against this backdrop of deprivation and suffering, members of bands such as Black Dyke could earn a comfortable living, certainly throughout the summer, giving concerts in parks and at the sea-side. Companies like John Foster's and Foden's, and collieries which had bands – such as St Hilda's and Creswell – were delighted to see the backs of the bandsmen for a few weeks as it reduced their wage bills. Band fees would, of course, be subsidised by the ratepayers of the towns visited, and by the thousands who flocked to hear the bands.

Brass Band News remained at eight pages. It generally steered clear of political debate or news of happenings outside the brass band world. Nevertheless, in June 1926 it stated that 'The industrial upheaval played havoc with May contests and many had to be postponed or cancelled'. Earlier in the year there was a list of 14 first-class contests that had disappeared. They included New Brighton, Hawes and Halifax.

1926 was a poor year for contesting for Black Dyke, with only Belle Vue and Crystal Palace attended. Though William Halliwell's bands won 1st, 2nd, 3rd and 6th prizes at Belle Vue and 1st, 3rd, 4th and 6th at Crystal Palace, Black Dyke's only prize this year was a 6th at Crystal Palace.

Despite problems on the contest front, nothing affected the band's concert activities. Black Dyke played in Southport from 6-12 June and in Liverpool on the 23rd and 24th. From 4-31 July it was on tour in Scotland. This so-called Scottish tour took in Glasgow, Airdie, Alloa, Newcastle(!), Aberdeen, Glasgow, Motherwell, and Bonnybridge, along with a week in Edinburgh and further moving around Scotland between the 20th and the 31st. On 1 and 2 August the band played in Mansfield, Nottingham, for the start of an English tour that was to last through most of August.

All of this must have been quite exhausting, but preferable to the kind of life being led by many other working men.

There were several changes within the band during 1926. Elijah Boam left after playing solo trombone for three and a half years; Harold Pinches also left, his immediate replacement being George Crossland.[50] Ernest Shaw moved onto solo trombone whilst his brother, Percy, a former solo euphonium player of Foden's now took up a similar position with Black Dyke. A few years earlier these two brothers had occupied the solo euphonium seats in two leading rival bands. They now occupied the solo euphonium and solo trombone seats in Black Dyke; but not for long.

---

[50] George Crossland had been in Black Dyke since 1922 as assistant to Harold Pinches. He died in 1979.

Early in 1927 Owen Bottomley was appointed principal solo cornet player. He had played in this position with Black Dyke for a short period towards the end of the War and now took over permanently. A 17-year-old 'discovery', Haydn Robinson, came in as the solo trombone player[51] and Ernest Shaw moved back to solo euphonium, Percy moving down to second. This move was short-lived, however, as Ernest left shortly afterwards for business reasons, having founded a family business making and selling mineral water.

Touring continued unabated, though there was now a slight expansion in the band's contesting activities. These brought but modest results, however, with a 3rd prize in Douglas, Isle of Man and a 2nd in Plymouth.

The early part of 1928 saw more changes in personnel and Percy Shaw moving back to solo euphonium. Tours continued. This year's highlight was a win at Crystal Palace. For only the second time, Black Dyke Mills Band became the National Brass Band Champion of Great Britain – the first time having been in 1902. The band's solo horn player, Herbert Abrahams was taken ill a few days before the contest and the young Joe Willie Wood was promoted.

The welcome home accorded to the band by the people of Queensbury was said to be quite extraordinary. Bandsmen were surrounded by 'an enthusiastic throng of factory lasses' wearing funny hats, and greeted by the shrieking of the factory siren. It was Monday afternoon, the mill yard was thrown open to all, bunting was hung across the roads and there were flags and pennants everywhere.

Shortly after the contest John Henry Iles came to Queensbury to officially present the trophy and the medals

* * * * *

The Halifax district notes in *Brass Band News* were supplied by a new correspondent from January 1929. The previous one wrote under the pseudonym 'Moderato'. From now on, the news was covered by one 'Pondasher'. Perhaps it was not a new correspondent after all!

---

[51] Haydn Robinson was born into a banding family in Denholme in 1909. He was in a church choir and took piano lessons from the age of nine. He played at Crystal Palace in 1926 with Clayton Silver Band and, following private lessons with Elijah Boam, was playing solo trombone with Black Dyke within two years. He was also an accomplished pianist, and in the winter months ran his own dance orchestra.

The 1928 band with the 1,000 Guinea Trophy. Owen Bottomley is to the left of the trophy and Mr. Pearce to the right; Percy Shaw is seated next to Mr. Pearce

John Henry Iles presenting the impressive trophy. Iles is to the left of the trophy and Captain Ronald Foster to the right.

Coverage of Black Dyke news was quite full and took a slightly different slant. It revealed, for example, that some of the travelling was now done in 'their beautiful saloon bus'. It was also revealed that several of the band's concerts were being given in theatres and cinemas. Touring continued in 1929, but it is also clear from the new columnist that the band played regularly in Queensbury and that for many years it had taken part in the town's Whitsuntide processions.

Amongst the more 'long-range' engagements this year were two visits to Dublin – both in connection with horse shows. A quartet was still performing in concerts and contests and now rejoiced under the name of the 'Premier Quartet'. Contests drew a blank this year. Due to its Southport engagement, Black Dyke again stayed away from Belle Vue and despite the boost gained in 1928 there was no prize at Crystal Palace in 1929. Mr Halliwell was not available this year, so the band was trained and conducted by the bandmaster.

A quartet party c. 1922 – Fred Haigh, Joe W. Wood, Percy Shaw and Bram Chatburn

Broadcasting and recording continued. Broadcasts were made both from home and whilst on tour. The three made in 1926 went out from Leeds, Aberdeen and Birmingham; of those made in the following year one came from Leeds and the other from Savoy Hill, London; whilst the two 1928 broadcasts came from Manchester and the Lord Street Bandstand, Southport. There were four broadcasts in 1929. The first, lasting an hour and a half, came from a studio in

Manchester whilst the second, an evening programme, came from the Bingley Hall, Birmingham. The third came from the Newcastle Exhibition and the fourth, a tea-time programme, again came from Southport's Lord Street Bandstand. Of course, there was no pre-recording in those days, therefore, all broadcasts were 'live'.

Black Dyke recordings made between 1926 and 1929 included the four Crystal Palace test pieces for those years – *An Epic Symphony, The White Rider, A Moorside Suite* and *Victory*, as well as some lighter items.

* * * * *

Social conditions in the country were still not improving. The decade now approaching has been labelled by some historians 'The Hungry Thirties'. Though life became a little easier for some in the years following the general strike there was a world-wide depression in trade – 'The Slump'. This had serious repercussions in Britain, with unemployment escalating to three million. Textiles, coal and the heavy engineering industries were badly hit – all present in regions where brass bands thrived. Many bands now folded, meaning fewer contests, and hard times for instrument makers, uniform companies and music publishers.

Black Dyke continued with its annual round of concerts and tours, though 1930 seemed to mark a turning point in the number of engagements. For example, the Southport series was suspended for this year, depriving most of the top bands of at least one week of concerts. There seems also to have been a larger proportion of local or semi-local engagements, though these were spiced with a number of higher-profile concerts. For example, the band participated in a Celebrity Concert at Belle Vue, and performed to an audience of 4,000 in the Tower Ballroom Blackpool. Even the quartet gave a concert in Huddersfield Town Hall. Again the band did not attend the Belle Vue contest, but was awarded 2nd prize at Crystal Palace.

News of Black Dyke's concert activities during the early thirties is rather sparse. In most years the season ended with Christmas carol playing around Queensbury and a charity concert for the poor children of Bradford.

Early in 1930 the band said goodbye to one of its longest-serving members – the last of the dynasty of the Bowers. Fred Bower retired following a broadcast on 5 January. He had begun playing the trombone at the age of 13, joining Black Dyke Juniors. Progressing to the senior band three years later, he played 2nd trombone for the next nine years and was then promoted to solo trombone, serving in that capacity for almost a quarter of a century before stepping back to second trombone for the remainder of his playing days. He was the only Black Dyke player to play in the band's two winning Crystal Palace performances. He had also helped the band to eight Belle Vue September contest wins and had competed in 150 contests, 63 of which had been won. Along with his father (Phineas) and his two uncles (Harry and Alfred, a long-serving E flat bass player) Fred had contributed to 150 years' service to Black Dyke by the Bowers; there had been at least one Bower in the band for the past 62 years – quite a record. Fred was honoured in a ceremony in the Victoria Hall on 2 February, receiving presentations from both the band and the company.[52]

In 1931 there was a week's engagement at Belle Vue following the band's success in the Celebrity Concert the previous year. There was also a month in Scotland and towards the end of the year the band was in London preparing a series of seasonal recordings. There was but one broadcast this year. The only new member of note introduced was a young man named Bernard Burns. 'Buddy' had played soprano cornet in the Juniors and was now brought into the senior band as a solo cornet player, from 1934 succeeding Gershom Collison as Black Dyke's soprano player. A bright spot on the contest scene was a win at the Glasgow International Contest, held in May. Belle Vue was yet again given a miss, and there was no prize for the band at Crystal Palace.

Amongst the week engagements during 1932 was the first of a number of visits to Hyde Park, London. Local correspondents almost inevitably sang the band's praises so it was good to see a more independent report, by the London correspondent, on the band's second appearance in Hyde Park, in 1933.

> Black Dyke attracted large crowds to Hyde Park, where they gave some magnificent performances. Bandmasters and bandsmen from all parts of the Metropolis were to be seen night after night listening and taking notes of the finer points for which this band is famous.

Cornwall was added to the list of places visited in 1933, but whilst the band continued its annual visits to Scotland and to some south coast resorts, there is a noticeable absence of engagements in the

---

[52] Fred Bower died on 8 January 1955.

northern towns, a reflection of the economic climate. There was, however, a one-day engagement in Southport. A rather different engagement this year was playing at Valley Parade Rugby Ground at a match between Bradford Northern and the touring Australians. This took place on a Monday and the band paraded through the city to advertise the game.

The fact that the band was now less busy is substantiated by the fact that there were three quartet parties – including a trombone quartet, and also that solo euphonium player Percy Shaw was accepting adjudicating engagements.

There were regular reports that the band was keeping to the fore with new repertoire, though this probably meant new arrangements or transcriptions. Specific pieces were rarely mentioned, but what would nowadays be regarded as a 'rave review' of a concert given for Blackpool Co-op appeared. This eulogized about a performance of what was said to have been the complete *Symphony No 4* of Tchaikovsky.[53]

There was a 1st prize at Glasgow in 1931; 1932 brought the band a 2nd prize at Crystal Palace, whilst 1934 brought a 4th prize from there, as well as a 3rd from a contest at Skegness. However, the best news was that Black Dyke, competing at Belle Vue for the first time in eight years, was rewarded with 2nd prize. 1935 was the best contest season for many years, with a win at Belle Vue and 3rd prize at Crystal Palace. The band also now returned to the scene of the Whit Friday band contests, winning 1st and 2nd prizes in each of the years 1933, 1934 and 1935.

Commercial recordings all but dried up for the band during the early thirties, with just four 10-inch discs released in 1931-32. Amongst the items recorded were Liszt's *Hungarian Rhapsody No. 2* and the cornet solo *Shylock*, played by Owen Bottomley. Broadcasts remained fairly stable, with two each in the years 1932 and 1934 and four in 1935, the year of the Belle Vue win.

1935-1945

In 1935 the nation rejoiced at the Silver Jubilee of King George V but mourned his death in the following year. Then followed the

[53] This must have been the Weston Nicholl arrangement made for Black Dyke in 1911, a mere 33 years after the completion of the Symphony by Tchaikovsky. It is not, in fact, the complete Symphony; it opens with the famous 'Fate' theme from the 1st movement and then moves into complete transcriptions of movements 2 and 4.

accession of King Edward VIII, followed by his abdication. The brass band world mourned the death of William Rimmer and was stunned with the news that Crystal Palace had been destroyed by fire, on 30 November 1936. There was much wailing and gnashing of teeth at its loss, but much rejoicing when Iles announced that the National Championships would continue, re-located at the Alexandra Palace.

1937 was a rather happier time, with the Coronation of King George VI and Queen Elizabeth. A celebration on a smaller scale took place marking the 25th year of Arthur O. Pearce's bandmastership at Black Dyke. This was a remarkable achievement and he was honoured with a number of presentations. In his response to the various speeches he intimated that his term of office was nearing its end. In fact, he was to serve for a further 11 years.

Coronation year provided extra engagements for bands and a temporary upturn from the doldrums in which many found themselves. Another positive step was Denis Wright's appointment to the staff of the BBC. Through his influence new broadcasting policies emerged.

A warning signal that problems were not confined to local bands came in 1938 with the disbanding of the famous St Hilda's. It had existed as a professional band for a decade since the closure of the pit. Its owner now decided – partly because there were fewer engagements and partly because he was finding it increasingly difficult to find players of the right calibre – that the time had come to 'call it a day'. Another piece of bad news in 1938 was of the bankruptcy of John Henry Iles. Despite feelings to the contrary in some quarters, he had been a generous benefactor to the brass band movement. Though his enthusiasm for it continued, he was now unable to help financially.

For Black Dyke there was a gradual erosion in the number of engagements. with a corresponding increase in its contest activities. Further, in 1938 and 1939 there was an upturn in the number of commercial gramophone recordings made and, following Denis Wright's appointment at the BBC, there were more broadcasts, with more substantial pieces included in programmes.

There were several changes to Black Dyke's key personnel during this period. Late in 1936 Owen Bottomley was replaced by Harold Jackson. Harold had begun his playing career at the age of eight when he joined Haworth Band, conducted by his father. He was playing solo cornet by the time he was 12. At 15 he became principal solo cornet with Harton Colliery, succeeding the legendary Jack Mackintosh who had joined the BBC Symphony Orchestra. At Harton, Jackson came under the influence of William Halliwell. Following two years playing with Horwich RMI Band, on Halliwell's recommendation he became principal solo cornet of Black Dyke.[54]

Harold Jackson left Black Dyke in May 1938 and though it was announced that Owen Bottomley was to take over, this proved to be but a temporary move as later in the year Willie Lang became the band's principal, at the age of 17. Born in 1920, he played with Norland Band as a boy, joining when he was 10. Four years later he joined Bradford City and at 16 came to Black Dyke as assistant to Harold Jackson. Now, greatly helped by Owen, he began what was to be an illustrious career in brass bands prior to building an equally illustrious career as an orchestral trumpeter.

There was also a change of solo euphonium, Percy Shaw being replaced in 1935 by Rowland Jones. Born in South Wales in 1913, Rowland commenced his playing, at the age of 12, with Gwaun-cae-Gurwen Band. He was auditioned there by Arthur Pearce and offered the job of solo euphonium at Black Dyke. He also had a fine singing voice and, following a solo on the euphonium, he generally sang his encore. He left Black Dyke in 1938 to join Bickershaw Colliery, but later became a principal tenor at Sadler's Wells.[55]

Another change took place around this time as Haydn Robinson moved down to make way for the 15-year-old Jack Pinches. Jack was the second son of Harold, and a product of Black Dyke Juniors, which he joined at the age of 11, becoming its solo trombonist two years later. He moved into the senior band in 1937 as 2nd trombone player, taking over the solo trombone chair a year later.

Black Dyke was never out of the prizes at either Belle Vue or the Nationals between 1936 and 1939, though it was unable to secure a win. Its best performances were 2nd prizes at Crystal Palace in 1936 and Belle Vue in 1938. A few other contests were entered but the only success of note was at the West of England Brass Band Festival, held annually in the Cornish village of Bugle. In 1937 the date of the

---

[54] After leaving Black Dyke, Harold Jackson played for a while with Besses. He played in the R.A.F. Central Band during the war and then became a professional trumpet player, playing in the newly-formed Philharmonia Oorchestra. He died in 1986, aged 73.

[55] Rowland Jones was to appear as a guest singer with the band a number of times over the next few years. He died in 1973, aged 60.

contest coincided with the band's Southern tour of that year. Conducted by William Halliwell, Black Dyke won 1st prize.

Whit Friday contests were still being attended but the first spectacular results did not occur until 1939 when, from six contests attended, the band won five 1st prizes. A significant factor in these successes was that the band played a new march, composed by James Kaye, a well-known euphonium player. It was named *Queensbury*.

The band still toured. Scotland and London remained regular engagements up to 1939, but touring was less of a full-time occupation than in earlier years.

Broadcasts were becoming slightly more frequent, the majority coming from the Leeds studios. There were four from there in 1935 plus one from Morecambe, four from there in 1936 plus one from Derby, with similar figures in 1937. There was then a slight cutback to a total of four per year in 1938 and 1939. These included a broadcast from the Glasgow Exhibition and two from London – one of them from Broadcasting House and the other from Maida Vale. Repertoire was also more adventurous and records of the programmes, kept by Arthur Pearce, tell us more about what the band was playing than do the reports of concerts and tours. Included in the earlier broadcasts from this period were such items as *Rossini's Works, Weber's Works,* a selection from *Lucrezia Borgia* and Alexander Owen's *Heroic Fantasia.* Transcriptions included the overtures *William Tell, Marinarella* and *Zampa,* as well as Liszt's *Hungarian Rhapsody No. 2,* Guilmant's *First Organ Symphony* and Tchaikovsky's *Capriccio Italien.*

A particularly interesting programme in 1936 told the story of the 1860 Crystal Palace contest and featured some of the music played there. Another 1936 programme featured *Oliver Cromwell* and extracts from *An Epic Symphony, A Downland Suite* and *A Moorside Suite.* That was a programme of genuine contemporary brass band music of the time.

A 1938 broadcast consisted of arrangements made and conducted by William Halliwell. The first broadcast performance of what was to become Black Dyke's signature tune, *Queensbury,* was included in a Maida Vale broadcast on Sunday, 30 July 1939.

From 1938 the band had a contract to record for HMV. Only two discs were released in that year, the second featuring two hymn tunes, *Abide With Me* and *Deep Harmony* – recordings still popular through a re-release on a 7-inch EP (extended play) disc. In 1939 twelve 10-inch discs were released – 10 of them recorded in 1938. Owen Bottomley was the featured cornet soloist on two, playing *Silver Threads, The Lost Chord, The Rosary* and *Softly Awakes My Heart.* There were also a number of marches and lighter pieces, two more hymn tunes and the overtures *Poet and Peasant* and *Orpheus in the Underworld* – the latter arranged by Arthur Pearce. The war put the brakes on somewhat, with only three discs cut in 1939 – all released in 1940. Amongst the pieces recorded in this batch were the overture *Light Cavalry* and two trombone solos featuring Jack Pinches – *The Acrobat* and *The Jester.*

However, all was doom and gloom now as gas masks were issued, air raid shelters erected, the blackout descended on the streets and once again war was declared on Germany – on 3 September 1939.

* * * * *

Early 1939 had been a relatively happy time for many people. Some two million of them flocked to hear bands in London's parks. On the other hand, the Territorial Army was being built up and Civil Defence organizations established. Bands were, consequently, being affected even before the outbreak of war.

Once it started and conscription began to bite, a number of bands had to break up, unable to cope with the loss of players to the armed forces, the effects of Civil Defence duties and the demands being made on factory workers, some of whom were working 12 hours per day, seven days per week. Bands that survived were generally made up of men too old for military service and boys not yet old enough. Some works bands thrived due to their parent companies being on essential war work and able to keep a stable work force. Learners' classes became the order of the day and bands that had junior sections (such as Black Dyke Juniors) were at an advantage.

Entertainment came to a temporary halt as many engagements were cancelled, partly due to severe travel restrictions. The National Championships were abandoned and the Belle Vue September contest postponed until the end of the month. Soon, however, concerts were being organized either as fund-raising events or to entertain troops and workers. The blackout meant an early finish for most events.

It was some time before the seriousness of the war became apparent, but with the Dunkirk evacuation in June 1940, followed by the Battle of Britain and the Blitz, what had been called the 'Phony War' suddenly became the 'People's War'. By June 1941 over two million homes had been destroyed or damaged and within a few more months it was calculated that more civilians had been killed than military personnel. Of the towns and cities which were virtually destroyed, Coventry and Clydebank each had well-established bands. Both were stretched to the full to keep going. The offices of the *British Bandsman* in London were damaged eight times in bombing raids, and those of *Brass Band News* in Liverpool were affected in the Merseyside Blitz.

In mid-1940 the Home Guard was formed. This was a part-time militia force organized to resist possible invasion. Bands initially helped with parades and recruiting drives and soon many became Home Guard bands. In addition to the two Black Dyke bands Queensbury also had its Home Guard Band, conducted by Harold Pinches.

Other points to note from these war years were the many fundraising efforts such as War Weapons Week and Spitfire Week. Bands were invariably involved, as they were in Holidays at Home – programmes of events organized during the summer, aimed at discouraging people from going away for their annual holidays.

A less savoury aspect of the war was the ever-increasing range of rationed goods. This even stretched to clothing, and in the event of a band needing to buy a uniform it could only do so if a member gave up some precious clothing coupons. Musical instruments, if and when available, were subject to purchase tax which, in some cases, doubled their cost. During 1940 the sizes of both *Brass Band News* and *British Bandsman* were reduced due to a shortage of paper.

Against this wartime background, Black Dyke Mills Band continued to function. Most of its engagements were local and, following the 1939 Belle Vue contest, it chose not to attend any more contests. However, despite inevitable and frequent changes in personnel, standards were maintained and broadcasting became one of its most essential functions. During the war years broadcasting was very important both as a means of communication and as a vehicle for keeping up the spirits of the British people.

Black Dyke made over 100 broadcasts during the war. Most were made in the Leeds studio and most went out on what was called the 'BBC Home Service'. Music played was generally of a light, cheerful nature and on 3 April 1941 Black Dyke made its first contribution to the series 'Music While You Work' – a half hour non-stop programme of music relayed to factories and homes throughout the country each morning and afternoon. A flavour of the type of music played in this series can be gleaned from this particular programme:

March	*Honest Toil*	Rimmer
Xylophone solo	*Tarantella de Concert*	Greenwood
Soldier's Chorus from *Faust*		Gounod
Humoresque	*March of the Manikins*	Fletcher
The Tiger's Tail (from Suite *Americana*)		Thurban
Selection	*Cavalcade*	Noel Coward
Savoy American Medley		Debroy Somers

A second 'Music While You Work' programme, broadcast on 9 July 1941 began and ended with the Eric Coates march *Calling All Workers.* This became the programme's signature tune which, broadcast four times per day for many years, added considerably to the fortune made in royalties by this popular composer.

In January 1942 Black Dyke was allowed to travel to London to take part in a massed band concert in the Royal Albert Hall, along with Foden's and Besses. The concert was in aid of the Red Cross and the chief guest conductor was Sir Adrian Boult. The largely patriotic programme included *Land of Hope and Glory,* sung by the audience of some 7,000. Also in the programme was the first performance of Denis Wright's arrangement of *Themes from Symphony No. 5* (Beethoven). This had become something of a symbol of victory, its opening notes recalling the morse code signal for the letter 'V' (three dots and a dash). The arrangement was selected as the test piece for the 1943 Belle Vue contest and became a very popular programme item. The pieces conducted by Boult formed a half-hour broadcast, transmitted from 4 to 4.30 in the afternoon.

There was a further massed band concert in March, in which the same three bands were joined by Fairey Aviation. This took place in the King's Hall, Belle Vue, but seems not to have been broadcast.

On 29 May 1942 Black Dyke made the first of several broadcasts to specific overseas countries. Being 'live', they had to be made at a time convenient to the particular country. This programme, relayed to Africa, was performed from 9.45 to 10.15 in the evening. Nine days later, however, the band played the same programme again, for transmission in North America, but on this occasion playing from 3 to 3.30 in the morning!

Sir Edward Elgar (3rd from the left on the front row) listening to Black Dyke perform some of his music in the Victoria Hall, in March 1921. On Elgar's left is is Mr. Herbert Foster.

On 21 March 1943 the band performed its 100th broadcast. Included in the programme was the march *Queensbury*, the *Gloria in Excelsis* from the 1860 Crystal Palace contest and an arrangement of *Themes from the 1st Symphony* of Elgar, arranged for Black Dyke by J .A. Greenwood back in 1919.

The next broadcast of special interest was part of a massed band concert staged at Belle Vue on the afternoon of Sunday, 26 September 1943. The other bands taking part were Fairey's, Foden's and Bickershaw Colliery. The guest conductor was once again Sir Adrian Boult and this programme included the first performance of Denis Wright's transcription of the *Introduction to Act III 'Lohengrin'* by Wagner.

By now some programmes were being pre-recorded and could therefore be made at times more convenient to the bands.

Massed band concerts became very popular and often provided an opportunity to involve a famous orchestral conductor. We have already seen examples of Boult's involvement, and in March 1944 Malcolm Sargent conducted another concert from Belle Vue, featuring the same four bands as were in the 1943 concert. The leading orchestral conductor of the time, Sir Henry Wood, was the next 'prize', and he directed a concert in the Royal Albert Hall featuring six bands – Black Dyke, Foden's, Fairey's, City of Coventry, Luton and Enfield Central. The finale of this concert was Denis Wright's new arrangement of *1812* – the first of literally thousands of performances of this version of the spectacular Tchaikovsky overture.

Yet another Belle Vue massed band concert, in March 1945, introduced John Barbirolli to brass bands. He spoke in glowing terms of the musicianship of the bandsmen of Black Dyke, Bickershaw, Fairey's and Foden's.

June 8 1945 (VE Day) saw the end of the war in Europe but not until August was the war finally ended – on VJ Day. Black Dyke's last special wartime broadcast came from the Philharmonic Hall, Liverpool where, on Sunday, 3 June, Sir Adrian Boult conducted Black Dyke, Foden's and Fairey's, along with the Liverpool Philharmonic Choir. A substantial part of this concert was broadcast.

Commercial records were still being made during the early war years, for Regal Zonophone. Only one was made in 1940 but there were six in the following year. These included solos by Willie Lang – *Bless This House, Serenata* and *Jenny Wren.* Jack Pinches also recorded *In an Old Fashioned Town.* The two recordings of 1942, the last for several years, were a selection from Sullivan's *Yeomen of the Guard* and two famous marches – *The Standard of St George* and *Queensbury.*

Amongst the player changes within Black Dyke during the war, Owen Bottomley returned to replace Willie Lang, who spent much of the war in North Africa as a tank commander. Following the departure of Rowland Jones there were several solo euphonium players, most of whom were in the forces within a short time of taking up the position. The first of these was Henry Davis who, like Jones, came from Gwaun-cau-Gurwen. He was followed by Arthur Atkinson, a member of a well-known Bradford banding family. Then came two brothers, each a product of Black Dyke Juniors. Charlie Emmott had played solo horn in the Juniors, but had come into the senior band on 2nd euphonium before moving up when Arthur Atkinson left. Charlie was succeeded by his brother, Jack, a future Black Dyke bandmaster.[56]

---

[56] Charlie Emmott eventually moved on to E flat bass and became one of the most respected members of the band. As a boy he had been a member of Black Dyke Juniors. He joined the seniors in 1936 and served for 31 years. For much of this time he played E flat bass and was also a member of the octet. He died in 1968 and the band played at his funeral.

Jack Pinches was also called up, but instead of being drafted into the services he was selected as a Bevin Boy – which meant that he had to become a coal miner. The bright side of this is that he was 'posted' to Carlton Main Frickley Colliery and played solo trombone with their band for the duration of the war. After this he turned professional and became principal trombone of the BBC Symphony Orchestra. His place in Black Dyke was filled by Haydn Robinson, the player who had stood down for him in the first place.

Away from Black Dyke two other events are worth recording. The first was that during 1942 Harry Mortimer joined the BBC as Supervisor of Brass and Military Band Broadcasts – bands now had two allies in the BBC. The second was the awarding of the OBE to John Henry Iles, announced in the King's birthday honours of 1944. Iles was the first of many members of the brass band movement to be so honoured. However, even as this was happening he was looking towards the end of the war and wondering how the National Championships could be revived, the last having taken place in 1938 at the Alexandra Palace.

The end of an era.

The solution appeared even before the end of the war. Iles had been wooing the managers of a national newspaper, *The Daily Herald*, trying to persuade them to organize and fund the championships. On 27 January 1945 the owners announced that they would 'organize and sponsor a series of area contests'. They would provide trophies and cash prizes and every part of Great Britain would participate. There would be categories for bands of all levels – as there had been in the pre-war Nationals – but the highest placed bands in each section would meet in a series of Finals later in the year. There was a certain amount of resistance to the idea of having to qualify for these but Iles made it clear that this was a 'take it or leave it' situation and that turning it down would mean no more National Championships. The offer was accepted.

There were six English regions, called 'Areas', plus Scotland and Wales. All were required to send two bands to the Finals in each section. Finals for the top section would be held in the Royal Albert Hall, London and those for other sections at Belle Vue. Initially there were just three sections but in the following year this was raised to four and, many years later, to five. One other essential ingredient was that, following the top section Finals in the Royal Albert Hall, there would be a Festival Concert featuring soloists and a number of bands, with a guest conductor from the orchestral world. Though there have, inevitably, been changes as the Championships have evolved, they have always adhered closely to the pattern established in 1945.

Black Dyke won its Area contest in 1945 under Arthur Pearce, but failed to secure a prize in the Finals – won by Fairey Aviation conducted by Harry Mortimer. Worse was to come, the band not even qualifying in 1946. As they did not compete at Belle Vue in these years the 1945 Area win was the only tangible reward for the first two years of post-war contesting. Though the band had remained at the forefront in concerts and broadcasting throughout the war years it had fallen behind bands such as Fairey's which had remained virtually at full contesting strength.

Something had to be done, and that something, on the face of it, was appointing Harry Mortimer as professional conductor early in 1947. Harry Mortimer (1902-1991) had already become William Halliwell's successor as the leading brass band conductor. Born in Hebden Bridge, Yorkshire, he began playing the cornet at the age of eight, taught initially by his father, Fred. Fred Mortimer (1879-1953), had begun his conducting career with Hebden Bridge Band. He had come under the influence of both William Rimmer and William Halliwell and it was at the suggestion of the latter that the Mortimer family moved to Luton in 1910, where Fred became bandmaster of Luton Red Cross Band. After the war – during which he served in the army – with Halliwell as professional conductor, Fred Mortimer as bandmaster and his sons – there were now three – Harry, Alex and Rex all playing members – Luton developed into the

Harry Mortimer, The Doyen of the Brass Band World

leading southern band. In 1923 it became the only band from the South of England ever to win the National Brass Band Championships. In the following year the Mortimers moved again – this time to Sandach in Cheshire, home of Foden's Motor Works Band. Alex was the first to move, to take up the position of solo euphonium. He was followed shortly by the remainder of the family – once again at the suggestion of Mr Halliwell. Harry, as principal solo cornet player with Foden's, now established himself as one of the finest cornet players, not only of his generation, but of all time. He also took up the trumpet and from 1926 played professionally, initially with the Hallé Orchestra and later with the Liverpool Philharmonic and the BBC Northern orchestras. He became musical director of Fairey Aviation Works Band when it was formed in 1937 and built them into the leading war-time brass band. By the time he came to Black Dyke ten years later he had already conducted the winning band at the Belle Vue September contest on five occasions – three times with Fairey's and twice with Bickershaw Colliery. He had also led Fairey's to the title of National Champions in the first post-war contest. He had joined the staff of the BBC and was, therefore, already a powerful brass band figure.

His appointment as professional conductor at Black Dyke brought the required result, with wins both in the Area and at the Finals of 1947. However, one needs to look further than the appointment of a new conductor. He can, after all, only work with the material he has. The band, having lost most of its promising young talent during the war, was growing old. Many of its players were past their best and anyway, styles had changed.

A new influx of young players was required. Some of these came from Black Dyke Juniors, including at least three who were to influence the band's future. They were John Slinger, Gordon Sutcliffe and Geoffrey Whitham. All were put on secondary parts initially, but were ultimately destined to fill key positions.

However, the first major addition to the ranks was Denzil Stephens, who came to the band in 1946 and who, after a very short time, was given the position of solo euphonium. Denzil hailed from Guernsey and had come to the North of England during the war as an evacuee. He had a Salvation Army background and was soon playing in the Halifax SA Band. A member of Black Dyke heard him playing in a talent competition and suggested that he should apply for an audition. Mr Pearce recommended a course of private lessons, after which Denzil was admitted to the band. Later in 1946 Willie Lang was demobbed and returned as principal cornet player. Thus, the two most important positions were satisfactorily filled. Meanwhile, Geoffrey Whitham was playing baritone, whilst in 1947 Gordon Sutcliffe succeeded Joe Wood as solo horn player. Thus, Harry Mortimer had a new-look band to work with, and much credit must go to Arthur Pearce for integrating all the changes and providing Harry with what had once again become a top class band.

The band had other things to rejoice about in 1947, as Willie Lang became the All-England Solo Champion and the band's quartet won the Quartet Championship of Great Britain, which took place annually in Oxford. The members were Willie Lang, Frank Hiley (another young player recently brought into the band), Gordon Sutcliffe and Denzil Stephens. They were trained and conducted by Joe Wood who, along with Owen Bottomley, received a long-service award that year, the former for 25 years and the latter for 30.

The hat-trick Quartet of 1947-48-49 – Willie Lang, Frank Hiley, Gordon Sutcliffe and Denzil Stephens

In 1948 there was a repeat of the quartet's success, the joy of which was added to by the fact that the band's 'No. 2' quartet took 3rd prize. By virtue of its 1947 win in the National Championships, the band was given a bye and not required to compete in that year's Area contest. However, it went to the Royal Albert Hall and won again, giving Arthur Pearce a wonderful birthday present, as he was 77 on the day of the contest. The contest performance was conducted, of course, by Harry Mortimer. Black Dyke was one of nine bands which played in the evening concert, when the conductors were Sir Malcolm Sargent (recently knighted) and Harry Mortimer.

Whit Friday contests were revived in 1946, when Black Dyke was awarded two 1st prizes, four 2nds and a 3rd. In the following year the tally was a remarkable six 1st prizes from six contests and in 1948 there were five 1sts and a 2nd.

News of concert engagements was very sparse during these years. There seem to have been very few in 1946, with rather more in the following year – perhaps one in most weeks. They were more plentiful in 1948, when the band spent most of July on tour in Scotland.

Broadcasts continued to take place regularly after the war. The first of note was part of the 1945 Festival Concert, when Black Dyke joined Foden's, Fairey's, Scottish CWS and Creswell Colliery on stage in the Royal Albert Hall. The broadcast part of the concert was conducted by Sir Adrian Boult. Another special broadcast took place in Queensbury on Sunday 30 December, when the guest soloists were Jack Pinches and the veteran cornet player John Paley.

There were 14 broadcasts in 1946, mainly from Leeds, though one came from the Philharmonic Hall, Liverpool, with Black Dyke, Brighouse & Rastrick and Foden's, along with the Philharmonic Choir. The conductor was Stanford Robinson and the guest soloist the famous concert pianist Louis Kentner, who performed the 1st Movement of Schumann's Piano Concerto – with band accompaniment. On 26 October Black Dyke seems to have made its first contribution to the long-running series 'Listen to the Band' – with its famous Lionel Monckton signature tune of the same name.

In 1947 there were – unbelievably these days – 17 broadcasts by Black Dyke. The first was a 'Sounding Brass and Voices' programme with Colne Valley Male Voice Choir and the tenor singer Frank Titterton. The conductor was Leslie Woodgate and in addition to the band items there were six vocal numbers, all accompanied by the band. Later broadcasts this year included a massed band concert from the City Hall, Sheffield – when Black Dyke was joined by St Hilda's[57] and Creswell under Denis Wright's baton, and part of the 1947 Festival Concert from the National Championships, with seven bands conducted by Sir Adrian Boult. There were also three further 'Sounding Brass and Voices' programmes as well as the straight band broadcasts.

1948 brought a mere(!) 15 broadcasts. During one from Huddersfield, John Henry Iles presented Arthur O. Pearce with the Iles Medal of the Worshipful Company of Musicians – the first such

---

[57] This was neither the colliery band nor the professional band that developed from it, but a new band using the same name under licence, based near Bradford and formed in 1946.

award to be made. A broadcast during August from Cumnock in Ayrshire marked the opening of a new branch of John Foster & Son Ltd there. The Royal Albert Hall concert this year again featured nine bands, along with the London Men's Choir, with Sir Malcolm on the podium. On 16 November came the band's official 200th broadcast. The next, on Christmas Eve, from 7.15 to 8pm was Arthur O. Pearce's last broadcast, and his final appearance as bandmaster of Black Dyke Mills Band. It must surely have been a very emotional occasion.

A cursory look at music played during these broadcasts shows the vastness of the band's repertoire, through original works, transcriptions, selections, solos and a whole range of lighter items. Nor does it take an Einstein to realize how much the BBC – through the influence of Harry Mortimer and Denis Wright – was doing for brass bands at that time.

Joe Willie Wood, a faithful servant

Conversely, commercial recording remained almost at a standstill. The only Black Dyke release during the years 1942-1948 was a live recording of the band's winning performance of Hubert Bath's *Freedom*, from the Royal Albert Hall in 1947.

With the retirement of Arthur O. Pearce came the end of an era for Black Dyke. Apart from the final two years it had not been particularly memorable for its contest successes. However, the band had enhanced its reputation no end in its broadcasting and concert performances, and for much of the period it was virtually a professional band – work in the mill being something to be indulged in only when the band did not have an engagement.

By the time of his retirement in 1948 Mr Pearce had become known as the 'Prime Minister of Brass Bands'. Black Dyke had won

51 first prizes, 37 seconds and 17 thirds during his 37 years as bandmaster, amassing prize money of some £12,000. The band had made about 50 gramophone recordings and given over 200 broadcasts. He had been the first of many recipients of the Iles Medal of the Worshipful Company of Musicians – for services to bands.

Towards the end of 1948 there was an announcement regarding Mr Pearce's successor. It was to be the band's long-term solo horn player and, more recently, the 'guardian' of the band's quartets – Joe Willie Wood.

* * * * *

Arthur Oakes Pearce died on 13th January 1951, aged 79. He was given an impressive funeral. Black Dyke Mills Band attended a private service at Mr Pearce's home before leading the cortège to the chapel and the graveside. Friends came from far and wide and there were 16 Rolls Royces in the procession that passed through the town.

CHAPTER 6

The Geoffrey Whitham years – a time of change

THE NEXT period to be discussed covers the years 1949-1965, years that saw significant changes in many aspects of life in Black Dyke Mills Band. Not least of these was the fact that in a relatively short time-span there were five different professional conductors and five bandmasters. There was also a change in the work situation. Hitherto, the company had employed all bandmasters and virtually all players. This was normal for leading works bands and was the reason why they could go on tour whenever and wherever engagements dictated.

Geoffrey Whitham, euphonium soloist and bandmaster

During the 1950s this changed, and with the swing away from a demand for time off work came a comparable change in the work status of the players. Gradually, fewer and fewer of them worked for John Foster & Son Ltd and, indeed, fewer of them were now what could honestly be described as 'working men'. This trend was to spread through the whole brass band movement as the old definition of a brass band being the 'working man's orchestra' became less accurate, with teachers, company directors and even doctors now in membership. Along with these changes, the autonomy of Black Dyke's bandmaster was eroded as players began to have more say in the running of the band, both with regard to acceptance of new members, and which and how many engagements were to be undertaken.

However, though conductors came and went, a number of players remained throughout this period. Gordon Sutcliffe, the solo horn player and a very strong character did so and was highly influential. John Slinger, though with a less dominant personality, was thought by many to be the finest musician in the band and contributed considerably to the band's musical development. Both of these players came up through Black Dyke Juniors. However, I have chosen Geoffrey Whitham to head this chapter for a number of reasons. As the all-important solo euphonium player from 1950-1963 he had a huge influence. In addition, he combined this post with that of conductor of Black Dyke Juniors from 1960 after which, relinquishing both positions, in 1963 he became Black Dyke's eleventh bandmaster. Though moving on after three years, he remains to this day an ardent Pondasher. His grandfather, Charlie Tinker, was a member of Black Dyke's bass section from 1913 to 1933 and therefore Geoffrey's connections with Black Dyke, and his encyclopaedic knowledge of it, cover over 90 years.

Geoffrey Whitham (b. 1932) began his playing career with Black Dyke Juniors in 1942. He played euphonium from the very start, transferring to the senior band as its 2nd baritone player in 1947, moving to 1st baritone in the following year and to solo euphonium in 1950. He remains, therefore, one of only a handful of surviving players who served under Arthur O. Pearce. His audition for entry into the band concerned not only Geoffrey himself, but his parents, who were also interviewed by 'Mr Pearce'. He demanded their assurance that they would see to it that their son was properly turned out at all times, that he would never be late for a rehearsal or engagement, and that Black Dyke Mills Band would be the first priority in Geoffrey's life.

Having survived all of this, Geoffrey recalls that younger members of the band were required to attend half an hour before rehearsal time so that Mr Pearce could 'instruct' them in matters concerning the band. These instructions were largely the reminiscences of an old man, but they made the young bandsmen aware of the responsibilities that went with the privilege of membership of Black Dyke. They were also made aware that they were custodians of a great tradition.

* * * * *

As was seen at the end of Chapter Five, Joe Willie Wood was named as successor to Arthur Pearce as bandmaster. Joe had commenced his playing days with Brighouse Boro' Band in 1901, staying there until its disbandment in 1907. He was then a member of Clifton & Lightcliffe until 1912, playing solo cornet and soprano. Now he returned to Brighouse – but to Brighouse & Rastrick Temperance Band, becoming the solo horn player in 1914, and acting as bandmaster for a year before leaving at the end of 1921 and moving to Black Dyke.[58]

Joe had thus been a member of Black Dyke since 1922 and its highly respected solo horn player since 1928. However, it is difficult to move successfully from being a playing member to bandmaster – especially in a band such as Black Dyke, and it should be noted that at this time Black Dyke had been National Champions for two years so they were at the top of their form. Whilst Joe had the respect of his colleagues as a player he was unable to earn it as bandmaster. His reign, therefore, was short-lived – lasting only from January to September. It is quite significant that Harry Mortimer, as professional conductor, conducted several concerts and broadcasts during this period.

Joe Wood's successor as solo horn player was Gordon Sutcliffe. Like so many other members of Black Dyke, Gordon served his apprenticeship in the Juniors. He came into the seniors on the 2nd horn chair in 1943 and succeeded Joe Wood on solo horn in 1947.

As reigning champions Black Dyke did not compete in the 1949 Area contest and as they did not attend Belle Vue there were no band contests during Joe's term of office. There was, however, a busy concert season. This began with a massed band concert in Halifax, when Black Dyke combined with Brighouse & Rastrick, a band that Arthur Pearce conducted during his early years, to mark his retirement. Harry Mortimer conducted and Haydn Robinson made a presentation on behalf of the band. One of the items in the concert was a cornet duet, *Ida and Dot*, played by Willie Lang and

---

[58] Joe W. Wood died in 1962 at the age of 71.

Harry Mortimer. It was conducted by Fred Mortimer. The proceeds of the concert were donated to the Bandsmen's Empire Memorial Fund, a charity very much in the news at the time.

Another concert of note took place in Rochdale. It was a Police Charities concert in which Black Dyke's former euphonium soloist, Rowland Jones – now with Sadler's Wells – was the guest soloist. Again, Harry Mortimer conducted.

However, Joe Wood conducted the band in most of its concerts. As well as local engagements, Black Dyke visited Kettering, Birmingham, Grimsby, Darlington, Chesterfield, Nottingham and York. There was also a visit to the South West, where the band appeared in the Royal Cornwall Show at Falmouth as part of a week's tour of Cornwall. The band also toured in South Wales and played in Bath and Eastbourne. Hardly comparable to some earlier seasons, this nevertheless represented a very successful time for the twice-Champion Band of Great Britain. The principal soloists at this time were Willie Lang, Denzil Stephens and Haydn Robinson.

Though the band did not contest during the Joe Wood period its quartet, under his direction, completed a hat-trick at the Championships of Great Britain. Nevertheless, it was announced that Alex Mortimer was to become bandmaster of Black Dyke Mills Band with effect from 1 October 1949, with Joe Wood continuing as manager of the business side of the band's activities.

The Mortimer years

Alex Mortimer (1905-1976), like his elder brother, Harry, was born in Hebden Bridge but moved to Luton in 1910. In 1924 he was the first of the Mortimers to move to Foden's, where he played solo euphonium for 20 years, becoming one of the finest of all euphonium players. He left in 1944 to become principal tuba player of the Liverpool Philharmonic Orchestra, but five years later became musical director of the Scottish CWS Band. However, within a few months he had been appointed bandmaster at Black Dyke.

Having won the Nationals in each of the last two years of Arthur Pearce's bandmastership, the band went on to complete its hat-trick in 1949, the first year of Alex Mortimer's period of office. This, of course, was under the baton of Harry. Prizes were presented to the winning conductors on this occasion by Princess Elizabeth (later to become Queen Elizabeth II) during the evening concert – her one and only appearance at the Nationals.

The band did not compete at Belle Vue in 1949, 1950 or 1951 and through its London wins was not required to appear in the Area contests of 1948, 1949 or 1950. It was barred from the Nationals in 1950 due to the hat-trick and therefore contesting was not a big issue during these years.

A fresh start was called for in 1951. Winning 2nd prize in the Area meant that the band qualified for the Finals. Conducted by Alex in both events, the band went on to win the Championships again – a triumph for the younger Mortimer.

At around the time of Alex's appointment Black Dyke appeared in a spectacular Celebrity Concert promoted by the *Daily Herald* in the highly prestigious London Palladium. Conducted by Harry Mortimer, the band took the audience by storm with its performance of Liszt's *Hungarian Rhapsody No 2.*

One of Alex's first appearances with Black Dyke was in a Brighouse & Rastrick massed band concert in Huddersfield Town Hall. Along with Brighouse, the bands appearing were Foden's and Black Dyke, conducted by father and son in their 'solo spots'.

From now on Alex conducted most of Black Dyke's concerts and broadcasts. In addition to the many local engagements undertaken in 1950 there was a fortnight's tour in the south, taking in Eastbourne, Plymouth and Cornwall, where an audience of some 10,000 assembled on the football ground at Camborne to hear the band. This seems to have been the only tour this year, but during October the band played in Enfield, Dagenham and Luton, *en route* to the Finals, as well as appearing on television from Alexandra Palace in a programme with Sir Malcolm Sargent, demonstrating brass band instruments. Though not involved in the National Championships this year, Black Dyke was one of the nine bands to appear in the Festival Concert.

There were some significant changes in personnel during 1950; Haydn Robinson was replaced by Lance Winn, who hailed from Easington Colliery Band in the North East; following call-up at the age of 21, Denzil Stephens was replaced on solo euphonium by Geoffrey Whitham. It was announced in December that Bernard Bygrave was to replace Willie Lang as principal solo cornet player. Bernard had had some experience in the solo cornet section of Creswell Colliery and latterly had played principal cornet with Brighouse & Rastrick. Willie was going to play trumpet with the West Riding Orchestra.

The 1951 band, with Alex Mortimer seated behind the 'Daily Herald' trophy – Willie Lang and Charlie Emmott are to his left, and Bernard Burns and Denzil Stephens to his right

Black Dyke's Quartet in the early 1950s, showing from right to left – Alex Mortimer, Bernard Bygrave, Alwyn Pinches, Gordon Sutcliffe and Geoffrey Whitham

Early in 1951 Bernard Burns, Black Dyke's soprano player, retired from playing in order to take up the baton – moving on to conduct Butterfield's Tank Works Band in Shipley.[59] He was replaced by Tommy Waterman, who came to Black Dyke from City of Coventry. This was Festival of Britain year and many bands found extra engagements. Black Dyke was on tour for nine weeks this year – almost like old times! The tour began with a week at an Exhibition in Hull. It included two weeks in Eastbourne, a week in Plymouth and further touring in Wales and in the vicinity of Bath.

A very special engagement this year was the first performance of a new work by the English composer Thomas Wood, commissioned by the Arts Council. Frank Wright scored the work and Sir Adrian Boult conducted this first performance, in the Royal Albert Hall. The work was called *The Rainbow* and its text was based on a story connected with the Dunkirk evacuation. It required six bands and huge vocal forces.

By early 1952, the year that saw the death of King George VI, Willie Lang was back in Queensbury and Bernard Bygrave had left. There were fewer band concerts this year and the only long-range engagements for Black Dyke seem to have been the annual trip to Plymouth and a few days in Cornwall. Were bands losing their appeal?

The National Championships of 1952 and 1953 were held at Earls Court, where the seating capacity of the Empress Hall was considerably larger than that of the Royal Albert Hall. Black Dyke were awarded 3rd prize there in 1952, following a 5th at Belle Vue, but in 1953 the only prizes won were a 1st at the Area and 3rd at Belle Vue.

1953 was Coronation Year and there was a decided upturn in band engagements. New uniforms were issued, in a less formal style than that of traditional uniforms. They were made from cloth produced at Black Dyke Mills. In addition to the many local and 'middle-distance' concerts this year, the band appeared in Southampton prior to sailing to the Channel Islands for a week's engagement in St Helier. This was followed by a week in Worthing. On a weekend in June the band travelled 450 miles in three days, with a Friday broadcast in Leeds, a Saturday concert in Aberystwyth – which included another performance of *The Rainbow*, and ending with a Sunday concert in Doncaster.

---

[59] Bernard Burns died in 1991, aged 82.

An unusual concert took place in Bolton, when Foden's, Fairey's and Black Dyke were the bands, and the conducting was shared by three of the famous Mortimers – Fred, Harry and Alex.

Though the band won the Area contest in the spring, tragedy struck, as one of the band's solo cornet players, Albert Brown collapsed and died the following morning. He was only in his early 40s. By a strange twist of fate Brighouse & Rastrick also lost a player on the same day. Albert Portrey, a BB flat bass player collapsed upon leaving the stage following the band's performance. He was taken to hospital where he also died the following morning.

The number of broadcasts undertaken by Black Dyke during these years remained buoyant, though there was a dip to 10 in 1949. There were 12 in 1950, 13 a year later, a high of 15 in 1952 but something of a slump to nine in 1953. The only broadcast of any note in 1949 was part of the London Palladium concert, mentioned above. Other broadcasts in 1949 and throughout 1950 seem to have been quite ordinary, with rather mundane programmes. There was more variety in the 1951 broadcasts, with one or two original works and some orchestral transcriptions. There were also quite a few broadcasts in the 'Sounding Brass and Voices' series. Despite the surge in the number of broadcasts in 1952 their content was again quite ordinary, and the high number made by Black Dyke contrasted with a general reduction in band broadcasts. The 1953 broadcasts, though fewer in number, followed a similar pattern to that of the previous year.

There were no Black Dyke commercial recordings from 1942 until 1950, when JAMCO released 14 Black Dyke discs. Amongst the repertoire included in these were *Hungarian Rhapsody No. 2*, *Queensbury*, *A Comedy Overture* (John Ireland), various selections, solos by Willie Lang (*Facilita*, *Trumpet Tune* and *Arbucklenian Polka*) and Denzil Stephens (*Rondo from Horn Concerto No 4* – Mozart), and a rare duet, *The Troubadours*, with Lance Winn and John Slinger. Being on such a minor label, these will now be collectors' items.

Alex Mortimer was taken into hospital during the early part of 1954 with what was described as 'internal trouble'. He had recovered from this, but it came as a shock to read in *British Bandsman* of 13 February that he had been appointed musical director and manager of CWS (Manchester) Band and that he would take up his duties in March. Health was given as one of the reasons for the move and it must be admitted that the wilds of

Queensbury are no place for anyone who does not have a strong constitution.

There was now once again a vacancy for the all-important position of bandmaster at Black Dyke. By a strange co-incidence Fairey's and Foden's were each in a similar situation. Rex Mortimer, the third son of Fred, accepted the challenge at Foden's whilst a former principal cornet player, Elgar Clayton, took over for the second time at Fairey's.

There was an overlap in Alex Mortimer's conducting duties, as on 10 April he conducted his new band in a broadcast and took his old band to the Area contest the following week. Oh dear! Having what was described as an 'off day', Black Dyke failed to qualify for the 1954 Finals. Once again, the band was going through what, by its own high standards, must be described as a bad patch.

Not until 19 May was the announcement made in *British Bandsman* that the new bandmaster of Black Dyke was to be Edmund Hoole.

* * * * *

Edmund Hoole had recently been making a name for himself with Wharncliffe Silkstone Band, based in South Yorkshire. They had been prize-winners in many local contests and had done well in the Belle Vue May contests of 1952, 1953 and 1954. His playing career began at the age of six, with a local Salvation Army Band. He joined Wharncliffe Silkstone on commencing work at the colliery when he was 13, and became its conductor 10 years later. Now, at the age of 35, he had achieved his life's ambition, to conduct Black Dyke Mills Band.

The busy 1954 season included, once again, a week in Jersey. Following a rough sea crossing the band played from 19-26 June on the new bandstand in St Helier's Howard Davis Park. Edmund (Ned) Hoole seems to have been a big success, his charismatic personality scoring with the audiences. The soloists at this time were Messrs Lang, Whitham, and Winn. In July the band returned south to give two concerts in Plymouth.

There were now some important changes in personnel. Willie Lang left to join the recently-formed Ferodo Works Band at Chapel-en-le-Frith in Derbyshire. Shortly after this Lance Winn left to join John White's Footwear Band in Northamptonshire. David Pratt, already a member of the cornet section moved onto the principal's chair, whilst 14-year-old Colin Monkman was brought in as the new solo trombonist. The band's final summer engagement of 1954 was at Buxton, where the soloists were now Messrs Pratt, Whitham and Monkman.

In February 1955 Edmund Hoole suffered a severe blow when his young daughter died, following a short illness. This, understandably, caused serious family problems. Though it was announced that he would conduct both Black Dyke and Wharncliffe at the Area contest, Harry Mortimer took Black Dyke – and won.

The band was now 100 years old. There were concerts and social events to celebrate this, and each bandsman was presented with a pewter tankard to mark the occasion. Later in the year the band appeared on television to mark the centenary. There seems to have been a move to boycott Belle Vue this year, as neither Black Dyke, Munn & Felton's, Foden's, Fairey's nor Brighouse & Rastrick attended. At the Nationals, Black Dyke took 5th prize. There was a return to the Whit Friday march contests this year – the band's first appearance there since 1948. It was rewarded with a 1st prize and two 2nds.

1955 seems to have been a relatively quiet year, with many routine engagements but no long-range tours. Indeed, with several band members not working at Foster's it became difficult or even impossible to accept such engagements.

The following year began with the announcement that Edmund Hoole was to leave. No specific reasons were given but it is understood that his daughter's death had made it difficult for his family to settle in Queensbury. Therefore, they returned to their former home and Edmund returned to Wharncliffe Silkstone Band.

It was announced in March 1956 that Jack Emmott was to be the new bandmaster. He was a former member of the band, having played euphonium from 1940 to 1944, then being in the army for 12 years where he received training as a bandmaster. He was still a young man, aged only 31. Joe Wood now took the opportunity to retire and Jack took over the secretarial duties.

There were soon reports that the band was settling down well with Jack. They won the Area under his baton and in the Whit Friday march contests picked up two 1st prizes and two 2nds. Yet again Black Dyke did not compete at Belle Vue but was placed sixth at the Nationals. As Area champions they were one of the nine bands to appear in the Festival concert at the Royal Albert Hall – this time with Karl Rankl conducting.[60] Black Dyke had had another busy concert season but again there were no tours. The most prestigious engagement this year was a return to Cumnock in July, when the Queen visited the factory of John Foster's and the band provided appropriate music.

By 1957 bands generally were losing their popularity. Adverse comments about brass bands in parks escalated and, worse, several works bands which had been founded within the previous few years were now disbanded.

Maurice Murphy, an oustanding talent

The big news at Black Dyke early in the year was of the appointment of a new principal cornet player, his name – Maurice Murphy. Maurice, born in Hammersmith, moved at a very early age with his family to the North-East. Showing exceptional promise, he became the All-England Juvenile Solo Champion in 1947 at the age of 11, and whilst still a boy, played with Crookhall and Harton Colliery bands. In 1951 he moved to Bradford to join the YEWCO Works Band, and on its demise in 1956 moved to Stockport to become assistant principal cornet player with Fairey's. On his appointment as principal cornet player of Black Dyke the Yorkshire correspondent of *British Bandsman*, writing as 'Moorlander', had this to say:

---

[60] Rankl was guest conductor at a number of brass band concerts. Austrian-born, he had settled in England in 1939. He was music director of Covent Garden Opera Company from 1946-1951 and in 1952 became principal conductor of the Scottish National Orchestra.

> Maurice Murphy is settling down well, and we anticipate that this boy will be one of England's leading cornet players in the near future.

What a prophet!

Playing at a Festival Concert following the East Anglian Brass Band Association's annual contest, the band's soloists were now Messrs Murphy, Whitham and Monkman. Surprisingly, Black Dyke was not in the top three at the Area contest and therefore did not qualify for the Finals. Following this disappointment, the band showed an improvement in the Whit Friday march contests, with three 1sts, two 2nds and a 3rd prize.

Easily the most exciting event for Black Dyke during the summer of 1957 was a visit to Moscow by its octet – a chamber group formed for the occasion from the band's key players. The group left Queensbury during the last week in July to participate in a 15-day Festival, the object of which was 'to promote peace, friendship and understanding between all nations'. Some 33,000 people from 149 different countries were present. The octet gave nine performances, to great acclaim, and there was speculation about a Russian tour by the whole band. Unfortunately, this did not materialise.

Broadcasts during these years, though highly satisfactory when compared to figures of the present day, were showing signs of decline. The totals were eight in 1954, seven in 1955, eight again in 1956 and a return to better days with 12 in 1957.[61]

Programmes were generally of a light nature and included much popular band music of the time, along with the occasional original work or old-fashioned selection. Colin Monkman made his broadcasting debut playing Hespe's *Melodie et Caprice* in a programme recorded in Decemeber 1954.

The band's centenary broadcast, from Leeds on Friday, 17 June 1955 was a rather traumatic experience for the members. Harry Mortimer should have conducted but because of a chill he was unable to attend. Then, shortly before the broadcast, two cornet players were involved in a motor cycle accident, one being detained in hospital. Maurice Murphy was brought in from the YEWCO Band to fill the gap in the cornet section and Edmund Hoole conducted. The programme included two original works – *On the Cornish Coast*

---

[61] No records of broadcasts were kept between 1949 and 1953 but I was able to compile a list from entries in *British Bandsman*. Hoole kept records from 1954 and Emmott kept some from March 1956.

(Bath) and *Severn Suite* (Elgar), as well as a performance of the *Gloria in Excelsis* – played by Black Dyke in 1860 at Crystal Palace. There was also a cornet solo, *Passing By*, featuring David Pratt, and the marches *Queensbury* and *BB&CF*.

Virtually the same programme was played for a centenary television programme that went out at 10pm on Friday, 9 October, though the cornet solo was replaced by *Melodie et Caprice*, played by young Monkman. On this occasion Mortimer and Hoole shared the conducting.

A BBC recording for *Bright and Early*, made on 9 March, was Jack Emmott's first official engagement as bandmaster, whilst Friday, 28 September saw what was probably Black Dyke's first appearance in the still popular 'Friday Night is Music Night'. This came from St George's Hall, Bradford, and along with the band featured Bradford Police Choir, the singer Vanessa Lee and, of course, the BBC Concert Orchestra.

The Willcocks years

Though Jack Emmott was now undertaking all of the band's conducting duties, there had been a long tradition at Black Dyke of engaging a professional conductor to take the band to major contests. Harry Mortimer had served the band well in this capacity but he was now a very busy man, and there was a feeling that a new face would be advantageous.

A year earlier, due to Harry being on the other side of the world adjudicating, Fairey Aviation had engaged Major G. H. Willcocks to take it to the Nationals, which it duly won. However, Fairey's had just recently won the Belle Vue September contest, their quartet were the British Champions, and relatively little was made of this 'military man' who stepped in and had the 'good fortune' to steer the band to its seventh major title in a decade.

One man who took rather more notice than most was Maurice Murphy, the number two solo cornet at Fairey's in 1956, but now number one at Black Dyke. Major Willcocks was invited, through the link with Maurice, to conduct the band in the forthcoming Belle Vue September contest, an invitation he happily accepted.

Major George Henry Willcocks, MBE, MVO had spent a lifetime as a military musician. He joined the Royal Fusiliers as a band boy in 1915 and took up his first appointment as a bandmaster in 1926 – with the 2nd South Wales Borderers. His principal appointment came in 1938, however, when he was commissioned and made Director of Music, the Band of the Irish Guards. He remained with the 'Irish' until his retirement from the army in 1949, by which time he had become the Senior Director of Music, the Brigade of Guards. After three months in Southern Rhodesia he returned to England and from 1950 was director of music of the Ford Motor Works Military Band, based in Dagenham.

G. H. Willcocks – 'The Major'

Mid-1957 witnessed what must have been one of the best-kept secrets in all brass band history. The appointment of Major Willcocks at Black Dyke seems to have created not the slightest ripple of interest, no mention of it being made by any correspondent in *British Bandsman.* Not even when his name appeared alongside Black Dyke in the list of bands entered was there any comment. There was not much in the way of prophecy here, because during his five years with Black Dyke, the band won once at Belle Vue, twice in London, and picked up three Area titles – in three attempts.

Due to the octet's Russian trip, a broadcast and other engagements, 'the Major' had a mere four rehearsals on the Belle Vue test piece, a new work by Helen Perkin – *Carnival.* This was quite unusual as a test piece, calling for restraint rather than bombast and musicality rather than pyrotechnics. There was an immediate bond not only between 'the Major' and the band but also between 'the Major' and the music. The performance at Belle Vue introduced the vast, hushed audience to a new kind of brass band playing, especially in the work's 2nd movement, 'Pavane'. This demonstrated a degree of delicacy and refinement new to bands and their audiences. Black Dyke's performance was nothing short of stunning. The composer, Miss Perkin, had this to say in *British Bandsman* of 21 September:

> The winning band was, of course, superb, and I must congratulate Major Willcocks on a uniquely sensitive and full-blooded reading of 'Carnival'. Every tiny change of mood was understood and expressed in a most telling manner, and not a point was missed. Bravo to the players, too! It was magnificent. The *Pavane* nearly broke my heart.

A week earlier than this, a somewhat begrudging 'Moorlander' wrote in *British Bandsman*:

> Heartiest congratulations to Black Dyke Mills Band on their great and undisputed victory at Belle Vue on Saturday last: and also to Major Willcocks, who conducted so magnificently. As I have written recently, I had heard them in rehearsal and knew they would play *up to standard.* (My italics, R.N.).

So, the new partnership was established and Black Dyke was back in the super-league of contesting bands.

It was reported during March 1958 that Major Willcocks had been seen as a listener at recent Area contests, and towards the end of the month he led Black Dyke to victory in its own event. Then, though

The 1957 band with the Belle Vue shield. Jack Emmott is seated behind the shield and on his right are John Slinger and Geoffrey Whitham. (Maurice Murphy and Major Willcocks are not in the group).

taking 3rd prize at Belle Vue,[62] the band was not amongst the prize-winners in the Nationals.

In the 1959 Area contest Black Dyke, under the Major, again took 1st prize. Once more Black Dyke did not compete at Belle Vue – only 16 bands did! But it went on to create one of the most memorable performances of all time at the Nationals, playing Lalo's overture to the opera, *Le roi d' Ys* – (*The King of Ys* – pronounced 'eess'). Black Dyke had not been in the top four places at the Nationals since its 3rd prize in 1952, so the win this year must have tasted very sweet. The editorial comment in the following week's *British Bandsman* included the following:

> Black Dyke's performance was received with a roar of applause – it was one 'out of the bag' as the idiom goes – and the roar came again when the result was announced.

I was privileged to be in the audience that day. I can still savour the magical sound of the baritones and basses in the opening bars, the oboe-like sound of Murphy's muted cornet, the beauty of Sam Smith's flugel solo[63] and, above all, the superb playing of Whitham – along with the wonderful E flat bass obbligato, played by Charley Emmott. Frank Wright, who transcribed the overture for brass band and who was one of the three adjudicators, wrote:

> It is obvious that the euphonium soloist is an artist. He plays this famous, but enormously difficult solo with tenderness and touching simplicity. Perhaps singers of this 'Rosenn' aria might take a lesson from him.

In 1960 the band was given a bye at the Area because of the 1959 win, but was once again placed third in the Finals.

Black Dyke now faced 1961, little realising that this was to be its last year with Major Willcocks and Maurice Murphy. It began with a

---

[62] At Belle Vue this year a different system of adjudicating was tried out. When every band had played, the adjudicators nominated six to return to the platform for a final play-off. The winning band was Carlton Main Frickley Colliery, enjoying the most successful period in its history. The 'play-off' system was never used again at Belle Vue.

[63] Sam Smith played flugel horn at Black Dyke from 1953-65. His father, Harry, had also been a member. Shortly after leaving Black Dyke Sam emigrated to New Zealand. He died there in 1995, aged 67.

quite amazing performance of William Rimmer's arrangement of Liszt's *Les Preludes* at the Area contest. Prior to this performance Black Dyke and Brighouse & Rastrick had each won the Area contest seven times, but now Black Dyke's total was eight.

The run-up to the Finals did not augur well for Black Dyke. Maurice and the Major were involved in a motor car accident just a few weeks before the contest, resulting in the latter being detained in hospital for several days. Then, *en route* to London for the contest, the coach in which the band was travelling was hit by a car. Some of the instruments were so badly damaged that they were rendered unplayable. Further, one bandsman had to be taken to hospital. To cap it all, in the draw for the order of play, Black Dyke drew number 13!

However, instruments were loaned to the band by Boosey & Hawkes, the injured player arrived at the Royal Albert Hall in time to play and unlucky 13 became lucky 13 as the band produced another 'out of the bag' peformance. The test piece was *Les francs juges* – better known to bandsmen as *Judges of the Secret Court* – by Berlioz, and the announcement of Black Dyke as winners for the second time in three years was almost a foregone conclusion.

Black Dyke's good form in the major contests during these years was reflected in its Whit Friday march contest result:

1957	3 x 1st, 2 x 2nd, 1 x 3rd	1960	5 x 1st, 1 x 2nd
1958	3 x 1st, 1 x 2nd	1961	5 x 1st, 1 x 3rd, 1 x 4th
1959	5 x 1st, 3 x 2nd	1962	5 x 1st, 1 x 2nd, 1 x 3rd

Reports of concerts this year were very sketchy. There seems to have been a minimum of contact between Black Dyke and the various correspondents in the band press. One thing that was apparent, however, was that the octet was now established as a performing group. Its frequent appearances suggest that demand for the band had waned. Occasionally the octet would play a few pieces in one of the band's concerts.

Park engagements were certainly disappearing as 'watching telly' became a time-consuming business for the masses. Because of this, many of the evening concerts were cancelled in park engagements that had traditionally been afternoon and evening affairs.

There were, however, occasional concerts of note. One, in October 1958, took place in the Salvation Army Citadel in York. The programme was mainly serious, and included *Kenilworth* (Bliss) and music from *La Traviata*. This concert was a sign for the future, when closer links were formed between Salvation Army bands and what they called 'outside bands'.

Towards the end of 1959 there was a Celebration and Presentation concert in the Victoria Hall, Queensbury, following the band's success in the Nationals.

Probably as a result of this success, the band seems to have been rather busier in 1960. The outstanding concert this year took place in the Royal Festival Hall, London. Here, the band participated in a BBC outside broadcast event designed to promote new music. A composer's competition had been held, and six pieces selected to be played in the concert. Black Dyke were engaged, as National Champions.[64]

The 1960 concert took place on 18 June. Jack Emmott conducted in most of the first half of the concert, though there was a performance of a new arrangement by Denis Wright of Handel's *Hallelujah Concerto*. Wright himself conducted this and the organist was George Thalben-Ball. The second half, conducted by Harry Mortimer, featured the six new compositions and the first performance of Peter Yorke's suite, *The Shipbuilders*, commissioned for the occasion by the BBC and destined to become immensely popular.

As Area Champions Black Dyke were again involved in the Festival Concert following the National Championships. There were six bands and once more Karl Rankl was the chief guest conductor, though Herbert Howells conducted a performance of his *Three Figures* – which had been the test piece for the Championships. As this year saw the centenary of the first Crystal Palace contest, in 1860, the *Gloria in Excelsis* was included in the programme.

1961 saw the first of Black Dyke's own concerts – another sign that there were uncomfortable spaces in the band's diary. Organised by what was called the band's 'Social Committee', it was built on the lines of the BBC 'Sounding Brass and Voices' programmes and in it the band was joined by Keighley Vocal Union. The conductor was Major Willcocks. Several Black Dyke promotions took place during the next 20 years or so.

---

[64] Similar events had been held previously; Munn & Felton's were the guests in 1958 and Foden's in 1959 – each band appearing as reigning National Champions.

A nice gesture was noted in September 1961, when the senior band linked up with Black Dyke Juniors in a fund-raising concert for them, in the Victoria Hall. Geoffrey Whitham was now conducting the Juniors and he, Jack Emmott and Major Willcocks shared the conducting.

Black Dyke's first engagement after its success at the Nationals of 1961 was a week-end in Maryport, Cumbria, organised by the Dearham Band. Members of Black Dyke were 'billeted out' with families. This became an annual weekend outing for the band for many years and several lasting friendships were forged.

Other concerts late in 1961 included one in Eastbrook Hall, Bradford, with the band's former euphonium player, Rowland Jones as guest soloist, and a massed band concert in Newcastle City Hall featuring Black Dyke and Brighouse & Rastrick.

An average of just over nine broadcasts per year was maintained during these years. They demonstrated a reasonable mixture of modern and traditional band music. Programmes such as 'Brass Band Parade', 'Listen to the Band' and 'Friday Night is Music Night' were still in vogue, and two new concepts appeared – 'Out and About' and 'Saturday Night on the Light' – in which a brass band appeared as part of a more general multi-appeal programme. There were also a number of Saturday afternoon programmes lasting 45 minutes, in which the band appeared with a soloist – a singer or an instrumentalist – in one case Tommy Reilly, the celebrated harmonica player.

There were occasional broadcasts with a special interest. One of these was a 'Friday Night is Music Night' from St George's Hall, Bradford. The special feature in this was *Cornish Holiday* – a work for orchestra and band by Denis Wright. For the performance of this, Harry Mortimer conducted the combined BBC Concert Orchestra and Black Dyke.

In 1960 the Royal Festival Hall concert, referred to above, provided two broadcast sessions on the night, live, from 7.30 to 8.15 and from 9 o'clock to 10. Additionally, a recording of excerpts from the concert was broadcast later. Incidentally, the winning composition was *Off the Cuff*, by Patrick Rivers. This, and another piece from the six, *Tarantella Chromatica* by Frank Stokes, remained in Black Dyke's concert repertoire for some time.

There were also broadcasts in the BBC's General Overseas Service. 'Winning Band' broadcasts were not yet the norm, but a special late night 15 minute broadcast took place on 20 November 1961 when the band played *Judges of the Secret Court* and a new march by Major Willcocks – *The Champions.*

Though Black Dyke had not been on tour for a number of years some other bands had – notably CWS (Manchester), Fairey's, Foden's, Munn & Felton's and Carlton Main Frickley Colliery. The same could be said about commercial recordings. Though there had been a general lull since about 1950, Harry Mortimer's All-Star Band was recording regularly from 1952, whilst Fairey's, CWS (Manchester), Foden's and Munn & Felton's each made recordings between then and 1957,

The old 78 rpm disc had now been superseded by the 7-inch EP (extended play, running at 45rpm) and the 10-inch and 12-inch LP (long play, running at 33rpm). These had revolutionised recording, allowing much longer pieces to be recorded without break, giving a much better sound quality, and facilitating editing. Harry Mortimer's All-Star Band had been producing these regularly since 1957, Fairey's since 1958, and CWS and Foden's since 1959.

The first Black Dyke recordings in the new format did not arrive until 1960, when three 7-inch EPs were made. They included recordings of *Le roi d'Ys, The Pondashers* – another march by Major Willcocks dedicated to all Black Dyke supporters, and a cornet solo, *Will o' th' Wisp,* composed by the Major for Maurice Murphy and played by him on the recording. There were also a number of other light pieces. 1961 saw two more 7-inch EPs and in 1962 there was a 10-inch LP. All of these were released on the Paxton[65] label, the Major conducting on the three early ones and Jack Emmott on the others. Jack's final recording with the band was on a 7-inch EP, released by EMI in 1963.

The only major change in band personnel during this period was the replacement of Colin Monkman by Grenville Richmond on solo trombone. Grenville was a former member of Brighouse & Rastrick and had played in the Band of the Royal Signals during military service. A new member of the bass section was Peter McNab, also a former member of Brighouse. Peter was to be the band's compère for many years.

---

[65] A subsidiary of Novello, Paxton published and recorded many brass band pieces during this period.

After such a memorable year it was worrying to learn, late in October, that the Major was in hospital again. He had been to Leeds to conduct a Winning Band broadcast, shortly after which he suffered a severe heart attack. He died on 12 January at the age of 62. Black Dyke had lost its beloved Major. The devastated bandsmen made the journey to his hometown of Dagenham for the funeral. The Ford Motor Works Military Band, of which he had been musical director for a decade and the Pipes of the Irish Guards provided music for this.

* * * * *

It was noted in 1959 that long service was an important feature of Black Dyke. Wilfred Kershaw had completed 25 years and Harry Beckwith had just retired after 44 years' service. Arthur Oldfield had left after 37 years with the band and Joe Wood after 34. Haydn Robinson, Harry Nelson and Bernard Burns had each given over 20 years' service and, of course, Arthur O. Pearce was bandmaster for 37. Still in the band were Ernest Keeton, who had served for 38 years and Owen Bottomley, with 37 to his credit. It was further noted that Arnold Sharpe, a director of John Foster & Son had just died. He had been responsible for the band's welfare since 1947 and had been highly respected. Peter Lambert, who was to be the link between band and company for the next 20 years or so, replaced him.

Long-serving members had contributed to the stability of the band in the past but changes in family life-styles were militating against the trend. There were still some players who had been at Black Dyke for a long time but only about four of them were to pass the 20-year mark. First-class banding was becoming a young man's game.

The remaining years covered by this chapter witnessed a very unsettled period for the band, with many changes. Following the death of Major Willcocks, Leighton Lucas was appointed professional conductor for 1962. Though well known in the orchestral world – particularly in the sphere of ballet, he did not really understand the workings of a brass band and had little conception of the musical standards required in top level contests. He survived for just the one year.

His successor was George Hespe – a former professional tuba player and a widely experienced band conductor. He had composed

The 1961 band (photographed early 1962). Leighton Lucas is on Jack Emmott's left. Behind Leighton is Maurice Murphy and behind Jack is soprano cornet player Tommy Waterman

the 1953 Belle Vue test piece (*The Three Musketeers*) and had conducted the winning performance there in 1955 (with Ferodo Works Band). However, the poor man was not enjoying the best of health. Shortly after conducting the band's performance of the overture *Rienzi* in the 1963 Area contest he collapsed, suffering from a heart attack. Though recovering from this, it effectively ended his conducting career.[66]

Meanwhile Jack Emmott resigned the bandmastership in the following June, after just over seven years.[67] In August it was announced that the band's long-serving solo euphonium player, Geoffrey Whitham, was to be Black Dyke's new bandmaster and that he would conduct the band at the Belle Vue September contest.

However, early in 1964 Major (later Lieut-Colonel) Cecil H. Jaeger was engaged to conduct the band at the Area contest. He was Director of Music, the Band of the Irish Guards – so was following in the footsteps of Major Willcocks in the worlds of both military and brass bands. Affectionately known to everyone as 'Jiggs', he was an

[66] Hespe died in 1979, aged 79.

[67] Shortly after this, Jack emigrated to New Zealand where he worked for many years with bands, choirs and orchestras. After his death, at his own request, his ashes were returned to Queensbury and interred in the grave of his brother, Charlie.

immediate hit with the band and was to be its professional conductor for the next three years. An inspirational conductor, he produced many fine performances with Black Dyke. Unfortunately, the all-important winning performance in the major contests eluded him.

'Jiggs', an inspirational conductor

Reverting now to 1962: about four months after the death of Major Willcocks the band suffered another body blow with the announcement that Maurice Murphy was about to turn professional and become principal trumpet of the BBC Northern Orchestra. He had led the band with distinction for six years and his departure was a great loss; he had also been a key member of the octet. His last appearance as principal cornet was at a concert in St George's Hall, Bradford, on 13 May.[68] In July there was speculation that Jim Shepherd, principal cornet player of Carlton Main and the reigning British Solo Champion was to succeed Maurice. However, he changed his mind and remained – for the time being – at Carlton Main.

John Clay, already a member of Black Dyke's cornet section and a future highly successful flugel horn player, moved into the 'hot seat' and was, for a time, the band's principal cornet player. This was seen as a temporary solution to the problem and in the spring of 1963 the 33-year-old Keith Caldwell became Black Dyke's principal cornet player. He was from New Zealand, where he had been Cornet Champion. In England he had previously played with CWS (Manchester) and Ferodo. His first appearance with Black Dyke was at a concert in Huddersfield Town Hall in March.

---

[68] After a number of years with the BBC Northern Orchestra Maurice moved to London to play principal trumpet with the LSO, sitting alongside his predecessor at Black Dyke, Willie Lang. Maurice now earned a reputation as one of the world's leading trumpet players. He was later joined in the LSO by another former Black Dyke cornet player, Rod Franks.

This also proved to be a temporary appointment and in April it was finally agreed that Jim Shepherd would become Black Dyke's principal cornet player. Jim had begun his playing career at the relatively late age of 13. His first band was Newbiggin Colliery and during military service he played with the RAMC Staff Band. He had been with Carlton Main for the last two and a half years, was now 26 years old and was to give distinguished service to Black Dyke for the next decade. He began his Black Dyke career at a concert in Queensbury marking the Centenary of Queensbury itself.

Another vacancy was created when Geoffrey Whitham became bandmaster. A number of potential successors were tried but eventually the mantle of solo euphonium fell on John Clough. John had joined Black Dyke in 1960, having played principal cornet with Bradford Victoria Band since 1953. At first he played cornet at Black Dyke but later moved onto 2nd baritone, from which he made the enormous leap to solo euphonium, a position he held successfully for 25 years.

At around the same time Grenville Richmond left the band. He was replaced by a trombonist from the Lindley Band – Frank Berry. Frank had been brought up at Lindley but had also played with the Duke of Wellington's Regimental Band during his military service. He was to remain at Black Dyke for almost 20 years. There was thus, now, a completely new team of primary soloists in the band – Messrs Shepherd, Clough and Berry. They were to develop into a formidable team, bringing great credit to the band.

Despite these highly significant changes – as well as other moves on inner parts – the band continued to make its mark on the contest scene as well as maintaining its reputation in concerts and broadcasts.

Having won the 1961 Nationals, the band did not need to compete in the 1962 Area contest. It took four 1st prizes on Whit Friday under Jack Emmott, but under Leighton Lucas collected only a 6th prize at Belle Vue, failing to score at the Nationals.

In 1963 the band was not in the frame at the Area contest under George Hespe and therefore did not attend the Finals. However, there were three Whit Friday wins and 3rd prize at Belle Vue, all under Geoffrey Whitham.

There was a brilliant win at the 1964 Area contest under Major Jaeger followed by five Whit Friday 1st prizes under Geoffrey. In the Nationals, with an outstanding performance of *Variations on a Ninth,*

~~*Frank Berry*~~
Jim Shepherd - cornet

~~*John Clough*~~
Frank Berry
trombone

~~*Jim Shepherd*~~
John Clough
euphonium

A formidable team

the band was 'pipped at the post' by GUS and had to be happy with 2nd place. This was the first time that a serving Director of Music had conducted in the Nationals.

The 1965 Area contest saw a second outstanding win for Major Jaeger and Black Dyke and, conducted by Geoffrey Whitham, three Whit Friday wins and 3rd prize at the Edinburgh International Contest – Black Dyke's one and only appearance there. On this occasion, for the first time in a decade, the band undertook a week's engagement, playing in Edinburgh during the Edinburgh International Music Festival week.

There was, at this time, a campaign by the instrument manufacturers to persuade brass bands to adopt the same playing pitch as other branches of music – orchestras, military bands and choirs, as well as pianos and organs. Hitherto, bands played in what was called 'high pitch' and there were tuning problems if they wished to combine with other musical forces. Black Dyke, like many other bands, purchased special tuning slides to bring the band's pitch down. The bandsmen were not satisfied with the results, however, and returned to high pitch. In June Boosey & Hawkes

The 1964 band, Geoffrey Whitham bandmaster. Jim Shepherd is on the middle row, 4th from the left, Frank Berry is on the middle row, 4th from the right and John Clough is on the front row, 3rd from the left.

triumphantly announced that Black Dyke had ordered a full set of new low pitch instruments. They were the first contesting band to do so.

The new instruments arrived only a few weeks before the Nationals, where Black Dyke was not in the prizes. How much this had to do with the new instruments, how much it had to do with the band's dreaded number one draw, or how many other reasons there were, we shall never know.

* * * * *

As was seen earlier, Jim Shepherd joined Black Dyke in 1963. He had won the title of Champion Soloist of Great Britain earlier in the year and, indeed, had also won it in 1962. He was, therefore, up for the hat-trick in 1964. This he duly completed, but not only that. A new quartet was formed, comprising Jim, Stephen Thornton, Brian Wood – all relatively new to Black Dyke – and John Clough. They became the new Quartet Champions of Great Britain. In addition, Jim won the special award for best instrumentalist in the Quartet category.

In 1965 Black Dyke sent two quartets to Oxford – 'A', the standard group and 'B', a trombone quartet, made up of Frank Berry, Derek Southcott, Colin Hardy and John Slinger. The Trombones were declared winners and the 'A' team came second. So, though Black Dyke won the title twice in succession it was not considered to be a double win as the groups were different.

The concert calendar was now beginning to take on a slightly different shape. I have frequently referred to 'routine' engagements. These would include annual marching jobs such as those connected with Remembrance Day and the various Whit walks. There was often some playing at around Christmas time and during the summer there was the round of park or seaside bandstand engagements. Some variants of these included New Brighton, Morecambe and Adwick-le-Street. The evening concert at New Brighton was held in a theatre; there was no evening concert at Morecambe, so this became a family day out; and at Adwick-le-Street the evening concert was in the Miners' Welfare Hall. Thorne and Scarborough were standard afternoon and evening park concerts. At Scarborough the bandsmen were rowed out to the bandstand, built in the middle of the lake in Peasholm Park.

The summer season, as was seen in earlier chapters, had diminished considerably, and continued doing so. However, a trend was now taking shape where there were more indoor concerts – many of them in reasonably good class halls. Black Dyke was regularly appearing in St George's Hall, Bradford, the Victoria Hall, Halifax and in Huddersfield Town Hall. It was also visiting places such as Derby, Leicester and Swansea. There was a growing trend for contest organisers to book a leading band to give an evening Festival Concert following the contest. These were to become very successful. There was a ready-made audience, little extra cost apart from the band's fee and a varied programme, well played, after what might have been a day of heavy listening. A concert in Oxford Town Hall in 1965, following a contest organised by the local band, was one of the first of this type of concert to be given by Black Dyke.

Black Dyke's octet was still in demand throughout these years, and as larger halls came into use there were more concerts with choirs. Black Dyke also continued to organise its own concerts.

A 1962 engagement, which calls for special comment, was participating in the procession known as the Lord Mayor's Show, in London. This was a large procession passing many of London's famous landmarks. It took 25 minutes to pass a given point and Black Dyke – just one of many bands – headed the Milk Marketing Board's part of the procession.

Broadcasting continued to form an important part of the band's music-making, though I have not been able to log all broadcasts, as there were periods when they were not reviewed in *British Bandsman.* There were, however, one or two of special interest. Under the title 'Miniature Brass' the octet had its own programme in September 1962. In November there was a broadcast from Sheffield City Hall, part of the celebrations commemorating the Centenary of the BBC's North Region. Black Dyke were joined by Foden's, Fairey's, CWS (Manchester) and the Sheffield Philharmonic Choir. Charles (later Sir Charles) Groves was the conductor and amongst the guest soloists was Willie Lang. He performed two movements from Haydn's *Trumpet Concerto,* and also included in the programme was Ireland's *Comedy Overture* and the Grand March from Verdi's *Aida.*

In July 1963 there was a rare appearance on television. This was from a tele-recording in Huddersfield Town Hall, along with Keighley Vocal Union and conductor Stanford Robinson.

1970 saw the 70th birthday of one of brass band's leading personalities, Dr. Denis Wright, OBE. As one of the pioneers of band broadcasting he was offered a broadcast of his own music, to be conducted by himself with a band of his choice. He chose Black Dyke and directed them playing his *St Nicholas Eve*, the *Canzonetta* and *Rondo* from the *Cornet Concerto* – with Jim Shepherd as soloist, the *Scherzo* from *Music For Brass* and one of Wright's most successful compositions, *Tintagel*.

Only one further commercial recording was made in this period and it was the famous 12-inch EMI recording on which the conducting was shared by Major Jaeger and Geoffrey Whitham. The programme was a mixture of old and new and included the overtures *Poet and Peasant* and *1812*. The march *Knight Templar* was also included, having brought the band most of its Whit Friday successes.

* * * * *

Other things happening in the wider world of brass bands at this time concerned the National Brass Band Championships and the BBC.

In 1964 Harry Mortimer retired from his position at the BBC as Supervisor of Brass and Military Bands. He was now 62 years old and was, in fact, two years beyond what should have been his retiring age. To everyone's consternation he was not replaced and it was decreed that each Region would be responsible for its own band broadcasts. This was a mixed blessing. In the North we had Bill Relton on the BBC staff. He was a life-long supporter of brass bands, was born in Queensbury, and had been a member of Brighouse & Rastrick in his youth. He was, therefore, well equipped to look after our interests, but in many other regions there was no one on the staff who cared a hoot about brass bands.

It was something of a relief, therefore, in mid-1965, when it was announced that Geoffrey Brand was to become responsible for all BBC band programmes that originated in or were sponsored by the London Region. Geoffrey was a senior member of the BBC's staff and was able to influence band broadcasting not only through his allocation of air time to bands within his region, but also by creating special programmes and bringing leading bands from other regions to London. Over the next few years Black Dyke was to benefit from this.

Co-incidentally, also in 1964, the *Daily Herald* withdrew its sponsorship of the National Brass Band Championships. Happily, a sister Sunday newspaper, *The People* took over the Championships with immediate effect. However, after the following year's events this paper withdrew its support of the Area contests. This meant that Area Committees were responsible for funding as well as running their own contests – no great problem in the stronger regions but creating difficulties for some of the others.

Back on the Black Dyke front, during late 1965 Geoffrey Whitham was invited to become musical director of Hammonds Sauce Works Band. This entailed directing the band both in its concerts and its contests and becoming the band manager, charged with bringing what was really a second class band into the upper echelons. He accepted the challenge and left Black Dyke at the end of the year.

So ended another era in the annals of Black Dyke Mills Band. It was a little while before the news broke, but in *British Bandsman* of 15 January 1966 there was an announcement of Geoffrey's move and on the front page on 22 January the following appeared:

> The new Bandmaster of the John Foster and Son Limited Black Dyke Mills Band is to be Mr Roy Newsome. He succeeds Mr Geoffrey Whitham, who is now Bandmaster of Hammonds Sauce Works Band.

This is where I came in!

CHAPTER 7

The Roy Newsome years – an eye-witness account!

AFTER a couple of trial rehearsals with the band I was asked to take the octet in a Huddersfield Town Hall lunchtime concert as my final audition. The players seemed happy with this and after a meeting with Peter Lambert my appointment as bandmaster of Black Dyke Mills Band was confirmed. By coincidence, my first official engagement was also with the octet, in a BBC television *Look North* news programme from Bradford.

Roy Newsome (photograph: Studio Tristan)

It soon became evident that there were vacancies in the horn and cornet sections. Gordon Sutcliffe, having served for 23 years – most of them on solo horn – decided that the time had come to retire. His number two, Wally Shaw also left, on doctor's orders, after 24 years with the band. Brian Wood, who had played 2nd horn, was moved up to solo horn, Allan Holdsworth, a Queensbury lad, filled the 1st horn position and Kevin Wadsworth, a 14-year-old from Lindley, came in on 2nd horn.[69] David Horsfield, a former principal cornet player with Brighouse & Rastrick, was recruited to strengthen the cornets.

---

[69] As all bandsmen know, the three horn positions in a brass band are designated Solo, 1st and 2nd and not, as might be expected, 1st, 2nd and 3rd.

Major Jaeger was still the band's professional conductor and in March he completed his personal hat-trick at the Area contest, known then, incidentally, as the Yorkshire Championships, following the changes in the structure of the Nationals. In September he was promoted to the rank of Lieutenant-Colonel and at the start of his next rehearsal at Queensbury the band surprised him by playing *Colonel Bogey* instead of *Le Carnaval Romain* – the test piece he had come to rehearse for the Nationals. His response was quick and typical – 'You B . . . ers!'

This year the band came fifth at Belle Vue and was again placed second in the Nationals – a bitter disappointment to Jiggs, who had led the band into the runner-up position two years out of three, narrowly missing the win he desperately wanted for the band.

During my first year as bandmaster we made three BBC recordings, the first of which was a full-length programme of the music of George Hespe. During the preparations for this I visited Mr Hespe at his home in Sheffield. There was also a 'Friday Night is Music Night' broadcast from the Camden Theatre in London, on the eve of the National Championships. These were always exciting events, with the BBC Concert Orchestra, star singers, and the front man, Jimmy Kingsbury. We also recorded the music for the preliminary rounds of a new BBC knockout competition, 'Challenging Brass', to be heard on the radio early in 1967.

There were about 30 concerts this year, some in park bandstands but most in concert halls or town halls, during the early and later parts of the year. There were also six octet concerts. One special event was another visit to Cumnock – celebrating the town's centenary. The band played an important part in a week of festivities, as guests of the Scottish branch of John Foster & Son Ltd.

In the Whit Friday contests we notched up six wins and two 2nd prizes. As was customary, we played George Allen's excellent contest march, *Knight Templar*. At Stalybridge the band won 1st prize for the 10th consecutive year, playing to a crowd estimated at 3,000 – and that was at just one of eight contests attended.

There was a rare appearance by Black Dyke this year at a contest other than Belle Vue, the Nationals or Whit Friday. This was at the Teesside International Industrial Eisteddfod, a one-off contest held in a huge marquee just outside Middlesbrough. The band achieved a joint 1st and a 2nd prize, its two quartets won 1st and 2nd prizes in the ensemble class and several solo prizes were won by individual members of the band.

Colonel Jaeger resigned in January 1967 and we were without a professional conductor for a time.[70] Nevertheless, the band again won the Yorkshire Championships and also 'Challenging Brass', becoming the first 'BBC Band of the Year'. Due to the re-organising of the National Brass Band Championships, touched on in Chapter 6, there was a separate Area contest this year to determine which bands would represent Yorkshire in the Finals. The band took 3rd prize here. This was a tough time for the band, with three contests in just over two weeks, each with a different test piece, with no professional conductor and with something of a 'rookie' at this level in the position of bandmaster. A rule in vogue at this time meant that the 1st and 2nd prize-winners automatically qualified for the Finals and that if, in the opinion of the adjudicator, the band which came third had given a performance 'of outstanding merit', a recommendation could be made that the band giving it should be invited to the Finals. Frank Wright, the adjudicator on this occasion, made such a recommendation and, to the relief of the band, it was accepted.

The band's second LP was released in March. In the Pye 'Golden Guinea' series, it was called 'The Virtuoso Band'. The three corner men – still Jim Shepherd, John Clough and Frank Berry, were all featured on the recording, which also included such old favourites as *Les Preludes* and *Hungarian Rhapsody No. 2* and the Willcocks march, composed for the band, *The Champions.* Two more LPs were made in November for release early in 1968.

On Whit Friday this year, we tried out an alternative march, John Carr's *Bramwyn.* We played that at two contests and the old faithful *Knight Templar* at six. The eight contests netted five 1st prizes and three 2nds. Not a record, but not bad.

It was announced in July that Geoffrey Brand was to be the band's new professional conductor. The immediate consequence of this was a win at the Nationals – the first since 1961. Geoffrey boosted the band's confidence and this was an important element in this success,

---

[70] In December 1968 Lieut-Colonel C. H. Jaeger, O.B.E., Mus. Bac., A.R.C.M., L.R.A.M. became Director of Music of the Royal Military School of Music, Kneller Hall. Sadly, he died on 27 September 1970, aged 57, only hours after conducting at the Welsh and Grenadier Guards Bands at Windsor Castle in music from the previous year's iInvestiture of H.R.H. The Prince of Wales.

for which it produced a memorable performance of Eric Ball's *Journey into Freedom.*

Geoffrey had a Salvation Army background but after studies at the Royal Academy of Music he became a professional orchestral trumpet player. He toured America as a member of Sir Thomas Beecham's Royal Philharmonic Orchestra and then joined the orchestra of the Royal Opera House, Covent Garden. In 1955 he joined the BBC as a music producer, 10 years later taking on responsibility for all band broadcasts from London, alongside his other work for the BBC Light Programme, which included such programmes as 'Friday Night is Music Night'. During the sixties he conducted a number of brass bands, not only in England but also in Denmark and Sweden. Early in 1967 he became Music Advisor of the National Youth Brass Band of Great Britain and took over the Editorship of *British Bandsman.* He was, therefore, a leading personality in the brass band world when he came to Black Dyke.

Geoffrey Brand, a great motivator

Broadcasts in 1967 went up to 15, partly due to being BBC Band of the Year and possibly partly due to Geoffrey's influence. The broadcasts included two for America in the BBC's Overseas Transcription Service. These were produced by Denis Wright, who was present at the sessions, but who died about two months later. There was also the final round of 'Challenging Brass', live from Huddersfield Town Hall, again won by Black Dyke. The other finalists were Carlton Main and Markham Main. One of the more exciting broadcasts was of a concert from the Royal Festival Hall in a BBC Light Music Festival. Black Dyke was joined by BMC (Morris Motors) and the conductors were Harry Mortimer and the distinguished composer Malcolm (later Sir Malcolm) Arnold. There

Geoffrey Brand conducting the title-winning performance in the Royal Albert Hall, 1972
(photograph: London Press Photos Ltd)

were two 'Friday Night is Music Night' broadcasts this year, one from St George's Hall, Bradford, and the other again from the Camden Theatre. There was also a 'Winning Band' broadcast from the Royal Albert Hall. I was beginning to appreciate the thrill of being bandmaster of such a famous band.

Items for the preliminary rounds of the 1968 'Challenging Brass' series were now recorded, along with a group of Commonwealth National Anthems. There was a rare appearance on BBC television, in a programme in the series 'Omnibus'. This traced the fortunes of three bands in their preparations for the National Championships. The other two bands were GUS (Footwear) and Woodfalls Silver, preparing for its first appearance at the Albert Hall.

The band did not compete at Belle Vue this year, but its win at the Nationals settled the on-going argument about low pitch, especially as the band which came second, CWS (Manchester), had converted and was also playing in low pitch.

During July, Ernest Keeton completed the remarkable feat of serving 50 years with Black Dyke Mills Band, his first appearance being at Belle Vue in 1917. He had been employed throughout by Foster's and had played euphonium and E flat bass. His half-century was commemorated with the presentation of a cheque from the band by a former member.

On a personal note, I was featured this year in the radio programme 'Down Your Way'. My home town of Elland was the subject of the programme and on finding out that the bandmaster of the famous Black Dyke Mills Band lived there, he had to go onto the list of visits. So, Franklin Engelman and his team visited my home in Church Street and my choice of music for the programme was Jim Shepherd playing *The Nightingale* – from our recently released LP.

* * * * *

The period covered by this Chapter is from 1966 to 1977. During those years I had two spells with Black Dyke – 1966-1970 and 1972-1977. Geoffrey Brand was professional conductor from 1967 until early 1975. It will be useful to see an outline of the band's contest record during those years, but first of all it is necessary to explain some of the changes which took place.

The National Championships were now in the hands of a private individual, Edwin Vaughan Morris. He had managed them during the periods when they were owned by the *Daily Herald* and *The People*, but now he was the owner. He was a great organiser and also a great innovator, and wanted to find a system whereby he could attract some of the growing number of overseas bands. He tried, with little success, to do this in the years 1968-1971. In the first two of these years he used the title 'World and National Championships' for the Royal Albert Hall event, ruling that any overseas band which could claim to be the National Champion of its own country and which had an instrumentation comparable to that used in Britain could apply. Only one did.

In 1972 he went a stage further, separating the titles National and World, setting up what he called the World Championships by inviting six British bands to enter, along with any overseas contenders. Again, only one overseas band appeared. The criterion for British bands was that they should have been National Champions more than once in the preceding 25 years. The bands which were eligible were Black Dyke, Brighouse & Rastrick, CWS (Manchester), Fairey's, Foden's and GUS (Footwear) – formerly Munn & Felton's. They would not take part in Area contests but would compete in a special contest following the National Championships. Apart from the extraction of the six bands, the Nationals continued as before, with Area contests and the winner of the Finals being declared National Champions. I do not propose to discuss the futility of this scheme nor the dubious use of the titles 'World' and 'National'. It was an experiment doomed to failure and to everyone's relief, normality was resumed in 1972.

The other situation I must explain is that by 1973 Geoffrey Brand, Black Dyke's professional conductor, was involved with the ownership of the National Championships and felt that, for the time being, he ought not to conduct there. Because of this it fell to me to

Roy Newsome acknowledging the hat-trick performance in the King's Hall, Belle Vue, 1974
(Photograph: Harry Newborough)

take the band to the contests of 1973 and 1974. However, the band was now looking to re-establish the system in which the primary function of the professional conductor was to conduct the band in major contests, and I was perfectly happy with this. Though my title had changed from bandmaster to resident conductor, the job was still the same as that which I had taken on in 1966 – to take the band on most of its concert engagements, to share broadcasts and recordings with the professional conductor, and to prepare the band for his visits in the run-up to contests. Much as Geoffrey would have liked to revert to the accepted system, he felt unable to do so, so he did the honourable thing and resigned, opening the door for the appointment of a successor.

Having explained all that, here now is a table showing Black Dyke's record at the two major contests during the Geoffrey Brand years:

	Belle Vue	**Nationals**
1967	did not compete	1st
1968	1st	2nd (World & National Championships)
1969	Unplaced	2nd (World & National Championships)
1970	4th	1st (World Championships)
1971	2nd	Unplaced (World Championships)
1972	1st	1st (Double)
1973	1st (R.N.)	3rd (R.N.)
1974	1st (R.N.)	3rd (R.N.)

Perhaps it is worth pointing out that the 'double' in 1972 was the first for Black Dyke since 1902 and that the Belle Vue hat-trick (1972-74) was Black Dyke's first there since 1879-81. The Belle Vue contest had now become known as the British Open Championships.

* * * * *

Having looked at contests we can now review some of Black Dyke's other activities, from 1968. This was a particularly interesting year; there were nine broadcasts, a recording of two programmes for German radio and four television appearances. Three of these were for the series 'Choirs on Sunday', produced by the famous Jess Yates of Yorkshire Television (YTV). One was in Leeds Town Hall with a 1,000-voice choir, one in Huddersfield Town Hall with Huddersfield Choral Society and the other in Sheffield City Hall with an augmented Sheffield Philharmonic Choir.

Black Dyke in a YTV production of Choirs on Sunday in the City Hall, Sheffield
(with acknowledgement)

Concerts continued as usual, but what a difference a title makes! As BBC Band of the Year and National Champions, the 'House Full' signs were up wherever we played, usually with hundreds turned away. The Nationals trophy, a magnificent piece of silverware, was invariably on display, creating much interest and each concert generated a sense of occasion. The most noteworthy concert this year was in York Minster, with an audience of 2,000. Special dispensation had to be obtained to allow applause.

Things were looking up on the commercial recording front also, with several more made this year. The inevitable titles were trotted out – 'The Champions', 'Champion Brass' and 'Champions Again'. But there were also two rather special discs. The first was of Gilbert Vinter's magnificent work for brass and voices, *The Trumpets.* This requires an augmented band – with six basses, four trombones, three euphoniums and extra cornets, as well as an off-stage trumpet, the organ and four percussionists. For the recording, we hired some special tubular bells, so large that they had to be suspended from the balcony, with a stepladder provided for the percussionist. The choir for the recording was an enlarged Huddersfield Glee & Madrigal Society and the conductor was Geoffrey Brand. Gilbert Vinter himself came to the recording and the whole experience was one never to be forgotten.

The other recording was totally different, but equally memorable. The world of pop music was passing through what was called 'Beatlemania', a certain group from Liverpool breaking all records. Paul McCartney (now Sir Paul) had been asked to write the signature tune for a television programme that was being planned. This featured the famous Stanley Holloway as a loveable but forgetful old man called Bob Bridge. The programme was to be called *Thingumybob,* and that was the title of the tune.

Paul had not previously written a purely instrumental piece and at first he tried it out with three brass players, but concluded that it

A historic photograph of Paul McCartney with Black Dyke (with acknowledgement)

needed a full brass band. On enquring which was the best brass band he was told that Black Dyke were National Champions. That was good enough for him and wheels were set in motion to engage the band and for Geoffrey Brand to score the music. It was also decided to have a march-like version of *Yellow Submarine* to fill Side B of what was to be an EP on the famous 'Apple' label.

A recording session for Paxton had already been arranged for Saturday 29 June in the Victoria Hall, Saltaire. The band was also booked to play at Adwick-le-Street on the Sunday afternoon and evening. Nevertheless, it was agreed that we would meet in Saltaire on Sunday morning to record the two McCartney pieces.

Little did the band realise what it had taken on. Bob Auger of Pye Records was the recording engineer but Paul McCartney, who had driven up from London in his Rolls Royce, had also brought along one of his sound experts, Peter Asher. The hall was already set up from the previous day's sessions and everyone imagined that after a couple of short runs through the two pieces, we'd record them and be on our way. Not so. Messrs McCartney and Asher were not happy with the sound emanating from the speakers in the control room.

Bob Auger reset the microphones and tried a different seating formation for the band. The two were now even less satisfied than before. They wanted a sound like you would get if the band was playing in a park bandstand – or so they said after about two and a half hours grafting through *Thingumybob*. Then the other Bob – Auger that is, at his wit's end, asked what he thought was a totally ridiculous question: 'Why don't we go out into the street?' Two faces lit up and Asher said, 'Can we?'

Windows were opened, microphone cables slung out and chairs carried into the street. A quick run-through, one 'take' and that was it. They'd got what they'd come for. Now for *Yellow Submarine*. By now we had quite a large audience, particularly of adoring young females. They needed little persuading to add the 'off-stage' effects to the piece for the flip side. Ten minutes later it was all over and the band was preparing for departure to Adwick-le-Street.

Despite the hassle, everyone had had a very pleasant morning. McCartney took to the band and the band took to McCartney. There would be more collaborations in the future.

The Whit Friday march contests were something of a let-down this year. It was usually possible to attend all eight contests that were being run at that time, though you needed a bit of luck. On arrival at each venue the band's 'runner' ascertained how many bands were waiting to play. If the band was really lucky it played immediately, but if there were a number of bands already there a decision had be taken whether to wait, or to move on and return later in the evening. We had had a series of delays this year and by quite late in the evening had played at only six contests. In an attempt to catch up we went up the hill to Dobcross and found just one band waiting. This wasn't too bad, so we formed up and as soon as this band had finished its contest performance we were away, playing the march *Slaidburn*. We must have been going at light infantry pace down that hill.

Arriving at the contest venue I was confronted by a rather small man who wanted to know where the 'Board Man' was. (It was normal for someone to walk in front of the band as it marched to the field carrying a board with the name of the band chalked on it.) We had committed the unforgivable sin of not waiting for this particular gentleman. It transpired that the small man talking to me was, in fact, the Board Man. Not only that, he was on the contest committee and said that as we had broken the rules we were disqualified.

I could stand no more, told the band to get back on the bus and off we drove to what would be our final venue. Horror of horrors, they had closed down. Our Whit Friday was ended. We had also again changed marches and had done pretty badly, winning only three contests. The ultimate bad news was that Brighouse & Rastrick had won four!

The band was exceptionally busy during 1969, with no fewer than 52 full band concerts. There were also 10 octet appearances, six broadcasts, two television shows and two more LPs recorded. The band also undertook its first overseas visit since the North American tour of 1906.

This was a trip to Roubaix in Northern France, for a ceremony 'twinning' the towns of Bradford and Roubaix. The outward journey was not without its problems, however. We first flew from Yeadon to London and then, through having to change terminals at Heathrow, eight members of the band missed the connecting flight. They had to fly to Paris and then travel to Roubaix by train – arriving there at five o'clock in the morning.

That apart, the weekend was a huge success. The band took part in a march through the town, played some national anthems in the Twinning Ceremony and gave a Saturday evening Gala Concert, during which it received several standing ovations. We were to learn over the next few years that though these were virtually unknown in Britain, they were quite common on the Continent.

On the Saturday afternoon there was a football match. Bradford City football team had also been flown out, to participate in a small tournament. They had played themselves into the final, but there they were beaten 1 – 0 by the locals. The band, however, suffered no such defeat. We played a few pieces before the match started, a few more during half time, and then the idea was to play some more while the crowd dispersed. But they wouldn't go. We played what we had planned to play and then gave encore after encore, but eventually it was the band that dispersed, leaving the crowd still applauding and shouting '*le Dyke noir*!'

Closer to home, we took part in a Royal Command Performance before HRH Prince Philip, Duke of Edinburgh, in the Alhambra Theatre, Bradford. The ever-popular Dave Allen compèred the show, which featured such luminaries as Ron Moody, Matt Munro and Freddie (Parrot-face) Davies – all at the very top of their careers. The band was last on, the show was running late, and we were cut down to two items. Jim Shepherd brought the house down with a characteristically brilliant *Napoli*, and we ended the proceedings with Offenbach's famous *Can-Can*. We were presented to the Duke backstage and when he came to Jim, remembering his stunning playing asked: 'Are you all right in there?' – pointing into his own mouth.

Geoffrey Brand conducted several of this year's concerts, one of which was in York University. An unusual piece on this programme was Edward Gregson's *Concertante for Piano and Band*, with the Huddersfield concert pianist, Keith Swallow. It was the first time this work had been performed outside Salvation Army circles. Band and piano combined in a second piece, the *Scherzo* from 'Concerto Symphonique' by Litolff. This was a Denis Wright arrangement and was played regularly in future concerts where a solo pianist was involved.

In earlier chapters I referred to the band's frequent appearances in the Festival Concerts following the National Championships. They had not been involved in these for a number of years but they returned in 1969. There were three other bands and the guest conductor was Vilem Tausky, a well-known orchestral conductor. Unusually for these occasions, each band was asked to play one item by itself. Vaughan Morris had previously asked me to write a piece for piano and band and it was my *Concerto for Brass Band and Piano* which was Black Dyke's solo item. Again, Keith Swallow was the soloist.

Perhaps I should mention that for a number of years there had been two concerts – one at five o' clock and the other at eight, with identical programmes. The bands did not like this. Following the tensions of the contest, it made for a very long, exhausting day. However, the demand for tickets was so great that the organisers persisted. That being so, my *Concerto* received both its first and second performances in the Royal Albert Hall that evening.

Another interesting concert this year was organised by Harry Mortimer in Wolverhampton. It was the first in an annual series called 'Champion Brass'. In it, he brought together the British Open and National Champions – in this case Black Dyke and Brighouse & Rastrick. Each band played a half-hour programme under its own conductor and then they combined under Harry Mortimer.

Television appearances this year were also quite interesting. In the first one, a number of bands had been filmed – including Black Dyke – in an actual concert, and individual members were then interviewed by that master of chat, Michael Parkinson. The other programme was in a new series called 'Stars on Sunday'. This had taken over from 'Choirs on Sunday'. The stars participating in this particular programme were Moira Anderson, Sir Ralph Richardson and Harry Secombe. The band joined forces with Huddersfield Choral Society and the Town Hall's grand organ in an impressive performance of *Dies Irae* from Verdi's *Requiem.*

Another choral society was involved in one of the band's two commercial recordings made this year. Bradford Festival Choral Society were old friends of Black Dyke, the two groups having regularly appeared together in concerts. Now they combined in a seasonal recording, 'Christmas Festival for Band and Choir'.

1970 proved to be another eventful year. The number of concerts was down slightly, but there was a weekend in Belfast and five days in the Netherlands. Two more LPs were made, there were 10 broadcasts, a television appearance, and the band again became BBC Band of the Year.

The Finals of this were held this year in the Royal Festival Hall, London and they led to a famous BBC 'boob'. Black Dyke played first in the competition and, in the interests of anonymity for the adjudicators – listening over a radio link, listeners knew us merely as 'Band A'. Our opponents were Carlton Main, identified as 'Band B'.

Time was running out as the results were being given over the air and amidst all the excitement the winners were announced simply as Band A, without the name being given.

We stayed in London overnight and on Sunday morning travelled to King's Lynn to give an afternoon concert. On our arrival there we were greeted with the question, 'Well, did you win?' Our fans in King's Lynn knew only that 'Band A' had won. Some suspected, through our programme, that that was us, and were very relieved to learn that they were right.

This was the start of what might be called the Three Capitals Tour. Having played in London for the Finals, we were in Belfast the following weekend and Cardiff the weekend after that.

The Belfast visit was quite an occasion. The 'troubles' were at their height and few visitors were arriving in Northern Ireland. We were, therefore, given a very special welcome. We shared a concert on the Friday night in Wellington Hall with Belfast's four leading choirs, and on Saturday gave a full-length band concert in the well-appointed Belfast City Hall. A party for the band and the choirs followed the Friday concert. Two members of the band fell in love with two young ladies from one of the choirs and eventually these colleens married and settled here in Yorkshire. Such is the power of music!

On the following weekend we gave a concert in a building in the Sophia Gardens in Cardiff. It was, in fact, a converted aircraft hanger, but it held 2,000 people and was packed to suffocation for the concert, part of a festival run by the Excelsior Rope Works Band, with a contest during the day, followed by a Festival Concert. This was the second time we had been there. After a night's sleep in Cardiff we were bussed to Evesham where, on our way home, we gave a Sunday afternoon concert.

Two weeks later we were off to the Netherlands for five days in connection with the 25th anniversary of the country's liberation from Nazi occupation. We gave four concerts and took part in a most moving ceremony on 5 May, the day after actual Liberation Day. In all the places in which we played the memory of hostages being taken away and shot was still fresh. Liberation Day itself was treated with great reverence – there were strictly no concerts anywhere. Despite the sombreness of the occasion, the band was greeted with great enthusiasm, and it was reckoned that we averaged five standing ovations per concert!

The British Open Championships made history this year. The test piece was *Spectrum*, by Gilbert Vinter and for the first time in a major contest, percussion was used. We had something of an off-day and ended in eighth place – to no one's surprise. Not so in the London event – the first of the so-called World Championships. Here, with an exhilarating performance of *Benvenuto Cellini*, Black Dyke took 1st prize and the title. As a result of this win the band was invited to appear on the popular children's television programme *Blue Peter*. In order to do this the band was flown to London – at the BBC's expense.

There were no changes on the principal chairs during these years but in 1968 Tommy Waterman, soprano player at Black Dyke for 17 years, had to give up playing for health reasons[71] and was replaced by David Hirst. David started his banding career with Holme Silver at the age of nine. At 15 he moved into the top league, joining Yorkshire Imperial Metals. He was a music student in Huddersfield. Brian Wood remained on solo horn almost till the end of 1967, when he was replaced by Kevin Wadsworth, moving up from 2nd horn, as Brian had done two years earlier. Kevin went off to college in 1970 and David Essex, who came from Coalville in Leicestershire and who had been playing 1st horn for a few years, moved onto the solo horn position. On Kevin's return in 1973 David reverted to 1st horn.

However, for some weeks I had been going through a personal crisis. My 'day job' was as head of music in a local grammar school – a full time job in itself. On top of this, running the band both administratively and in most of its musical activities, was becoming difficult. In addition, there were tensions and undercurrents in the band which, under all the circumstances, I was unable to deal with, and my health was being affected.

There seemed to be only one course open to me and that was to resign from the band, which I did. My last duty as bandmaster was to go onto the stage at the Royal Albert Hall to collect the trophy on the band's behalf. It was with a very heavy heart that I drove home the following day with my wife, Muriel. My connection with Black Dyke had ended.

* * * * *

---

[71] Tommy Waterman died in 1971.

For the remainder of 1970 the band was preoccupied with auditioning for the vacancy created by my departure. Early in January it was announced that my successor was to be Denis Carr, well known in brass band circles and son of John R. Carr, a highly respected conductor, composer and adjudicator. Something of a child prodigy, Denis had played a duet with Willie Lang in the Royal Albert Hall in 1948 – at the tender age of 10. He later switched to euphonium, playing with a number of bands, and for a time played solo euphonium for Brighouse & Rastrick. He was a tutor with the National Youth Brass Band of Great Britain and conductor of the Yorkshire Schools Brass Band, and had also been assistant conductor of Yorkshire Imperial Band. He was a highly educated musician and since 1965 had been a Senior Lecturer at Leeds College of Education.

On the face of it this was a very sound appointment but it proved to be rather short-lived. In the issue of 20 March, *British Bandsman* announced his resignation due to pressure of work at College and a spell of ill-health. A new job-title was found on Denis's appointment; instead of being bandmaster, he would be known as the 'resident conductor' a title more in keeping with the times. The next resident conductor was Wilfred Heaton, who took the job on in June. Wilfred was a first rate musician with orchestral experience as a french horn player. He was a fine conductor and a highly respected composer with a strong Salvation Army background. He and I had collaborated in a few concerts early in 1967 when he came to Black Dyke as a guest conductor.

Amongst this year's concerts was one run by the band in its series of 'Music for Pleasure'. It was given in Huddersfield Town Hall during February and commemorated the centenary of the birth of Arthur O. Pearce. It featured Rowland Jones as soloist. Rowland had, of course, played solo euphonium under Arthur Pearce, and was now a principal tenor at Sadler's Wells. Another interesting concert took place in the City Hall, Newcastle. The compère was the famous footballer and local lad made good, Jack Charlton – then of Leeds United and England. Jack had become a great fan of Black Dyke's and was involved in several concerts over the next few years. Denis Carr and Jim Shepherd were also both on home ground, having been brought up in the North East.

Reflecting the growing interest in British style brass bands in Switzerland, Black Dyke this year undertook the first of several tours there. It lasted eight days and was mainly in the French-speaking region. As anyone who has toured Switzerland with a band will know, the food, hospitality and scenery left nothing to be desired.

Wilfred Heaton, an outstanding musician

There were only three broadcasts in 1971, but again the band made two commercial recordings – 'World Champion Brass' and 'Highlights from Handel's Messiah', the latter with Bradford Festival Choral Society.

Towards the end of 1971 there were rumours on the brass band grapevine that there was going to be yet another change in the Black Dyke residency. Wilfred Heaton had made it clear from the beginning that he was not prepared to do the secretarial work. The company now decreed that unless he did he could not continue as resident conductor. This, in my view, was a short-sighted policy which would, in fact, haunt the band until it was changed. Wilfred would not even consider taking it on, I suspect it was part of the reason why Denis Carr had such a short reign, and it had certainly been a contributory factor to my departure in 1970.

Nevertheless, despite all the problems, I was prepared to give the job another shot, and after discussions with Messrs Lambert and Brand I returned to Black Dyke – as resident conductor – from the beginning of January 1972. The 'pluses' for me were that I fully understood the size of the task and that having had five years doing it I now had that experience behind me. Nevertheless, the problems were to catch up with me again, as will be seen later.

Earlier in the Chapter I reviewed the band's contesting successes in the Geoffrey Brand era and explained why, through his involvement with the National Championships, he had to relinquish his position at Black Dyke. He was succeeded in mid-1975 by Major

Peter Parkes, Director of Music, the Band of the Grenadier Guards. Formerly a clarinettist, he had also been Director of Music for several other army bands, including those of the Royal Tank Regiment and the Royal Enginers. Like Geoffrey, Peter had immediate success.

Having just completed a hat-trick at Belle Vue we were not allowed to compete this year but under Peter's direction, Black Dyke went on to win the Nationals. Peter and I were together at Black Dyke for only two more years, during which the band completed a hat-trick at the Nationals (1975-76-77) and a double-double (1976-77) by winning both major championships two years running. I shall be concentrating on Peter's work at Black Dyke in the next Chapter, when I will show the phenomenal run of successes which he and the band enjoyed.

Meanwhile, here is a brief summary of some of the events that took place during my second term of office at Black Dyke.

Overseas visits continued almost on a yearly basis. The most ambitious for a long time came in 1972 when, on 30 June, Black Dyke, CWS, Fairey's and GUS, together with their respective resident conductors, and guest conductors Harry Mortimer, Eric Ball and Geoffrey Brand, flew direct from Manchester to Niagara Falls. This was for a Canadian Brass Band Festival featuring the four bands. There were two massed band concerts in Niagara Falls, in which the three guest conductors shared the conducting, and each band gave one concert in the town and others in nearby venues. Black Dyke played in Toronto and also in Buffalo, just across the Rainbow Bridge from Niagara, in the USA – retracing some of the steps of their forebears in the band of 1906.

In 1973 the band returned to Switzerland for another memorable tour and in 1976 visited both Switzerland and the Netherlands. This latter trip was to appear as guests of Vara Radio (one of four principal broadcasting companies) in a gala concert which followed one of the Dutch championships. On the following morning the band recorded a programme in the Vara Studios. This festival took place for many years and it was customary to feature a leading English band in the evening concert. In 1977 Black Dyke made its third trip to Switzerland.

There was, during these years, a general improvement in the number of appearances by brass bands on television. In 1972 there was a seven-week series called 'Where There's Brass'. Black Dyke

Andre Previn in a blustery Queensbury, with myself and three band members – Stephen Brooke, Alan Widdop and Mark Mosley

Edward Heath enjoying a break in the recording session. Brian Couzens of Chandos is on the right, with Peter Parkes and yours truly also in the picture (*with acknowledgement*).

appeared in one of these, filmed in St George's Hall. In the following year the band played two items in the daily programme 'Nationwide'. Both of these were on BBC television. A more substantial programme, 'Sounding Brass', was filmed for Granada TV in the same year. In 1975 the band took part in a series called 'Brass Roots' on the BBC, and spent three days recording inserts for a number of editions of 'Stars on Sunday' for YTV.

There was also another programme in the series 'Omnibus', called 'Previn Meets Brass Bands'. For this, the famous maestro travelled to Queensbury to meet the bandsmen and to see the band rehearsing in the bandroom and performing 'in concert' – to wives and friends in the Victoria Hall. Mr Previn was so impressed with the band that we were invited to take part in a concert with him and the LSO, in the Royal Albert Hall. Part of this was screened live. These were indeed balmy days for bands and television.

The band also did reasonably well for broadcasts, averaging over eight per year – and reaching 14 in 1973. Several went out live from important festivals, including a two-hour Saturday afternoon broadcast of original brass band music from Cheltenham. There were also live broadcasts from two of the famous Henry Wood Promenade Concerts – in 1974 and 1975. In this latter year the band was again declared 'BBC Band of the Year', though this was no longer through a knock-out competition. A panel of music producers selected what they thought had been the best band broadcast on Radio 3 in the previous year. Black Dyke won the vote again in 1976.

Commercial recordings also remained buoyant, with 'Brass to the Fore', 'Triumphant Brass' and two albums in the series 'Sounds of Brass' released in 1972-73. There were further additions each year. LPs of note included 'Black Dyke Plays Langford' – quite obviously featuring arrangements and compositions by Gordon Langford, but also featuring as soloist the inimitable trombonist Don Lusher. Then there was 'A Christmas Fantasy', with the Huddersfield Choral Society, 'British Music for Brass Band', and in 1977 we recorded the LP 'European Brass', with guest conductor the former Prime Minister, the Rt. Hon. Edward Heath.

* * * * *

The early part of the period 1972-77 was quite a turbulent one for the band. After a short 'honeymoon' period following my return the undercurrents which had been present in 1970 began to simmer again. For many years the whole band, known as the '25-man committee', had conducted band business. Though there were certain advantages in this system it could be unwieldy and, to put it mildly, it was difficult to handle. One of the senior figures at Pye Records commented in one of the financial papers that dealing with Black Dyke was not easy. 'It was like trying to negotiate with 25 Freddie Trumans', he said.

Attempts were made in 1972 to try to persuade the band to elect a small committee which, along with myself, would deal with the day-to-day running of the band, keeping the remainder of the band informed about decisions taken. The band was having none of it, however, and in 1973 the idea was abandoned. In this year, no fewer than nine players left, including Jim Shepherd who, after 10 distinguished years at Black Dyke was looking to further his solo career. He also wanted to build up the James Shepherd Versatile Brass, a 10-piece brass group that he had recently formed.

Phillip McCann was appointed as Jim's successor. Born in Bo'ness, Scotland in 1948, Phillip showed early promise as a cornet player. He was both junior and senior champion of East Scotland in three successive years and in 1968 became the Champion Soloist of Great Britain. He had been a member of the National Youth Brass Band of Great Britain and from the age of 14 was its leader (principal cornet player). Before coming to Black Dyke he had played principal cornet with both Yorkshire Imperial and Fairey's, and had also been the leader of Harry Morrtimer's Men o' Brass.

The departure of so many players within a short space of time made life difficult for the band. It was committed to concerts, broadcasts and recordings and these had to be fulfilled. New players had to be brought in and this disrupted the flow of rehearsals, as pieces that were familiar to the others needed to be rehearsed for the benefit of the newcomers. However, the band survived and maintained a good success rate in contests.

Triumphant returns to Queensbury continued. On completing the double in 1972 the streets of Queensbury were lined with cheering crowds as the band marched past with the huge trophy. It was reminiscent of a football team bringing the cup home. The 1973 Belle Vue win came in Phillip McCann's first contest, and as it was the first time he had helped win a major title he was rather pleased! On completing the Belle Vue hat-trick in 1974 we not only had the

The inimitable Phillip McCann

usual warm welcome in Queensbury, but there was a Civic Reception for us at Bradford Town Hall a few days later.

There was another change of player towards the end of 1974 when David Hirst, the band's soprano player since 1968 left. David Carder, who came to us from Excelsior Rope Works Band in Cardiff, replaced him.

A level of about 50 engagements per year was maintained, plus a handful of octet concerts. The quality of the engagements was, however, on the increase. Early in 1973 there were concerts in York Minster and the Royal Albert Hall – both on the same weekend, as part of the 'Fanfare for Europe', heralding the move towards membership of the European Economic Community (EEC). In these concert we combined with GUS (Footwear) Band and York Celebrations Choir and performed Vinter's *The Trumpets* as one half of each concert. In another York Minster concert Black Dyke and the Celebrations Choir gave the first performance of a new work for brass and voices, Gordon Jacob's setting of *Psalm 103*.

The band also played in a number of prestigious music festivals, including King's Lynn, Cheltenham and Norwich. There were concerts in Edinburgh's Usher Hall and one in Swansea's Brangwyn Hall. The strangest of all was a weekend in far away Cornwall, the band's first appearance there for 20 years. For this the hosts, St Dennis Silver Band, chartered a plane to fly us from Yeadon to St Mawgan aerodrome for two concerts on Saturday and one on Sunday. It was an odd experience for me when the pilot, having parked up and locked the cabin door of his Viscount asked, 'What time would you like me back tomorrow, sir?' It was also an odd experience for the band members to be ending a concert in Cornwall at half past four in the afternoon and then to be sat at home watching 'telly' before seven o' clock in the evening.

Even the Royal Albert Hall was becoming familiar to us. Following the Fanfare for Europe concert there early in 1972 we were there each year for the Championships, of course. In 1974 we took part in the evening concert, playing with the massed band and accompanying former principal cornet player, Maurice Murphy, in the first performance of a *Concerto for Cornet* by Ernest Tomlinson. There were also the Proms of 1974 and 1975, mentioned above. For these we joined forces with Grimethorpe Colliery Band, under the baton of Elgar Howarth, their principal conductor.

Moving from the sublime to the not-so-sublime, the Whit Friday march contests attracted only spasmodic attention from Black Dyke during this period. Following the debacle of the disqualification, described above, the band did not attend for the next few years. This was not due to the disqualification, I hasten to add, but rather because in some of these years the band was engaged in overseas tours. We did compete in the years 1973-76, the most successful being 1974, when there were five wins.

1977 was a special year, however, not least because it was the Queen's Silver Jubilee year. It was also the year of the London hat-trick and of the second successive double. The two events involving André Previn and the recording with Edward Heath have already been mentioned. In March there was a glittering ceremony in St George's Hall, when the band was granted the Freedom of the City of Bradford, a singular honour, not normally bestowed on a brass band. Many civic dignitaries were present and in the packed audience were some 70 former members of Black Dyke, many of whom had travelled great distances. Two weeks earlier St George's Hall had been the scene of another happy occasion. At the conclusion of the Area contest the members of Black Dyke were each presented with a medal and a certificate commemorating the 'double' of the previous Autumn.

During the 1977 Swiss tour, the band had the unique honour of playing in the Swiss Parliament Building. The business of the House was suspended to enable the Members to listen to the band. This event was to mark the Silver Jubilee of Queen Elizabeth. It was the first time a foreign band had been allowed to play in the magnificent building – in Berne.

At the conclusion of the Swiss tour the band flew into London to take part, along with four other bands, in a Jubilee Concert in the Royal Albert Hall. The guest conductors were Harry Mortimer and

Walter Susskind, a well-known orchestral conductor. Two weeks later the band returned to the Albert Hall for its concert with Previn and the LSO. In this concert Previn actually conducted Black Dyke in a performance of *The Corsair*, and the band combined with the LSO to play the Coronation March, *Crown Imperial*.

Finally, in this very special year, the band provided music for the visit of Her Majesty The Queen and HRH Prince Philip to Leeds Town Hall as part of the Silver Jubilee celebrations. Quoting from the official programme:

> On Her Majesty's entrance into the Victoria Hall, Trumpeters of the Royal Scots Dragoon Guards will sound a fanfare from the balcony followed by the National Anthem to be sung by the Huddersfield Choral Society, accompanied by the Black Dyke Mills Band, who will [then] play background music. ...

Following a Royal walkabout in the Hall, the Choral Society sang *Rose of England*, accompanied by the band, as the Royal couple departed.

* * * * *

So, this had been a quite remarkable year, but again there were dark clouds on the horizon for me. Early in 1977 I requested that a separate secretary/band manager be appointed. I was again wilting under the various pressures. My request was turned down and as tensions built up during the year, again I had no alternative but to call it a day. With a great deal of help from Peter Parkes I completed the year as resident conductor and then once again said farewell. My last broadcast with Black Dyke went out on 3 December and my final official engagement was a Christmas concert in Halifax, with the Halifax Choral Society.

Happily, that wasn't the end and I have been invited back as guest conductor on a number of occasions. I have a good relationship with the present band and its officials, and am always made welcome when I visit.

CHAPTER 8

Peter Parkes – the later years

AT THE END of my term of office the band had to vacate its beloved bandroom. It had rehearsed there since 1855 and the members believed that it was the particular acoustic of the room that produced the band's special sound. They argued that players, conductors and instruments were all changed periodically, and that the only thing that remained constant was the rehearsal room. I have to confess to finding it ideal from the conductor's point of view. You could hear every fault in the band's playing and at the same time you could build up this wonderful sound.

Peter Parkes, the most successful professional conductor

As the state of the building deteriorated over the years the company had regularly tried to move the band elsewhere but the members had always managed to resist. Now came the day of reckoning. The fabric of the bandroom was dilapidated and despite constant repair the building was unsafe.

Foster's very generously agreed to have the building pulled down and rebuilt to identical specifications. A firm of builders 'who knew all about acoustics' was called in and the band rehearsed in the works canteen while the work was being done.

Later in the year the band moved back to its old premises, hopefully to live happily ever after. Alas, though the shape and size of the room were the same, the materials weren't and the acoustics were totally different. There was an unacceptable ring to the band's sound, making it impossible to hear the detail in rehearsal. Miraculously, by adding curtains, carpeting and other damping materials, the sound was gradually restored to its former glory. Trial and error succeeded where science had failed.

* * * * *

After I left Black Dyke for the second time there were five different resident conductors in 11 years. It seems sensible therefore, for the sake of continuity, to base this Chapter on the remaining years of Peter Parkes's time as professional conductor rather than on the terms of office of the resident conductors.

As was seen in Chapter 7, Major Parkes came to Black Dyke in 1975. His early run of five 1st prizes from his first five contests was nothing short of brilliant. Obviously that rate of success could not go on indefinitely, but the achievements continued to be quite remarkable, as the table below shows. I have included the European Championships. Qualification for these was dependent on being a national champion or the defending European champion. These conditions were not always strictly adhered to but they give an idea of what was required. The European Championships were begun in 1978, remained in England until 1983 and then moved about the countries involved.

	European	**British Open**	**Nationals**
1975		Not there	1st
1976		1st	1st
1977		1st	1st
1978	1st	2nd	Barred
1979	1st	4th	1st
1980	2nd	Unplaced	2nd
1981	Not there	Unplaced	1st
1982	1st	Unplaced	2nd
1983	1st	1st	2nd
1984	1st	2nd	6th
1985	1st	1st	1st (The 'Grand Slam')
1986	2nd	1st	2nd
1987	1st	Unplaced	2nd
1988	2nd	2nd	Not there

Celebrating the 1975 Nations win – the Royal Albert Hall in the background
(with acknowledgement)

Thus, under the baton of Peter Parkes, Black Dyke won 18 major titles in 14 years. It is a measure of the band's consistency that it held at least one title in every year except two of those covered. The peak year was 1985, when all three titles were won – an achievement dubbed 'The Grand Slam'.

Major Parkes left the Army in 1979. He now had more time to work with brass bands and, in addition to increasing his workload at Black Dyke he had many successes with a number of other bands.

My successor as resident conductor was Michael Antrobus. He had been a chorister at Chester Cathedral from the age of nine, took up the trumpet a few years later and by the time he was 15 was in the National Youth Orchestra. He played in an RAF band for a time and then lived in southern England, playing professionally and teaching. In 1973 he returned north and took a peripatetic teaching post in St Helens. He was also now interested in conducting and had worked with several bands before his appointment at Black Dyke, on 1 March 1978. He was resident conductor for just over two years, his final appearance being at a concert in the Wembley Conference Centre on 29 March 1980. Backing up what I wrote earlier, he made a statement to the press to the effect that the secretarial aspect of his work was encroaching on time that he wished to spend making music.

During the time Michael was at Black Dyke there were two more overseas visits, both breaking new ground for the band. The first, sponsored by Boosey & Hawkes (the majority of the bandsmen played on B&H instruments) was in Southern Germany, in May 1978. The second was just a year later, when the band flew to Norway, giving concerts in Bergen, Hamar and Oslo.[72]

There were some interesting television appearances in 1979. The first was during a programme called 'Don Lusher's World of Music', in which the band were guests of the famous trombonist. Next, they appeared in a Michael Parkinson chat show. This featured Harry Mortimer and André Previn and I recall Parkinson asking the 77-year-old Harry how he'd like to die. H.M. replied that he'd be very happy to go whilst conducting *1812* or *Life Divine*. Previn quipped that it would need to be something the band could finish off without a conductor! Before the end of the year a third television programme came the band's way – 'Black Dyke's World of Music'. In this the band returned the compliment and invited Don Lusher back as one of its guests.

Broadcasts continued, though they were few and far between. However, the band was again declared BBC Band of the Year for 1979. There were now a number of new programme titles. Amongst those from this period one was called 'Sam on Sunday' (Sam being Sam Costa, who presented the programme) and another, 'Among My Souvenirs'.

There were a number of interesting record projects – two of them involving Paul McCartney. The first was a session with Paul and Wings, a pop group formed after the break-up of the Beatles. This resulted in Black Dyke appearing on one track in an actual Wings album. Early in 1980 a full LP was issued, with the title 'Black Dyke Plays Wings'.

---

[72] A few years after leaving Black Dyke, Michael Antrobus settled in Norway, becoming a leading figure in that country's fledgling brass band movement.

There were a few changes in personnel at this time. In 1979 Brian Broadbent left after 25 years' service, mainly on 2nd euphonium. He was to become bandmaster at Fairey's and was replaced by Peter Christian who moved on to 1st baritone in 1981. He had already played with a number of leading bands.

On the departure of David Hirst (for the second time), one of the 'greats' of the soprano cornet came in – Brian Evans. Brian had been with CWS (Manchester) for 10 years, Fairey's for two and had spent the last six years with Brighouse & Rastrick. Unfortunately, for business reasons, he had to leave Black Dyke within a few months. He was replaced by Derek Ruffels.

The band was still busy with concerts, travelling to places as far afield as Oxford, Felixstowe, Reading, Newcastle and Chatham. Perhaps the two most interesting ones during these years were in Worcester and Wrexham. The Worcester concert was part of the Three Choirs Festival and included performances of Denis Wright's *Cornet Concerto* and Elgar's *Severn Suite*. The Wrexham concert was with Don Lusher and the well-known radio personality, John Dunn. Black Dyke also featured in the 1978 Festival Concert in the Royal Albert Hall, not as part of the massed band, but playing 'solo' during the concert, performing *The Champions* and *Corsair*.

Another event during this period was the publishing of a booklet, *The Magic of Black Dyke*. Its author was Frank Dean, rightly described as the band's number one fan. He regularly travelled with the band, sold records, helped with loading and unloading the bus and doing all the other mundane jobs associated with concerts. The book, mainly anecdotal, was his tribute to a band that had contributed so much to the quality of life not only of Frank himself, but to thousands of Pondashers throughout the world.

In March 1980 it was announced that Michael Antrobus would be replaced by David Loukes. David had a Salvation Army background, but after studies at the Guildhall School of Music he moved into the music profession, joining the trombone section of the Hallé Orchestra and remaining there for several years. From 1976 he and I were colleagues as pioneers of the course in Band Musicianship at Salford College of Technology – the first such course in Europe, if not the world. David now also took on a series of conducting jobs with bands in the Manchester area, at one time being Associate Conductor at Besses, whose principal conductor I became after leaving the residency at Black Dyke. He also had spells with

Wingates, James Shepherd Versatile Brass and Rochdale Wilsons Band. Thus, he came to Black Dyke with a wealth of musical experience.

During his period at Queensbury the band had seven broadcasts. Recordings also came out quite regularly. By now Black Dyke had an exclusive contract with a leading record company, Chandos. Two LPs call for special mention – 'Volcano' and 'Black Dyke in Digital'. The former was a high quality recording of a high quality programme of original band music, Robert Simpson's *Volcano* being the title track. The latter disc reflected new recording techniques and was the first British brass band recording to be digitally produced.

Television programmes took a backward step, with only one Black Dyke programme in the whole period. It was in a YTV series for which I was music advisor. There was a common plan each year for three years, with six programmes, featuring three leading adult bands and three promising youth bands. Programmes for youth bands also included a leading adult soloist – names such as Jim Shepherd and Don Lusher spring to mind, whilst programmes involving leading adult bands featured one or more promising young soloists. These programmes were called 'Brass in Concert'.

The Black Dyke programme of 1981 provided an opening for Brian and Martin Winter – two highly talented brothers from Leicestershire. Both played cornet with Loughborough Youth Band – winners of the Butlin's Youth Band Championships. Later both played with Desford Colliery and other leading bands, Martin going on to become an orchestral trumpet player and a high profile soloist.

Both 1980 and 1981 saw further tours sponsored by Boosey & Hawkes. That of 1980 covered Southern Germany again, but also incorporated visits to Luxembourg and Brussels, whilst the tour of the following year took in Germany (yet again), Austria and parts of Northern Italy.

There was a slight dip in contest successes during this period. In 1981 the band was required to compete in the Area contest for the first time since 1969, qualifying with 2nd prize. However, the band went on to win the Finals. Incidentally, the National Championships were in crisis this year. The owner, Robert Alexander, was heavily in debt – notably to prize-winning bands and adjudicators at the previous year's championships. The future of the Nationals hung in the balance until Boosey & Hawkes came to the rescue, paying off the considerable debts and taking over the ownership.

In 1981 Black Dyke was one of the four bands taking part in the Royal Albert Hall Festival Concert. Harry Mortimer was the Chief Guest Conductor and I had the privilege to be the Associate Conductor. Together we visited the four bands in their rehearsal rooms, which made it considerably easier to put the concert together on the day. The highlight of the concert calendar for the whole of this period, however, was the band's third appearance in the Henry Wood Promenade Concerts. This was on Monday, 7 September 1981 and was again shared with Grimethorpe, playing under the baton of Elgar Howarth.

We were informed in *British Bandsman* of 12 December 1981 that David Loukes had resigned, 'for personal reasons'. In January it was announced that he would be returning to Rochdale Wilsons, but not until *British Bandsman* of 13 February 1982 was the world informed that Trevor Walmsley was to take over as resident conductor at Black Dyke.

This was a complete change of policy. All bandmasters/resident conductors since Arthur O. Pearce had been relatively young, but Trevor was in the autumn of his conducting days. He was highly experienced, having been involved in top class banding for over 30 years. Many of those years had been spent with Brighouse & Rastrick, but also on his conducting CV one would find the names Yorkshire Imperial Metals (with which he had won the British Open Championships twice), Wingates, CWS (Manchester) and Ever Ready. His playing days went back to the 1930s. During World War II he was a member of a bomber crew and received the award of the Distinguished Flying Cross (DFC).

At last common sense was prevailing within the company and a member of the band took over the secretarial duties, leaving Trevor free to concentrate on musical matters. The band seems to have hit a rather quieter period just now. Though engagements came and went few, if any, seem to have been particularly memorable. Tours continued – Austria and Switzerland in 1982 and Spain a year later – both again under the auspices of Boosey & Hawkes.

There were about five broadcasts during these two years but not one television appearance. The only LP to appear was the groundbreaking 'Blitz' – a digital recording of the spectacular work composed by Derek Bourgeois for the 1982 Nationals. Also on this LP were *Journey into Freedom*, *Tam o' Shanter's Ride* and *Pageantry* – all classic brass band original works. This recording was to re-appear some three years later as the first brass band Compact Disc (CD).

The band hesitated about attending the first overseas European Championships, held in Kerkrade, Holland, in 1983. Obviously, considerable expense was involved, as well as time off work for the players. Readers of *British Bandsman* of 5 February were assured that Black Dyke would compete, but a week later they were told that Black Dyke would not compete. By 5 March, however, all was well again and the trip was on – to the great relief of the organisers. The band went, and emerged as winners.

In 1982 soprano player Derek Ruffels and solo horn player Kevin Wadsworth both left the band. Kevin was replaced by Sandy Smith, a Scot who, like Kevin before him, was destined to become one of the finest horn players of his generation. Derek was replaced by David Carder, returning to Black Dyke for a second stint. Also in this year one of the band's stalwarts of many years died. This was Hermon Ambler, who kept the bandroom clean and tidy, made the draw for the band at contests, and was in charge of trophies won and LPs sold at concerts. His proudest moments were marching down Queensbury High Street in front of the band, helping carry the trophy after each of the band's major victories.

In November 1983 it was announced that Trevor Walmsley had been offered the post of Brass Band Consultant to Boosey & Hawkes' Advisory Service. He would leave Black Dyke at the end of the year having, like his two predecessors, served for two years. However, it was good to see that he was leaving 'on the friendliest of terms'.[73]

* * * * *

Not until September 1984 was there any news about the next resident conductor. The news was that it was to be Derek Broadbent and that he would take up the appointment after the British Open Championships. Widely recognised throughout the brass band world as conductor, composer and adjudicator, Derek had been associated mainly with Brighouse & Rastrick and had, in fact, led them to one victory in the Nationals and to second places in both the Nationals and the British Open Championships. He remained with Black Dyke until the end of 1986, when he returned to Brighouse as

---

[73] Trevor Walmsley died in 1998, aged 76.

Derek Broadbent

musical director. During this year the band's official name became John Foster Black Dyke Mills Band.

This was a particularly productive period for contest successes, a period which included the 'Grand Slam'. There were also two BBC Band of the Year awards.

In 1984 (prior to Derek's appointment), there was a highly successful tour of Japan, lasting from 17 May to 8 June. In the following year there was a long weekend in the Netherlands (31 May to 2 June), but the closest thing to an overseas tour in 1986 was a weekend in Douglas, Isle of Man, in November.

Again the band did quite well for broadcasts, with 11 in the period 1984-86 – though this figure includes some repeats. Despite a reported slump in the sale of records, the usual two LPs per year came out on the Chandos label. Of these, 'Black Dyke Plays Rossini' received an award from the Music Trades Association in 1984. One of the 1986 LPs was called 'The Complete Champions: 1985 – a year to remember'. Its programme included the 'Grand Slam' pieces – *Royal Parks* (European), *Salute to Youth* (British Open) and *Cloudcatcher Fells* (Nationals), and for good measure, *Contest Music* – which formed part of the programme that earned the title BBC Band of the Year.

There was an extra recording in 1985 featuring principal cornet player Phillip McCann. This was called 'The World's Most Beautiful Melodies' – 15 cornet solos. It proved to be a best seller and in 1986 Phillip made a follow-up LP – the first of several. Again there were 15 tracks, but to add variety to the sound, four were with organ accompaniment, six with the orchestra of St-Martin-in-the-Fields and five with Black Dyke.

Attending the European Championships had become a costly business since it moved to mainland Europe. Apart from the expense of getting there, it was now a two-day event, with the set test and own choice sections on different days, other events staged when the contests were not in progress, and a Gala Concert to round off the weekend. In 1985 Black Dyke gratefully received a grant of £2,000 from the West Riding County Council towards the cost of the trip to Denmark, where the European Championships were being held. Whilst there they presented an open rehearsal, directed by Peter Parkes.

Again, though the band remained busy and well travelled, there seemed to be fewer high profile concerts than there had been in the seventies and early eighties. Perhaps the concerts weren't there, or perhaps there was another reason. Television competitions had become popular – 'Granada Band of the Year' on ITV and 'Best of Brass' - a knock-out competition involving eight bands, organised by the BBC. Black Dyke refused to enter either of these, arguing that the Nationals, the British Open and the European Championships provided all the competitive events it needed. Whilst not criticising this decision, I must point to the television exposure that was not coming the way of Black Dyke. 'Best of Brass', for example, had an audience in excess of two million viewers, and the winning band played three programmes in each series. Despite its continuing excellent results in traditional contests, Black Dyke was missing out on this and was inevitably receiving less acclaim from the general public than some of its rivals.

One high profile concert did come its way, however, and that was an engagement at the conference of the International Trumpet Guild, held at the Guildhall School of Music in 1986. This was the first such Conference to take place outside of the USA. About 250 of the Guild's 3,400 members were present, plus a further 100 visitors. 'Not the largest, but probably the most knowledgeable audience we've ever played to', commented Peter Parkes. Included in the programme was a major original work, specially commissioned for the occasion by Black Dyke. This was Arthur Butterworth's *Odin – from the land of fire and ice*. In 1989 this was selected as the test piece for the National Championships.

As usual, there were changes in personnel during these years. Amongst them, Frank Berry retired from playing in 1985. He had been in the band since 1964 and up to 1983 had played 1st trombone, being succeeded by John Maines. In 1984 John also left, to be replaced by Norman Law. Both of these were highly experienced players, each with experience in several leading bands. John had played with Sun Life and Fairey's. Norman with GUS, Foden's and Brighouse & Rastrick.

At the end of 1986 Derek Broadbent left Black Dyke; his final appearance with the band was at the annual Christmas Concert in Huddersfield Town Hall. For reasons best known to the band and the company, there was no new appointment until January 1988, meaning that Peter Parkes was carrying all musical responsibilities, a situation which I believe he has since acknowledged was not a good idea. There is a common saying in leading bands that 'familiarity breeds contempt'. Until recently, the system employed by many of them was that the bandmaster or resident conductor bore the brunt of the musical responsibilities. The professional conductor came in periodically as a 'fresh face', and the players, metaphorically speaking, 'sat on the edge of their seats'. There can be little doubt that during 1987 Peter and the band saw more of each other than was good for either of them, and the mutual respect which had been the hall-mark of the previous 12 years was seriously eroded.

Despite this, the band was extraordinarily successful in the Whit Friday march contests, which it attended for the first time since 1979. The number of contests had now escalated to the point that only a

The 'Legends' – Willie Lang, Jim Shepherd, Phillip McCann and Murphy
(with acknowledgement)

relative few could be attended by any one band. There were now 18. The band attended seven and won them all.

During this year there were three broadcasts and another Phillip McCann recording, 'More of the World's Most Beautiful Melodies'. On this, a harp was introduced as the accompaniment to some of the solos, as well as band, orchestra and organ.

There was no tour this year, but one highlight amongst the band's engagements was participating in what was called 'The Concert of the Century' – an event held in the Free Trade Hall, Manchester, celebrating the centenary of *British Bandsman*. Other bands taking part were Besses and Yorkshire Imperial, and the Chief Guest Conductor was Harry Mortimer. One special feature in the programme was a new piece by Elgar Howarth called *Legends*. It brought together four legendary principal cornet players of Black Dyke. They were Willie Lang, Maurice Murphy, Jim Shepherd and Phillip McCann and they were, of course, accompanied by Black Dyke, with Peter Parkes conducting.

Even exceeding this concert in status, the band made another appearance in the Henry Wood Proms, this time playing 'solo' under Peter, in an early evening concert in the Royal Albert Hall on Saturday, 29 August.

There was also a so-called celebration of 150 years of Black Dyke Mills Band. I've never been able to work out the logic of this, which assumed the band's formation to have been in 1837!

A new award had been instituted a few years earlier, that of 'Euphonium Player of the Year'. In 1987 it was awarded to John Clough.

* * * * *

At the beginning of 1988 it was announced that David Hirst – Black Dyke's soprano player from 1968 to 1974 and again in 1978 – was to become resident conductor. He had a wealth of playing experience and had conducted several bands.

During this year Black Dyke undertook its most prestigious tour ever, with two weeks in Sydney, Australia, as guests of the New South Wales Brass Band Association, and participating in the country's bicentennial celebrations. The tour lasted from 27 March to 10 April, and though moving around New South Wales, the highlight for the band was a concert in the magnificent Sydney Opera House.

This was not a good year contest-wise. Sixth place in the Area contest signified the band's first absence from the National Finals for 25 years. There was some consolation, however, with 2nd prizes at the British Open and European Championships.

Shock waves had run through the brass band world in the previous November when it was announced that Phillip McCann had resigned. The resignation was later withdrawn, but only temporarily, as in May 1988 it was confirmed that both he and John Clough had left Black Dyke, Phillip after 15 years and John after 28 – 25 of them on solo euphonium. Ironically, both players joined arch-rivals Brighouse & Rastrick for a short time, though both continued with other bands for a number of years, with Phillip emerging later as one of the band movement's leading conductors.

Robert Childs, a distinguished euphonium soloist

Roger Webster replaced Phillip and Robert Childs took over from John. Both had commenced their playing days in junior bands – Roger in Grimethorpe Juniors and Robert in Tredegar Juniors. In 1973 Roger, at the age of 12, joined Carlton Main. He had also played with Brodsworth and Rockingham Colliery bands and had had two stints with Grimethorpe. For the six months prior to joining Black Dyke he had played principal cornet with Brighouse & Rastrick. Robert left his roots at the age of 16 to become a member of GUS, later playing with Grimethorpe, Brighouse & Rastrick and Hammonds Sauce Works before moving to Black Dyke.

Amidst all this turmoil the long-serving bass player, Derek Jackson also left, but the band nevertheless completed a weekend in the Netherlands. It is not often realised that engagements and tours are arranged well in advance and, come what may, commitments must be honoured. There were again two broadcasts this year and three CDs were released.

There were two interesting engagements in early 1989. One was in the Queen Elizabeth Hall, London. Geoffrey Brand was guest conductor and the famous trumpet player John Wallace was the soloist in the première of Thomas Wilson's *Cartoon for Cornet.* The other was when the band was involved in a revival of Denis Wright's transcription of Handel's *Messiah.* This was a kind of 80th birthday present for Harry Mortimer who, at some time in his life, had expressed the hope that before he died he'd have the opportunity to conduct *Messiah,* with Huddersfield Choral Society and Black Dyke. Well, the BBC did him proud. The two famous groups were there in Huddersfield Town Hall and so, for good measure, was one of Harry's other favourite bands, Foden's, though at the time sporting the name Britannia Building Society. Four top class singers were also there, as was Maurice Murphy, to play *The Trumpet Shall Sound,* and I was able to add a touch here and there on the splendid Town Hall organ. The whole thing was recorded by the BBC and broadcast at Christmas, with a repeat the following Easter. The programme was called 'Messiah in Brass' and Radio 4 also produced a documentary programme called 'The Making of Messiah'.

Roger Webster, the present incumbent of the 'hot seat'

There were further player changes; Derek Jackson returned but Kevin Crockford (soprano) left. He was replaced by Nigel Fielding, a former Salford student. However, the band was again approaching breaking point. Holland and Belgium were visited in early April and this was possibly the last time that Peter Parkes and David Hirst appeared together with the band. Following what was reported as a 'heated' Annual General Meeting, David resigned but it was agreed that Peter would continue as professional conductor. To my surprise, I was asked to return as temporary resident conductor. This I did, taking a few rehearsals, a couple of concerts and accompanying Peter and the band on another Swiss tour. Featured soloists at this time were Roger Webster, Sandy Smith and Robert Childs. However, in July Robert resigned due to a hectic work schedule, in particular with his brother, Nicholas, as The Childs Brothers – at the height of their popularity as a euphonium duo.

Whit Friday contests were less successful this year. Though the band collected 10 prizes there was only one win. There were a couple of broadcasts and by now many of the band's recordings were available as CDs.

In June a new course in band studies was launched in Barnsley, with Peter Parkes as course leader. This item of news was but a prelude to the bombshell that was to explode a month later, with the announcement that Peter was to become professional conductor of Fairey's. Implied in this, of course, was his departure from Black Dyke.

One of Black Dyke's most successful eras had ended.

* * * * *

The 14 years that Peter Parkes spent with Black Dyke was a momentous period, not only for Black Dyke, but for brass bands generally. Repertoire, both serious and light, had developed considerably; bands had had a reasonable amount of time on television; the CD had become established and many were now available featuring brass bands; and top bands were appearing with increasing regularity in major concert halls. Belle Vue had gone but the British Open Championships lived on, and the European Championships were well established.

Black Dyke was recognised more than ever as the leading contesting band, enjoying the most successful period in its whole history. It remains, for me, a privilege to have been a part of it.

CHAPTER 9

The David King years

ALONG WITH the news that Peter Parkes had left Black Dyke came the announcement that his successor would be the Australian-born David King who, at 32, was probably the band's youngest ever professional conductor.

David King, Black Dyke's youngest professional conductor

A former Australian solo champion, David came to England in 1982 as principal cornet player with Hawthorne City, the Australian National Champions, who were here to compete in the British Open Championships. He remained in England and enrolled on the course in Band Studies at Salford College of Technology (which was later to merge with the University of Salford). Whilst still at Salford, he joined Black Dyke, playing assistant to Phillip McCann for a number of years. Always interested in conducting, he helped form the short-lived but remarkable Swinton Concert Band, leading it from virtually nowhere up to North West Area Champions – in 1987.

David's musical talent was never in doubt but his lack of leadership experience at the highest level caused comment and a later report suggested that this was 'one of the most daring appointments in the history of the Queensbury band'. Coming in mid-1989, it was reminiscent of the appointment of Arthur O. Pearce as bandmaster in 1912.

As was seen in Chapter 5, Arthur Pearce arrived at a critical time in the band's history. There had been several changes in personnel and the band had not been doing well in contests during the previous two or three years. Changes in personnel continued into 1912 and beyond, and it would take time for the band to settle. It did not have the luxury of this time, however, as within two years Britain was involved in the Great War. Nevertheless, Pearce remained, and in spite of further changes and the problems created by the war for many years, eventually, things came good.

David King also took over during a period of changes in personnel and at a time when the band had been doing less well in contests. This is where the similarity between 1912 and 1989 ends. After a mere two and a half years David was dismissed by the company. His later successes with Yorkshire Building Society Band suggest that this may have been premature and that, given more time, the history of Black Dyke could have followed a different course. I suspect, however, that there were other factors and that the phenomenon known as 'player power' was reaching unacceptable levels as far as the company was concerned. This is pure speculation on my part, however, so I will return to the world of fact and give a brief outline of events at Black Dyke during David's term of office.

A young Morgan Griffiths, protégé of Geoffrey Whitham

David was in sole musical charge in the second half of 1989 and during the early part of 1990. In early February it was announced that Kevin Bolton had been appointed resident conductor, after having appeared as guest conductor in one or two concerts. Kevin, a former principal cornet player with a number of bands, including Fairey's, had also been resident conductor at Fairey's, and had conducted other bands. He also had good academic qualifications and was a widely experienced teacher. Nevertheless, he stayed at Black Dyke for less than a year, resigning at the end of 1989. He was not replaced and was, therefore, the band's last resident conductor.

At the end of 1989 two more long-serving members left the band – David Essex, who had been in the horn section for 20 years, three of them as solo horn, and John Slinger, who had completed 45 years with Black Dyke.[74]

Early in 1990 Robert Childs was replaced by the young Morgan Griffiths, a protégé of Geoffey Whitham's, who moved to Black Dyke from Hammonds Sauce Works, where he had been playing 2nd euphonium. A year later David Pogson retired after 23 years with the band. He joined as a cornet player, from Slaithwaite, played number two to both Jim Shepherd and Phillip McCann, but for 15 years had been the band's highly popular flugel horn player. His departure was followed by that of Derek Jackson, who had been with the band for 25 years – though with a couple of breaks. Derek was probably the last of the players to leave who had been in the band whilst I was resident conductor.

Norman Law resigned at the end of 1991 in order to pursue a conducting career. He had been the band's solo trombone player for six years and was replaced by Chris Jeans. Chris had gained early top class playing experience with Sun Life Stanshawe, had also played with Rigid Containers Group (the former GUS), and had been Desford's solo trombonist for the last 10 years, sharing in the band's greatest triumphs. Rehearsals involved a 208 mile round trip from his home to Queensbury.

There were also other resignations during the period, making continuity difficult and having an unsettling effect on the band as a whole. It is remarkable therefore that Black Dyke achieved as much as it did in contests at this time, with a 4th prize at the British Open, a 2nd prize at the Nationals (both in 1989) and two famous wins at

---

[74] John began his playing career at the age of 13, with Queensbury Modern School Band, progressing through Black Dyke Juniors to Black Dyke Mills Band in 1946, at the age of 16. He played most instruments in the band at one time or another, and in fact was a member of the trombone quartet that won the British Quartet Championships in 1965. However, he is chiefly remembered as the band's 1st baritone player for a period of 28 years. During his time at Black Dyke, the band won fourteen National, one World, seven European and ten British Open titles.

the European Championships (in Falkirk in 1990 and in Rotterdam in 1991). There was also a win in the Yorkshire Area contest of 1990 and in the Whit Friday march contests of 1991 Black Dyke won eight prizes, including five firsts.

Though there seem to have been no television appearances during David's period, the band was doing quite well for broadcasts, with a total of at least nine during his two and a half year stay. These included one on the BBC World Service, one from the Queen Elizabeth Hall, with Geoffrey Brand as guest conductor and one from the newly-instituted BBC Festival of Brass, in which a number of leading bands made live recordings[75] of substantial programmes, in Manchester's Studio 7. Similar concerts were being produced in Bristol's Colston Hall, organised by Bram Gay, with support from Yamaha. These also were recorded by the BBC and included Black Dyke in their list of bands.

Other high profile engagements in this era included a 'Brass & Voices' concert in Worcester Cathedral, a concert in the Lyons Concert Hall of York University and a concert in The Salvation Army's Regent Hall in London. Featured soloists were Roger Webster, Morgan Griffiths and Sandy Smith.

The contract with Chandos Records had not been renewed and Black Dyke had not made a commercial recording for two years. During early 1991, however, the band made a CD, released on the Polyphonic label, which included music by Peter Graham and John Golland. Later in the year the band broke new ground with a highly acclaimed CD made for Albany Records, internationally known as a classical recording company but not normally associated with brass bands. All works on this were by the distinguished British composer George Lloyd.

Following my own brief association with Black Dyke in 1989, as temporary resident conductor, I was occasionally asked to take a concert and was very honoured to be invited to accompany the band as guest conductor on its second Japanese tour. This took place in 1990 and amongst the places visited were Tokyo, Osaka and Hiroshima. Concerts were given in marvellous halls to large audiences, often with many school children present. The courtesy

---

[75] 'Live recording' was a term introduced at this time. It referred to the recording of a concert as it was being played, that is in a 'live' situation, with an audience, and normally without retakes.

Black Dyke in Japan, with David King, Kevin Bolton and Roy Newsome
(with acknowledgement)

extended to the band had to be seen to be believed. Boosey & Hawkes helped with sponsorship and two new works were commissioned for first performances in Japan. These were by Peter Graham and John Golland.

The company provided the band with new blazers as part of its 'walking out' dress for the Japanese tour. In a break with tradition the blazer badge displayed the company crest in place of the traditional stag's head.

David King, obviously keeping in touch with his cornet playing, had been the British Open Cornet Champion in the years 1988-1991. In 1991 he crowned this by also becoming the outright British Open Solo Champion and earning for himself a trip to New Zealand, there winning the title 'International Brass Musician of the Year'.

However, *British Bandsman* of 18 January 1992 carried the banner headlines: 'King ousted for Watson'. This news seems to have been totally unexpected in all quarters, not least by David himself, who said the decision had come as a total shock. No specific reason for the dismissal was ever made public, but the general perception was that the band was not winning enough major titles. How could anyone expect it to be otherwise, with the massive changes in personnel? Many of these changes were inevitable anyway, following a long period of exceptional stability. The *British Bandsman* report concluded:

> Contesting is only one aspect of brass band music-making and David King's brief reign at Queensbury has included successful concerts, tours and fine recordings. If continuing success in competition is an essential part of the Dyke philosophy, quite apart from all other possibilities that James Watson will bring to the band, he will no doubt be expected to keep the trophy cabinet well stocked.

The whole brass band movement was now agog awaiting further developments. It did not have long to wait.

CHAPTER 10

James Watson – Principal Conductor

JAMES WATSON, Black Dyke's new supremo from early in 1992, had the distinction of being the British Junior Solo Champion for three successive years and the double distinction of being both Junior Champion and Champion Soloist of Great Britain in 1966, at the age of 14. He was a member of Desford Colliery Band until 1971, playing principal cornet when only 11. Significantly, he also played trumpet in the Leicestershire Schools Orchestra, one of the country's most successful youth orchestras.

James Watson, principal conductor 1992-2000

He studied trumpet at the Royal Academy of Music and whilst there became principal cornet player of the City of London Band, a group formed by Geoffrey Brand, primarily for the benefit of students in the London area with brass band backgrounds[76].

On leaving the Academy, James was appointed principal trumpet of the Royal Philharmonic Orchestra. He also held similar positions with the London Sinfonietta and the Nash Ensemble. After five years

[76] Black Dyke's Kevin Wadsworth was also a member of this band.

with the RPO he left, to concentrate on solo and ensemble work, notably as 1st trumpet in the renowned Philip Jones Brass Ensemble. In 1983 he returned to the orchestral scene as principal trumpet player in the orchestra of the Royal Opera House, Covent Garden.[77]

He was also taking an interest in brass band conducting and his first important appointment was with Brighouse & Rastrick. He led them to 2nd prize in the 1983 British Open Championships and 4th prize there a year later. He returned to his old band, Desford Colliery, as conductor in 1987, taking them to four National titles, with a hat-trick in the years 1987-88-89 and a further win in 1991 after the year's 'bar'.

James Watson therefore came to Black Dyke with a fine musical pedigree. He chose the title Principal Conductor[78] and held the position from 1992 to 2000, leading the band to wins at the National Championships in 1994 and 1995 and gaining 3rd prize in 1996, along with wins at the British Open Championships in 1992 and 1995, and 2nd prizes in 1993, 1994 and 1999. There was also a win in the European Championships of 1995, completing the band's second 'Grand Slam', and 2nd prizes in 1992 and 1996.

He also saw the band through the trauma of losing the support of John Foster & Son Ltd which, along with the rest of the textile industry, fell upon hard times in and around 1994. Important changes were now secured in the management structure of the band whilst, as part of his programme-planning strategy, James introduced segments of music in the big band idiom, regularly featuring himself as a trumpet soloist.

* * * * *

John Foster Black Dyke Mills Band had survived a number of turbulent periods in its history but had probably never faced the kind of revolution which occurred in 1992. I mentioned player power in the last chapter and, from the outside looking in, it seems to me that with the appointment of James Watson the hitherto

---

[77] I well remember on a visit to Covent Garden, James spotted Muriel and myself in the audience during the moments when the orchestra was warming up. Out of his trumpet came the first four bars of the march *Queensbury*, no doubt its first (and last?) performance at Covent Garden.

[78] Later he preferred the title Artistic Director.

unstoppable force of the members was about to meet the immovable object in the shape of James Watson.

The prelude to this revolution was the band being out of the prizes at the Area contest. However, no one could have foreseen the sequel to this, and I do not suggest that there was any connection between the results and what happened next. In the following week James Watson dismissed two players and on the same evening five more walked out in protest. One other left, having planned to do so anyway. To add to the problems, Roger Webster was out of action due to illness and the unthinkable happened – an engagement was cancelled.

However, within a week eight new players had been enlisted, including Robert Childs and Kevin Crockford, both former members. Early in April two more members left but they also were replaced immediately, and on the 18th the band departed for a 10-day visit to Sierra Leone in West Africa, funded by the British Council. Plans for the visit had been in the making since January, when an appeal for old instruments was made. The result of this was that about 100 of these, along with a large amount of band music, were shipped out to Sierra Leone as part of the project. Eight concerts were given, but owing to the political situation the band was forced to make a hasty getaway. Tuba player Phil Goodwin commented: 'We've played to some pretty rough audiences over the years but when machine guns and mortars started going off we realised it was time to get out'.

There was a substantial article in *British Bandsman* of 25 April in which James Watson referred to another political situation – that within Black Dyke since his arrival there. Coolly, he commented:

> The first two and a half months have been very rocky, but I'm pleased to say that the patient has had major surgery, is resting comfortably and looks forward to a full and healthy life.

Within days of its return from Sierra Leone the band was defending its European title in Cardiff. It took 2nd prize and also performed in the evening Gala Concert in St David's Hall. This was a remarkable achievement for a band that had faced such an upheaval, but to go to the 1992 British Open Championships a few months later and win was nothing short of miraculous.

Concerts were now proceeding normally and the featured soloists at this time were Kevin Crockford, Roger Webster, Chris Jeans and

Robert Childs. Though not participating in the National Finals, the band was engaged to play 'solo' in the first half of the evening concert. On the previous evening Black Dyke joined forces with Enfield Citadel Band of The Salvation Army for a concert in Regent Hall.

Black Dyke was again featured in the BBC Festival of Brass in 1992 and took part in a series of broadcasts called 'A Century of Brass and Wind'. There was also a 'Listen to the Band' broadcast.

Two new CDs appeared this year, 'Broadway Brass', an EMI recording in the Music for Pleasure series and 'Slavonic Brass', on the Polyphonic label. In addition to these, Chandos brought out seven CDs, mastered from Black Dyke recordings made between 1975 and 1988.

On Thursday, 23 January 1992, the whole band world mourned the death of its famous and much-loved figurehead, Harry Mortimer, CBE. In April there was a concert in his honour in York in which Black Dyke were joined by Fairey's and Britannia Building Society, and on 6 September, the day following the British Open Championships, there was a Service of Thanksgiving for the great man's life in Manchester Cathedral. Music was provided by a composite band made up of players who had played for him in his lifetime, and these included several present and former members of Black Dyke. The conductor was Elgar Howarth.

Finally, during this year, the Stag's Head was restored as the band's symbol.

* * * * *

The years 1993 to 1995 were years of rebuilding as far as the band's contesting record was concerned, but the problems were not yet over. An inside view was given by Roger Webster, writing early in 1993:

> In March 1992, 20 playing members of the band were replaced with carefully chosen individuals who have now been moulded into a single unit – The John Foster Black Dyke Mills Band. As well as trying to play to, and beyond the standard expected of 'Dyke', the band personnel try to encompass the values and traditions of the past, whilst creating new values, standards and traditions for the future. For the first time in my five years as part of this band, I can now truthfully say that the atmosphere and camaraderie amongst the

> players is equal at last to the high standard of musical attainment. About time too!!

Nevertheless, changes continued, not least on the administrative side. John Clay, a former flugel horn player and an employee of John Foster & Son, had served as band manager during much of the David King era. There were now several changes both in the title and in the people who took over this important role. Three of these were, in fact, ladies, one of whom was from the British Council and another the company secretary of John Foster & Son plc.

There now followed a very worrying time as the company hit hard times. In May 1994 it was announced that though Foster's would continue to provide rehearsal facilities, the band's main sponsor was to be Bradford & Bingley Building Society, whose Chairman was Donald Hanson. Mr Hanson was not only a fine businessman but also an accomplished musician. The 'Bradford & Bingley' were to fund the band to the tune of £70,000 per year for three years. In the following April the third of the lady administrators arrived; she was a member of the marketing department at the Building Society. However, by the end of the year the band's administration was in the hands of another former band member and local businessman, Geoffrey Whiteley.

Back now to the band and its re-building programme. Despite Roger's article, quoted above, he left the band in May 1993. Earlier he had worked in the sales department at Black Dyke but had recently become unemployed. His intentions now were to build a solo career. Lee Rigg, a member of the cornet section, moved temporarily onto principal cornet until the arrival a few months later of Roger's successor, Ian Porthouse.

Ian, born in 1967, began his playing career on cornet with Flimby Saxhorn Band when he was eight. At 16 he joined Leyland, conducted by Richard Evans – a former Black Dyke member, and within six months was playing principal cornet. He was also in the National Youth Brass Band of Great Britain for several years, being its leader for three of them. More recently he had played principal cornet with Desford, helping that band to two of its wins in the Nationals. He had toured extensively and had performed in many countries world-wide. However, he was driving some 235 miles per rehearsal and following a car accident one evening on his way home, he decided to leave Black Dyke. That was in November 1994, a mere

18 months or so after his appointment. His replacement in the 'hot seat' was 22 year old Matt Baker from the Redbridge Band, near London. He was to remain in the position for the remainder of the century.

Amongst other notable changes, Ian Brownbill came in on flugel horn, Billy Rushworth on solo horn and Robert Blackburn on 1st baritone – all in 1992. Towards the end of 1995 Chris Jeans relinquished his position as solo trombone player in order to pursue his interests as a soloist and conductor.

The rebuilding programme in contests had got off to an inauspicious start with 4th prize in the 1993 Area contest, meaning that once again Black Dyke was out of the National Finals and of course this meant that it had no chance of qualifying for the 1994 European Championships. However, there was a 2nd prize at the 1993 British Open. The following year began rather better, with a 2nd prize in the Area, continuing with a further 2nd at the Open and then a win in the Nationals – the band's first since 1985. This enabled Black Dyke to compete in the European Championships of 1995, which it duly won, going on to win both the Open and the Nationals later in the year, completing its second 'Grand Slam' a feat previously achieved in 1985.

Despite the importance attached to contests, Black Dyke has always been heavily involved in other activities – concerts, tours, broadcasts and commercial recordings. These other activities were now, however, beginning to take on increased significance.

The 1995 'Grand Slam' band with principal trophies. Matt Baker is to the left of the Bradford and Bingley logo, Kevin Crockford and Robert Childs to the right
(photograph by Selwyn Green)

A major administrative step was taken in the early part of 1993 with the founding of the society known as 'Friends of Black Dyke Mills Band'. By August there were already 1,000 members, the first being Russ Abbott, the well-known radio personality and comedian. This organisation is still going strong. For a small annual fee 'friends' periodically receive a newsletter, *The Black Dyke Bugle* and are able to purchase memorabilia. They can also claim discounts on Black Dyke CDs and for certain concerts. This has become a massive publicity campaign for the band, has been a means of keeping its enthusiasts advised on the band's progress and informed about its history, and has also been a useful source of income, adding to the band's financial stability and independence.

Concerts continued apace. In an attempt to widen the audience range, James Watson designed his programmes so that they would appeal to people of all ages and with a variety of musical interests.

The big event for the band in 1993 was a visit to New York to give a concert in the world-renowned Carnegie Hall. Philip Smith, a former English Salvation Army cornettist, now principal trumpet of the New York Philharmonic Orchestra was the guest soloist, and a spectacular programme was prepared for the Americans. Whilst in New York members of the band gave masterclasses at the famous Julliard School of Music.

The trip was not without its difficulties, however. These started with the problem of getting the visas through in time. Various well-known people were enlisted for help and support, including former Prime Minister, Edward Heath who, it will be recalled, had conducted the band in 1977. Another skirmish arose over the band's name, in America a 'dike' being a lesbian. The band insisted on the band's correct name being used in publicity, however.[79] Despite these and other problems the New York trip was declared an unqualified success.

There had also been a weekend in Switzerland earlier in the year but the only other overseas visit during this period seems to have been for the European Championships of 1995, held in Luxembourg.

---

[79] We experienced a similar situation during the 1972 Canadian Brass Band Festival. On our arrival in Buffalo, U.S.A., it was noted that on a poster displayed outside the concert hall, we were called 'John Foster's Brass Band'. On asking about this the implication of 'Black Dyke' was explained.

Philip Wilby

Peter Graham

Musical Associates from the mid-1990s

The sponsorship received from the Building Society was important to the musical progress of the band. James Watson commented, at the time:

> We can do bigger concerts in bigger venues, increase our commissioning policy and generally get brass bands noticed and taken seriously.

There was certainly a move on the commissioning front, with the appointment of the band's first composer-in-residence. He was Nigel Clarke, a colleague of James Watson's on the staff of the Royal Academy of Music, where he was a composition tutor. Clarke was given a two-year contract, with a brief to compose three works for the band. These were *Atlantic Toccata, Concerto for Euphonium – The City Beneath the Sea* and *Concerto for Band – Pendle Witches. Atlantic Toccata* was first performed in the BBC Festival of Brass, 1994 and also at the Harrogate Festival later in the year, whilst the Euphonium Concerto was premièred at York University, with Robert Childs as soloist. *Pendle Witches* came a little later. It was around this time that Philip Wilby became a musical associate.

Music by the celebrated English composer, Sir William Walton, began to feature in Black Dyke progammes, in particular a transcription by Edward Watson (no relation to James) of music for the 1930s film *Henry V*, with narrator. There were several performances of this, one in Symphony Hall, Birmingham in the presence of Lady Walton, at an event called 'Brass Explosion' and another in the BBC Festival of Brass. A CD was released in 1995, featuring the music of Sir William and of course *Henry V* was one of the items recorded. This CD, called 'A Muse of Fire', was really a programme of patriotic music and was released to coincide with a VE Day anniversary. Made for ASV Records, it was produced by Paul Hindmarsh – a BBC Radio 3 music producer. It was later declared to be the outright winner in the Orchestral Concert category of the Music Industries Awards 1996, a rare honour and unique in the annals of brass band music.

This was a very good period for brass band CDs. Nine new ones were produced by Black Dyke between November 1993 and December 1995, including an album of solos played by James Watson and two CDs featuring the music of particular composers – the Walton CD and 'Gregson Brass Music, Volume 2'. Three companies were used during this period besides ASV Records – Polyphonic,

Egon (a new company with strong Salvation Army links), and Doyen, another newly formed company, based in Oldham and the brain-child of Robert and Nicholas Childs, Nicholas becoming the managing director. Black Dyke also appeared on compilation albums of major events such as the National and European Championships. There was now a much larger proportion of serious music being recorded by brass bands.

Broadcasts and concerts were also taking on new dimensions. In addition to ordinary concerts, and broadcasts such as 'Listen to the Band', the BBC Festival of Brass had become an annual event. 'Brass Explosion', mentioned above, was also an annual event for a few years, and featured a number of leading bands, including Black Dyke.

There was also an event that was quite special to me as Music Director of the National Youth Brass Band of Great Britain. This was part of a conference, organised in Manchester by Howard Snell, the culmination of which was a concert in the Free Trade Hall, with the NYBB, Black Dyke and Britannia Building Society bands. Each played individually and then combined in the finale, *1812*, conducted by yours truly. It was a very special experience to see Britain's finest youth integrated with these two famous bands, many of their members having been in the National Youth Brass Band during their own formative years.

Many Black Dyke concerts continued to make money for various charities, but I must concentrate on musical matters. Several concerts are worthy of a special mention. The first was a concert promoted by Black Dyke in the City Hall, Sheffield, where their guests were Enfield Citadel. Collaboration between Salvation Army and contesting bands was now on the increase, and SA repertoire was contributing significantly to brass band programmes, having been made available to contesting bands from the early nineties.

A new development in broadcasting came when Classic FM recorded Black Dyke concerts in Exeter and Hull, though these seem not to have led very far as far as brass bands are concerned. This is surprising, as one would have thought that good class brass band concerts could provide ideal material for this popular radio channel.

On the occasion of the National Finals of 1994, James Watson set out to demonstrate both the versatility and the stamina of Black Dyke. On the eve of the contest itself he took the band to the Royal

College of Music to perform a taxing programme of music for brass band by composers who had studied there. On the Sunday following the contest itself he took the band to the Barbican for a concert in collaboration with LSO Brass. Major works were involved here also and the finale was a performance of Elgar's *Severn Suite*, with band and LSO Brass alternating in the earlier movements and combining for the finale. Prior to this concert, the band had performed new modern works in a Sunday afternoon event organised by the Society for the Promotion of New Music (SPNM). The centrepiece for this energy-sapping weekend was, of course, the contest itself, held on the Saturday and won by Black Dyke.

Concert programmes continued to evolve. A medley called *Tribute to Ted Heath*, arranged by Bill Geldard and featuring James Watson on trumpet became very popular. Another format, used in 1995, was to play a fairly serious first half containing original band music and serious transcriptions, and in the second half a section headed 'Slavonic Brass' followed by a 'Soloist's Showcase'. The Harrogate Festival this year saw the band premièring a *Concerto for Percussion and Band* by Derek Bourgeois, with the renowned and profoundly deaf percussion virtuoso, Evelyn Glennie.

The traditional Festival Concert following the National Championships was dispensed with in 1995. In its place came a mini-concert, played immediately after the contest and before the announcement of the results. As defending champions Black Dyke gave the concert this year. It included the first performance of a new piece by Peter Graham commemorating the 50th anniversary of the post-war Championships. Called *National Heritage*, it was a kind of musical collage made up of extracts from some of the musical highlights from that half-century.

Other interesting events during 1995 included a concert in Sheffield in which Black Dyke shared the platform with local-born opera star, Lesley Garrett.

It was also at this time that Black Dyke first became involved with the Canford Summer School. For many years there have been summer schools for musicians of all types – several catering specifically for brass band players. Canford hosts a well-established summer school for classical musicians. In 1995, for the first time, it opened its doors to the brass band world by inviting Black Dyke to organise a class. James Watson and a group of key players did this, with tutorials and full band rehearsals, culminating in an end-of-course concert in which delegates were joined by tutors under the baton of James, in a programme of major works studied during the week.

* * * * *

The remaining years of James Watson's term of office produced little reward in terms of contest results. In fact, the band attended only six major contests between 1996 and 2000, mainly through a set of indifferent results in Area contests, which meant non-appearance at the Finals or at the European Championships. The six contests attended brought in only two 2nd prizes and a 3rd. There was also a problem with the British Open Championships in 1997. Due to the sudden death of Princess Diana a week before the contest and the fact that the funeral was held on the day scheduled for the contest, this was cancelled and re-arranged for 17 January 1998. Because of a prior booking Black Dyke was unable to attend. This was, incidentally, the first time the British Open Championships were held in Symphony Hall, Birmingham.

A feature of many engagements from now on involved key players staying overnight and, on the day following the concert, directing masterclasses for local band people. Such educational events also occasionally took place overseas. In September 1996 there was a mini summer school in Denmark involving the whole band and 150 delegates. These came from all parts of Denmark and Sweden, and some even came from the Faroe Islands. In addition to playing along with the delegates in a massed concert, Black Dyke also gave two concerts during the weekend.

In 1997, through the influence of James Watson, Black Dyke became Band in Residence at the Royal Academy of Music. This was based on a three-year contract, through which the band was to give one concert per term and also to direct masterclasses. The inaugural concert took place in October, on the eve of the National Championships.

There were major changes on the administrative side of the band during these years. Late in 1996 a consortium of seven people formed a company and bought the bandroom from John Foster & Son, now in serious financial trouble and having to sell off its assets. The reason for the purchase was to ensure that the building would be there for the sole use of the band. Within a couple of years the band itself had bought the bandroom and for the first time ever, owned its own premises. Away from Foster's now, the band became Black Dyke Mills Band. By the beginning of 1997 the mills had gone and the name became simply The Black Dyke Band. The company was registered as Black Dyke Band (1855) but for the time being, sponsorship from the Building Society was to continue.

The organisation was now registered as a charity and as such was able to do more for the charities that it supported. During 1997, its first year in charitable status, it raised some £20,500 for good causes. By 1999 the total exceeded £50,000.

In 1998 ambitious plans were formulated to create a 'Centre of Excellence', in which high standards of performance would be matched with high quality educational projects. An appeal was launched and soon donations were arriving from all over the world, mainly from the 'Friends'. Two applications to the Arts Council for assistance were both turned down. As part of the fund-raising, a commemorative plate was issued in 1999.

At around this time Donald Hanson stepped down as Chairman, though he continued as a trustee. He was replaced by Sir James Hill, an influential figure in the Bradford area. Mr Hanson then became President.

Concerts were now invariably given in prestigious halls to capacity audiences. Events such as the BBC Festival of Brass and 'Brass Explosion' continued. In 'Brass Explosion 1996' in Symphony Hall, Birmingham, Black Dyke gave a performance of the full *Planets Suite* of Gustav Holst in the transcription by Stephen Roberts, complete with harps, celeste and ladies' chorus. The band had already committed this to CD and this was the first live performance. It was Black Dyke's 'solo' contribution and for the event's finale, it combined with the other two bands involved, Brighouse & Rastrick and Fairey's.

In 1998 the BBC axed its Festival of Brass but, happily, the Royal Northern College of Music (RNCM) stepped in and created its own Festival. Ironically, the BBC broadcast the concerts from this series and, of course, Black Dyke was there. From 1999 the band became involved in another fine series, The Great Northern Brass Arts Festival, organised annually by Philip Biggs in the Bridgewater Hall, Manchester.

Overseas visits continued on a fairly regular basis. The 1996 Danish Summer School has already been mentioned, and in 1997

Black Dyke at Niagara Falls in 2000

the band crossed the Irish Sea to give concerts in Strabane. The band was a great success in Switzerland in 1999 at the 1st World Band Festival, held in Lucerne and was to return there annually. Another recurring visit, first undertaken in 2000 was to Canada and Bermuda. At a concert in Toronto many of the 'Friends' located in North America and Canada, and even as far away as California on the west coast, took the opportunity to meet the band in the flesh. For the Toronto concert the hosts were the famous Hannaford Street Silver Band, a professional group based in the city. In Bermuda the band performed in the annual Bermuda Festival.

At least eight CDs were produced during these years, including the recording of *The Planets*, with the ladies of the Hallé Choir. There was a CD of the music of Peter Graham, the band's musical associate since 1997, and three solo albums. One of these featured the band's solo euphonium player, Robert Childs, whilst another featured Douglas Yeo, bass trombone player with the Boston Symphony Orchestra. The 13 works recorded here contained five newly commissioned pieces and the title of the CD was 'Proclamation'. The Robert Childs CD, called 'Première, Classical and Modern', featured concertos by Clarke and Wilby and a number of transcriptions made by Robert himself, inspired by his studies for the degree of Master of Music (MMus) at Leeds University. Finally, there was 'Reflections in Brass', sub-titled 'Evelyn Glennie Meets the Black Dyke Band'.

One of the recordings had strong links with television. The popular gardening programme, 'Groundforce' was backed by music by Jim Parker, played by Black Dyke and James Watson. A recording of the music was issued and the band appeared on some of the programmes, which attracted a viewing audience of around 12.5 million.

This was just one sign of better times for the band on TV. It had appeared on a London Weekend Television programme in September 1997 providing the backing for the popular singer, Sir Elton John. The programme was called 'An Audience with Elton John' and attracted an audience of some 20 million. In 1999 the band appeared in the comedy series 'Dinnerladies' with the Lancastrian comedienne, Victoria Wood. The band also featured in some of the programmes in the popular Sunday evening series, 'Songs of Praise'.

New music continued to be an important part of the band's mission. In 1996 Robert Childs introduced Philip Wilby's *Concerto for Euphonium* to the world, with a first performance in the Bridgewater Hall, Manchester, and a first London performance at the Royal College of Music. The second movement of this now much-played

The band and James Watson with the Groundforce team – Tommy Walsh, Alan Titchmarsh and Charlie Dimmock (with acknowledgement)

work is a spectacular plate-smashing 'Greek Dance'. In 1997, as part of a BBC Music Live project, Black Dyke premièred a new work by Michael Ball called *Whitsun Wakes* in a broadcast from Bridgewater Hall. This was selected as test piece for the British Open Championships later in the year. Nigel Clarke continued as composer in residence and created his *Mechanical Ballet*, premièred at the Royal Academy in June 1998. Another *Euphonium Concerto* appeared towards the end of the period. This was by Kenneth Downie and was sub-titled *Eulogy for Euphonium*. It was first performed at the RNCM in February 2000.

Amongst the more unusual works performed, one was called *The Tyke's Progress, or Billy Ackroyd's Musical Adventure*. Based on an imaginary story of a Black Dyke fan it was performed, with narrator Christopher Timothy, in the British Open Gala Concert of 1998. Another work was even more unusual. This was an opera based on J. M. Barrie's *Peter Pan*. Called *A Little Bird Told Me*, it was performed in Leeds in December 1999.

The 'London' weekend of 1996 proved to be another marathon for the bandsmen. In addition to the National Championships on the Saturday, the band gave a concert in the Royal Academy of Music on the Friday evening. This included three substantial solo items – Matt Baker performing the Denis Wright *Cornet Concerto*, Simon Cowen performing Gordon Langford's *Rhapsody for Trombone* and Robert Childs giving another performance of the Wilby *Concerto for Euphonium*. On the Sunday there was a concert in the Queen Elizabeth Hall, with music by Arnold and Holst, the Nigel Clarke *Euphonium Concerto* and the band's popular Ted Heath sequence. Sir Malcolm Arnold himself was present, celebrating his 85th birthday.

Other concerts of note included the Gala Concert at the Royal Albert Hall in 1997, when the band was joined by the International Staff Band of the Salvation Army, with guest soloist James Morrison, an Australian who plays a whole raft of instruments to virtuoso standard. This was said to be the first time that this SA band and a contesting band had played together. There was another concert with Morrison at Symphony Hall, Birmingham, in December 1998. This was a Christmas Spectacular that also featured the BBC Big Band.

In February 1999 Black Dyke hit the headlines in the daily national newspapers. It had provided the backing for a song called *That'll Do*, sung by the pop star Peter Gabriel. This was so successful that it was nominated for an Oscar, and Black Dyke was invited to go to Hollywood to take part in the show. Unfortunately, the band was already booked to give a concert and a masterclass in Bournemouth. Tempting as the invitation to go to Hollywood was, the band did the honourable thing and fulfilled the Bournemouth commitment, an action that was widely applauded.

Changes in personnel continued – perhaps not surprising with the degree of commitment required. In 1999 the band appeared at the British Open Championships with no less than 15 recent changes. Several of the new members were women. This was a nine-day wonder and a complete break with tradition. Most brass bands depend on women to maintain both numbers and standards, but a number of leading bands, including Black Dyke up to this point, had remained all-male. There was something of a precedent, as a lady percussionst (the wife of John French, the band's 2nd euphonium player) had played with the band on a number of engagements, but becoming a member was different and caused quite a reaction, even to the point of one or two band members resigning. However, the women were there and they were there to stay. One of them was Lesley Howie, a Scot studying at the RNCM. She was appointed solo horn at Black Dyke in January 1999 and at the time of writing is still there, recognised as one of the band movement's finest tenor horn players. A few months later another key position was filled by Michelle Ibbotson, who played soprano cornet with Black Dyke for some four years. Several key places in the band have been held by female players and eyebrows are no longer raised.

Leslie Howie, Black Dyke's Lady of the Tenor Horn

Further drama came to Black Dyke in 2000, however, first with the resignation of solo euphonium player and assistant conductor Robert Childs, who had been offered the musical directorship of Cory's, in South Wales, a position he took and which he has since held with distinction.

Shortly after Robert's departure it was announced that the Bradford & Bingley sponsorship was to end. Though this was a serious blow, through good 'housekeeping' the band was still financially secure. The company (and indeed the band) hoped to retain the services of James Watson, ever conscious of his commitment to the band over the time he had been its principal conductor. However, they were unable to reach an agreement as to how the expenses involved could be managed – bearing in mind that James lived in Watford and was making the journey to Queensbury at least twice per week. The outcome was that he resigned with effect from 30 May.

The headlines in *British Bandsman* of 10 June read – 'James Watson Quits Black Dyke Band'.

Another era had come to an end.

CHAPTER 11

Nicholas Childs, moving towards the 150th

JAMES WATSON'S final concert with Black Dyke was at the Royal Academy of Music on 16 June 2000. Within days it was announced that Nicholas Childs was to be the next principal conductor. Like his brother, Robert, who had recently left Black Dyke to become conductor of Cory's, Nicholas began his playing days with Tredegar Juniors under the watchful eye of his father, John, himself a former euphonium player but at the time conductor of Tredegar Town Band.

Nicholas Childs, today's principal conductor

Leaving Tredegar, Nicholas played principal euphonium with a number of leading bands, notably Grimethorpe and Foden's. He also made a number of appearances on tenor tuba with the BBC Philharmonic and Hallé orchestras, received several major awards, and in 1986 was declared Euphonium Player of the Year.

Nicholas held teaching posts at the RNCM and the University of Salford, where he also gained the degree of Master of Arts (MA), majoring in conducting. He has regularly been a tutor for the National Youth Brass Bands of Great Britain, Wales and Switzerland, and was appointed music director of the National Youth Band of Denmark in 1996 and 1997. Continuing to develop his conducting skills, Nicholas was in demand both in Britain and in several European countries. He had been musical director of Foden's since 1997 and with them had won three consecutive Area contests as well as the National Championships of 1999. At the beginning of 2000 he became an associate conductor of the NYBB. In addition to all of this, Nicholas Childs is the managing director of Doyen Recordings Ltd.

* * * * *

Many tributes were paid to the work of James Watson; Nicholas Childs himself acknowledged the vision of his predecessor, particularly through the appointment of what he called the 'creative back room boys' – Philip Wilby and Peter Graham, both of whom were to remain at Black Dyke as musical associates.

David Thornton, today's euphonium soloist

Two major instrumental appointments were made soon after Nicholas arrived: David Thornton succeeded Robert Childs and Brett Baker succeeded Simon Cowen who had served for four years. Both were former principal players with the NYBB. At the age of 13 David became the first euphonium player to be accepted as a student at the famous Chetham's School of Music in Manchester, and from the age of 18 studied at the RNCM. He had played with a number of leading bands and came to Black Dyke from Fairey's, with a string of awards to his name.

Brett hailed from Gloucester, where Flowers had been his main band. In 1992 he became a student at Salford University, reading Business Economics. Whilst there he was a trombone tutor on the University's BA in Band Musicianship course. He was the British Open Trombone Champion in 1993 and 1994 and for a time had

Brett Baker, today's trombone soloist

played with Faireys's. He had also built up a worldwide reputation as a soloist, commissioning several new works and making a number of solo CDs.

There were other changes in the band at this time, but the next major one came towards the end of the year, when principal cornet player Matt Baker stepped down, making way for the return of Roger Webster after an absence of eight years. During this time Roger had developed into one of the best and most sought-after cornet players in the country.

So, with a new principal conductor and a complete change of primary soloists the band looked to the future with great optimism. The soloists, all well known on the international stage, were allowed to continue developing their solo careers, all of them taking time out from Black Dyke in order to do this.

More than 20 new CDs had been created by early 2005. Several were devoted to the music of a particular composer. Composers so honoured were Arthur Butterworth, Michael Ball, Peter Graham, Wilfred Heaton, Eric Ball and Edward Gregson. The Gregson CD included two of the composer's latest and greatest brass band works, *The Trumpets of the Angels* and *An Age of Kings*. This was voted 'CD of the Year 2004' by *British Bandsman* and *Brass Band World*. There were also three solo albums featuring, respectively, Roger Webster, David Thornton and Brett Baker. The one by David Thornton was selected by *British Bandsman* as its 'Solo CD of the Year 2004'.

Two other CDs, 'Epic Brass' and 'Jubilee Brass' also appeared in video form – filmed live in two of the Royal Albert Hall Gala Concerts (see below). There were also two DVDs – one shared with the International Staff Band of the Salvation Army in a 'Tribute to Eric Ball', and the other an enacted history of Britain in a presentation compiled in collaboration with the Leeds-based Royal Armouries, with music by Philip Wilby.

Current developments in the recording business included the Doyen catalogue being taken over by World of Brass – part of Salvationist Publishing and Supplies Ltd – and entry into the market by a Swiss company, Obrasso, which specialises in recording its own publications. Black Dyke has recorded several albums for this company and also, continuing with projects introduced in the James Watson era, volumes 2, 3 and 4 of 'Spectacular Classics' and volumes 3, 4 and 5 of 'Essential Dyke' have appeared. Another CD that received great acclaim was of Handel's *Messiah* in Denis Wright's transcription, with the band accompanying the Halifax Choral Society, and Maurice Murphy playing *The Trumpet Shall Sound*, under the baton of John Pryce-Jones.

There were two further ventures into the world of pop music during this period, one in 2000 when the band provided the backing for a single with the group 'Beautiful South', the other a year later when the band participated in the 'Back the Mango Festival', in conjunction with the National Museum of Film and Photography in Bradford.

Black Dyke continues to contribute to series such as the RNCM Brass Festival and the Great Northern Arts Festival. In the Northern Arts Festival of 2000 guest soloist Rod Franks performed with the band. Rod is a former assistant principal cornet player of Black Dyke and currently principal trumpet of the LSO, along with Maurice Murphy.

Black Dyke on stage at Symphony Hall, Birmingham, with Dalewool Auckland Band, of New Zealand *(with acknowledgement)*

In the 2001 RNCM Brass Festival Brett Baker performed Martin Ellerby's new *Concerto for Trombone* and David Thornton performed the well-established *Euphonium Concerto No. 2* by John Golland. In the 2002 Festival Roger Webster performed a new *Cornet Concerto* by the young Norwegian composer Torstein Aagaard-Nilsen, whilst the band gave the fist performance of Philip Wilby's Concerto Grosso for Brass Band, *Atlantic*. The RNCM series of 2005 saw Black Dyke performing Edward Gregson's *An Age of Kings*, conducted by Nicholas Childs. Also in this programme there was a performance of the full *Enigma Variations* of Sir Edward Elgar, in Eric Ball's celebrated transcription, plus a new work by the young English composer, Philip Harper. This is called *The Legend of Sangeet*, is based on a Hindu legend and calls for the use of the sitar – an Indian instrument described as a 'long-necked lute'. Black Dyke had earlier premièred this work at the King's Lynn Festival.

Black Dyke's connections with the RNCM were strengthened in 2001 when it became Band-in-Residence. The five-year residency features concerts and open rehearsals in the College. At around the same time Nicholas Childs became Head of Brass Band Studies.

By now, what were formerly regarded as 'prestige' events were becoming almost routine, more and more engagements being fulfilled in major concert halls. In September 2000 there was a concert called 'The World of Brass'. Held in Symphony Hall, Birmingham on the day following the British Open Championships, it featured seven bands, including Black Dyke, from four different nations. In this musical marathon, each band played its own individual programme and three of them combined for the finale. The post-British Open concert in the following year was called 'Best of British Brass' and in that of 2002, six bands celebrated the centenary of the birth of Harry Mortimer. Black Dyke was, of course, involved in both events.

Amongst other major concerts during this period, from 2001 the band has appeared annually in St David's Hall, Cardiff, in a series of fund-raising concerts on behalf of the Rotary Club of Cardiff. Following the National Championships of 2001, the band appeared in the Festival Concert, called 'Epic Brass', along with the International Staff Band and Symphonic Brass of London. The following year this concert was called 'Jubilee Brass' and featured Black Dyke, the International Staff Band and the Don Lusher Big Band. Both concerts were recorded and filmed for posterity, being released in DVD form.

In 2002 Black Dyke, in association with the British Trombone Society and the Society for the Promotion of New Music ran a competition for composers, with the most promising works being performed by the band at Leeds University.

2003 was the centenary of the birth of Eric Ball and a concert in celebration of this was given in the Royal Hall, Nottingham, with Black Dyke and the ISB. This was also the year of the Queen's Golden Jubilee. Black Dyke appeared in London on the day of the big parade, along with a number of other bands, playing celebratory music specially composed by Elgar Howarth. They also played in Leeds on the occasion of the Queen's visit there, performing a fanfare specially composed by Philip Wilby.

In 2004 Black Dyke participated in the 11th Oldham Walton Festival and also performed in a concert with the Band of the Royal Marines celebrating the 10th anniversary of Gramercy, Peter Graham's publishing company. This concert was relayed live on the internet and was thought to be the first such venture. The transmission was organised by the high-tech wizards of Salford University, where the concert was held. There was another great occasion in Symphony Hall, when Halifax Choral Society and Black Dyke, conducted by John Pryce-Jones performed *Messiah.*

There seems to have been a good relationship with the BBC during these years. There were several broadcasts for 'Listen to the Band', two of them recorded on location before live audiences. One was in the Nottingham Playhouse and the other in Huddersfield Town Hall. In 2001 there was a television programme as part of 'BBC Music Live', when 'Songs of Praise' was filmed in Leeds, with a 3,000-voice choir and a brass band of 650, led by Black Dyke. In 2004 Black Dyke was selected to accompany the finalists in a new competition devised to find the 'Radio 2 Young Brass Soloist'. These Finals took place at the RNCM.

Again the band was involved overseas. In 2001 it returned to Lucerne to perform in the World Brass Band Festival and in 2001, 2002 and 2004 again performed in the Bermuda Festival, on each occasion also spending some time in America. On the 2004 trip the band was accompanied by Peter Meechan, recently appointed Young-Composer-in-Association. Peter is a graduate of the RNCM. The one-year appointment requires two compositions for the band. The first of these, his *Euphonium Concerto,* received its first performance in Bermuda. Another highlight of this Bermuda visit was a performance by Roger Webster of the newly-adapted *Trumpet Concerto* of Elgar Howarth's.

There was a terrible piece of news in 2002 with the sudden death of a former member of Black Dyke, Fred Ellis. He was killed in a motor car accident in America whilst there on business. Fred joined the band around 1965 and was a member of the cornet section for some 20 years. He also served as secretary and treasurer. He was in the band throughout my time there and was one of the most gentle and yet highly respected members.

It was announced in 2004 that Michelle Ibbotson, the band's soprano player had left the band and that her place in the forthcoming contest would be filled by Alexandra Kerwin, currently living in New Zealand. In fact, Alex flew from there to play with Black Dyke both at the British Open and the National Championships. Following the contests, the legendary Peter Roberts became the latest addition to the ranks of Black Dyke. Peter had spent most of his playing days with Grimethorpe but for the last few years had been with Yorkshire Building Society.

There have been some prestigious awards during these last few years. In 2001 David Thornton became Euphonium Player of the Year and in 2003 Philip Goodwin became the first recipient of a new award – 'Pondasher of the Year'. Philip plays E flat bass and is currently the longest serving member of Black Dyke, having joined in 1985, previously playing with the famous CWS (Manchester) Band. In the same year Nicholas Childs completed his doctorate, studying at the University of Salford and being awarded the Doctor of Musical Arts (DMA). A year later Roger Webster also joined the ranks of the 'brass band doctors', with a PhD. His studies commenced at the University of Sheffield, but were completed in Salford.

Philip Goodwin – first Recipient of the 'Pondasher Award'

In August 2002 John Clay, a former member and also a former band manager took on the job of organising a reunion for

Trophies amassed on Whit Friday, 2003

Photograph taken at the National Championships of 2001 during Black Dyke's winning performance of 'Albion' *(Picture reproduced by courtesy Brass Band World magazine. Photographer Tony Carter © BBW)*

ex-members and current members. To date two of these have taken place and both have been very successful.

Black Dyke returned to the Whit Friday march contest scene in 2003, after an absence of 12 years. They took top honours, with six 1st prizes, a 2nd and a 3rd. There were no fewer than 25 contests, all held on the same evening. Coming right up to date, Black Dyke again participated in the 2005 Whit Friday march contests, attending nine out of this year's 23 events. With six 1st prizes, two 2nds and one 3rd, it also took the title 'Saddleworth District Open Champion'.

In the major competitions under Nicholas Childs the band is consistently what is generally described as 'there or thereabouts'. There have been two 2nd and two 3rd prizes in the British Open Championships and in the Nationals there have been two wins as well as a 3rd and a 4th prize. The first win was in 2001 and the second in 2004, meaning that Black Dyke entered its 150th year as National Champions.

* * * * *

The foregoing will, I hope, give a flavour of the music-making of Black Dyke band during the early years of the 21st century. An incredible amount of it was taking place and much of it is recorded in some detail in recent issues of *Black Dyke Bugle*, a most interesting publication and one which I thoroughly recommend to all who have found this book interesting. Of course, if you are a 'Friend of Black Dyke' you will probably have already read them all. If not, why not?

CHAPTER 12

The 150th year – Conclusion

THE STORY of this year is only partially unfolded as I write. The events of the rest will, no doubt, be related in due course. The year, however, has got off to a flying start, with a January concert in Halifax Parish Church, the RNCM Festival referred to in the previous chapter, a return to St David's Hall, Cardiff, in the series for Rotary, and again providing accompaniments for the finals of this year's 'Radio 2 Young Brass Musician'.

In competition there has been a 2nd prize at the Area contest, though as reigning Champions the band is ensured a place in this year's Finals in October. The 'big one' came at the end of April when the band travelled to Groningen in the North of the Netherlands to

Taken during the National Championships of 2004
(Picture reproduced by courtesy Brass Band World magazine. Photographer Tony Carter © BBW)

Photograph taken in the Bridgewater Hall, Manchester, during the 150th Anniversary Concert on 12 June 2005, with combined male voices choirs at the rear and Black Dyke Trustees standing on the left, with compère John Maines (Photograph © by Studio Tristan).

compete in the European Championships, along with the National Champions of eight other countries.

On the Friday evening each band performed the set test piece, a new work by the Dutch composer Johan de Meij, called *Extreme Makeover.* The piece contains several references to music by Tchaikovsky, but towards the end requires all the cornet players to blow into bottles, tuned by partially filling them with water. The players blow into the bottles in much the same way that flautists blow into their flutes. Each bottle is tuned to a different pitch, so that either melodies or chords are possible, and these provide an accompaniment to a marimba solo.

On Saturday afternoon each band returned to the platform to perform its 'own choice' test piece. Amongst the works heard were pieces by Peter Graham, Derek Bourgeois, Philip Sparke and Kenneth Downie. Black Dyke had commissioned a new piece by Peter Graham called *Journey to the Centre of the Earth,* which received its première in Groningen, to great acclaim.

There was an evening Gala Concert, the first half of which was given by Black Dyke Band, before a large, lively and multinational audience. Following a second half, which featured various Dutch groups, the results were announced. Black Dyke had won in both categories, taking a prize of 5,000 euros, a presentation banner for the band and an embroidered banner for the conductor. There was also the European Brass Band Association Trophy, to be held for a year. (For the record, Buy as You View – the former Cory Band – conducted by Robert Childs, was placed second and Stavanger Brass from Norway came third.) This was a splendid win and means that Black Dyke are now National and European Champions.

A busy season lies ahead, during which there will be a further visit to Lucerne. Amongst the many concerts two celebrate the band's 150th anniversary. The first of these was in the Bridgewater Hall, Manchester on 10 June, and the second will take place in York Minster on 1 October. Other major events planned include a celebratory concert in Ripon Cathedral in July and in August the band's first appearance at the newly-opened and much-publicised Sage Centre in Gateshead. The climax will come when once again Black Dyke Band appears in the Gala Concert at the Royal Albert Hall in October.

* * * * *

So ends my attempt to climb the Everest that is Black Dyke Band. The story of any such organisation is also a story of the people who made it what it is and what it has been. Regrettably, I've been able to refer only to relatively few of them. Perhaps one day someone will come along and paint a more detailed picture. John Clay, who I have referred to a number of times, has made an in-depth study of the band's history and has a collection containing all kinds of memorabilia – photographs, records, videos and the like. He is doing much to help perpetuate the memory of some of Black Dyke's many great moments and I commend his work to all who are interested in Black Dyke Band.

There are hundreds – perhaps thousands – who have contributed to the success of this world-famous institution. My book is humbly dedicated to all of them, whether or not they have found a place in it. Appendix D lists Black Dyke's conductors, under their various titles. Some principal players are listed in Appendices E and F, with approximate dates when they held those positions. There are many omissions and, no doubt, a few inaccuracies. For these, please accept my humble apologies.

Black Dyke Band is an institution. To be a member is to inherit a way of life and a mandate to ensure that its future is as great as its past.

APPENDIX A
1855 band books

1. Quick march
2. Cavatina
3. Waltz
4. Polka
5. Hallelujah Chorus (from *Messiah* – Handel)
6. Aria: *Anna Bolena* (Donizetti)
7. Quadrille: *Como*
8. Polka
9. Cavatina: *La Sonnambula* (Bellini)
10. *The Death of Nelson* (Braham)
11. Cavatina: *Attila* (Verdi)
12. Quadrille
13. Cavatina: *Lucrezia Borgia* (Donizetti)
14. Cavatina: *Torquato Tasso* (Donizetti)
15. Missing
16. Trio Coro
17. *Yorkshire Waltz* (Enderby Jackson)
18. *The Heavens are Telling* (from *The Creation* – Haydn)
19. Waltz
20. Overture
21. Polka
22. Waltz: *Gruss an Homburg*
23. Overture: *Tancredi* (Rossini)
24. Quadrille: *Bonnie Dundee* (arr. F Galloway)
25. Grand selection: *Norma* (Bellini)
26. Waltz: *Fair Star*
27. *Let Their Celestial Concerts* (probably by Handel)
28. Quadrille
29. Polka: *The Echoes of Mont Blanc* (Jullien)
30. Grand March
31. Galop
32. Quadrille
33. Grand selection: *Attila* (Verdi)
34. Waltz
35. Overture: *The Magic Flute* (Mozart)
36. Grand selection: *Linda* [di Chamounix] (Donizetti)
37. Grand scena: *Il Trovatore* (Verdi) (London f.p. 1855)
38. Waltz: *Mountain Daisy*
39. *The Soldier's Polka*
40. Grand selection: *La Traviata* (Verdi) (London f.p. 1856)
41. *The Wedding March* (Mendelssohn)
42. Overture: *The Caliph of Bagdad* (Boieldieu)
43. Quadrille: *Horton* (Jullien)

APPENDIX B
Engagements in Diamond Jubilee Year - 1897

Month	Date	Engagement
Jan	20	Halifax
Feb	10	Brighouse
	12-13	Huddersfield
	19-20	Halifax
	21	Wigan
	21	Manningham Park, Bradford
	28	Rochdale
March	6-7	Hull
	20	Bedford
	21	Luton
	28	Halifax
April	16	Theatre Royal, Oldham
	17	Nelson (contest - 1st prize)
	18	Halifax
	19	Kidsgrove (contest - 1st prize)
	22-24	Leicester Exhibition
May	4	Horton Park, Bradford
	5	Manningham Park, Bradford
	8	Frosterley (contest - 1st prize)
	11	Keighley
	16	Wibsey & Bowling
	18	People's Park, Halifax
	24	Cowgill Park, Shipley
	25	Leeds
	26	Akroyd Park, Halifax
	28-29	London (contest - 2nd prize)
June	1	Horton Park, Bradford
	2	Manningham Park, Bradford
	3	Halifax Park
	5-6	Blackhill (contest - tie for 1st)
	7	Queensbury
	11	Oldham
	14	Bowling
	15	Dewsbury
	16	Huddersfield
	17	People's Park, Halifax
	19	Keighley
	20	Armley
	21-26	Aintree, Liverpool (Jubilee)
	27	Hunslet
June 28-July 3		Glasgow
July	4	Halifax (Thrum Hall)
	5	Fenton (Staffs)
	6	Leeds
	7-9	Leeds Flower Show
	10	Keighley
	11	Leeds
	12	Skelmanthorpe
	13	Keighley
	14-15	Wolverhampton Fetes
	16-17	Buttershaw
	19	Leeds
July	20	Horton Park
	21	Manningham Park, Bradford
	22	Salterhebble Show
	23	Ulverstone Show
	24	Leeds
	25	Kildwick
	26	Bowling Park
	27	Tibshelf Show
	28	Halifax
	29	Hunslet (Leeds)
	31	Copley Show
August	1	Bradford
	2	Kidderminster Fete
	3	Bradford
	4	Alfreton Show
	7	Stockeld (Wetherby)
	8	Brighouse
	9-13	Bridlington Quay
	14	Ovenden Show
	15	Queensbury
	16	Peel Park, Bradford
	17	Elland Show
	18	Bramley
	19	Halifax
	20	Wakefield
	21	Buxton (contest - 1st prize)
	22	Elland Festival
	23	West Bromwich
	24	Dewsbury
	25	Manningham Park, Bradford
	28	Middleton-in-Tees (cont. 1st)
	29	Skipton
Sept	6	Manchester (Belle Vue)
	8-9	Hornby Castle (Lancaster)
	10-11	Chadderton Show
	12	Ovenden Festival
	19	Wibsey
	21	Horton Park

	26	Hyde (Cheshire)
Oct	2-3	Leicester
	10	Rochdale
	30	Yeadon's (Bazaar)
Nov	6-7	Workington
	22	Liverpool
	23	Birkenhead
	24	Blackburn
	27	Dewsbury
	28	Barnsley
Dec	11	Sheffield
	17-18	Huddersfield
	24-25	Halifax

APPENDIX C
Three brass band programmes

Black Dyke, 12th June 1901

March	*BB & CF*	J Ord Hume
Overture	*Poet and Peasant*	Suppé
Selection	*Cinq-Mars*	Gounod
Selection	*Spohr's Works*	arr. Gladney
Selection	*Messenger Boy*	Monckton
Selection	*Ruy Blas*	Lintz
Waltz	*Hydropaten*	Gung'l

Black Dyke, 16th June 1911

March	*Pomp & Circumstance*	Elgar
Selection	*Gems of Schubert*	arr. W. Rimmer
Largo from the	*New World Symphony*	Dvorak, arr. Nicholl
Overture	*Magic Flute*	Mozart, arr. Nicholl
Fugue in G Minor		Bach, arr. Nicholl
Tone Poem	*Finlandia*	Sibelius, arr. Nicholl
Selection	*L'Africaine*	Meyerbeer
Scotch Patrol	*Jamie*	Dacre*
Fantasia	*Rossini's Works*	arr. Round

Linthwaite, 9th August 1911

Grand March	*Impregnable*	J. Ord Hume
Overture	*The Viking's Daughter*	W. Rimmer
Valse	*Casino Tanze*	Gung'l
Selection	*Sullivan No 1*	
Euphonium Solo	*The Village Blacksmith*	Weiss
Intermezzo	*In the Twilight*	W. Rimmer
Selection	*Meyerbeer's Works*	
Valse	*Septembre*	
Selection	*Duchess of Dantzig*	Monckton
Hymn		*Abide With Me*

* This is the piece better known as 'Jamie's Patrol'

APPENDIX D
Black Dyke conductors

Professional Conductors		**Bandmasters**	
1855-1874	Samuel Longbottom	1855-1862	James Galloway
		1863-1870	William Rushworth
		1870	William Jasper
		1872-1874	William Jasper
		1874-1895	Phineas Bower
1877-1879	Joseph Fawcett		
1880-1888	Alexander Owen		
1888-1907	John Gladney		
		1896-1911	Harry Bower
1908-1909	William Rimmer		
1910-1911	J. Weston Nicholl		
1912-1921	J. A. Greenwood	1912-1948	Arthur O. Pearce
1922-1939	William Halliwell		
1947-1949	Harry Mortimer	1949	Joe Willie Wood
		1949-1954	Alex Mortimer
1954-1956	Harry Mortimer	1954-1956	Edmund Hoole
		1956-1963	Jack Emmott
1957-1962	Major G. H. Willcocks		
1962	Leighton Lucas		
1963	George Hespe	1963-1965	Geoffrey Whitham
1964-1967	Major C. H. Jaeger		
		1966-1970	Roy Newsome
1967-1975	Geoffrey Brand		
		Resident Conductors	
		1971	Denis Carr
		1971	Wilfred Heaton
		1972-1977	Roy Newsome
1975-1989	Major Peter Parkes		
		1978-1980	Michael Antrobus
		1980-1981	David Loukes
		1982-1983	Trevor Walmsley
		1984-1986	Derek Broadbent
		1988-1989	David Hirst
		1990	Kevin Bolton
1989-1992	David King		
Principal Conductors			
1992-2000	James Watson		
		Assistant Conductor	
		1996-2000	Robert Childs
2000-	Nicholas Childs		

APPENDIX E
Some of the principal players of Black Dyke (1)

Solo Cornet

William Rushworth 1860
Alexander Owen 1880-1888
George F. Birkinshaw 1889
John Paley 1891
George F. Birkinshaw 1892
John Paley 1893-1901
Ceres Jackson 1902-1909
Louis Allison 1909
Ceres Jackson 1910
John Paley 1911
Willie Wood 1911-1912
Louis Allison 1912
Harold Pinches 1912
Louis Allison 1913
Harold Pinches 1913-1917
Billy Rushworth 1917
Joe C. Dyson 1917-1918
Owen Bottomley 1918
Harold Pinches 1919-1926
George Crossland 1926
Owen Bottomley 1927-1936
Harold Jackson 1936-1938
Owen Bottomley 1938
Willie Lang 1938-1941
Owen Bottomley 1941-1946
Willie Lang 1946-1950
Bernard Bygrave 1950-1952
Willie Lang 1952-1954
David Pratt 1954-1957
Maurice Murphy 1957-1962
John Clay 1962
Keith Caldwell 1963
Jim Shepherd 1963-1973
Phillip McCann 1973-1988
Roger Webster 1988-1992
Lee Rigg 1992
Ian Porthouse 1992-1994
Matt Baker 1994-2000
Roger Webster 2000-

Solo Euphonium

John Taylor 1860-1866
Phineas Bower 1867-1892
John Bailey 1893-1897
Harry Waddington 1906
Joe Ambler 1907
Harry Sutcliffe 1908-1912
George Keeton 1912-1913
Ernest Shaw 1913-1925
Percy Shaw 1926
Ernest Shaw 1927
Percy Shaw 1928-1934
Rowland Jones 1935-1938
Henry Davis 1938-1939
Arthur Atkinson 1939
Charlie Emmott 1940-1943
Jack Emmott 1943-1944
Charlie Emmott 1945-1946
Denzil Stephens 1946-1950
Geoffrey Whitham 1950-1963
John Clough 1963-1988
Robert Childs 1988-1990
Morgan Griffiths 1990-1992
Robert Childs 1992-2000
David Thornton 2000-

Solo Trombone

Greenwood Firth 1855-1879
Edwin Stead 1879-
Sam Radcliffe 1886
Charles Jeffrey 1891-1898
Fred Bower 1898-1922
Elijah Boam 1922-1926
Ernest Shaw 1926
Haydn Robinson 1927-1938
Jack Pinches 1938-1941
Haydn Robinson 1941-1950
Lance Wynn 1950-1954
Colin Monkman 1954-1958
Grenville Richmond 1958-1964
Frank Berry 1964-1983
John Maines 1983-1984
Norman Law 1984-1991
Chris Jeans 1992-1995
Simon Cowen 1996-2000
Brett Baker 2000-

APPENDIX F
Some of the principal players of Black Dyke (2)

Soprano Cornet
Frank Galloway 1860-
William Jasper
Sam Hoyle 1873-1882
Joe Riley 1886-
J Hubbard 1891-
Samuel Simpson
Thomas Scatliff 1893-1910
Ives Fieldsend 1911-1912
Hubert Hepworth 1913-1915
Bram Chatburn 1916
J. H. Walker 1918
Hubert Hepworth 1918-1920
Gershom Collison 1920-1934
Bernard Burns 1934-1951
Tommy Waterman 1951-1968
David Hirst 1968-1974
David Carder 1974-1978
David Hirst 1978-1979
Brian Evans 1980
Derek Ruffels 1981-1982
David Carder 1982-1984
Kevin Crockford 1984-1989
Nigel Fielding 1989-1992
Kevin Crockford 1992-1999
Michelle Ibbotson 1999-2004
Peter Roberts 2004-

Solo Horn
John/Jonas Smith 1860-1868
Joe Naylor 1872-1893
Harry Charnock 1902-1909
Ernest Ambler 1911
George Downs 1912-1914
Herbert Abrahams 1915-1928
Joe W. Wood 1928-1939
Albert Drake 1939
Joe W. Wood 1939-1947
Gordon Sutcliffe 1947-1965
Brian Wood 1966-1967
Kevin Wadsworth 1967-1970
David Exley 1970-1973
Kevin Wadsworth 1973-1982
Sandy Smith 1982-1992
Billy Rushworth 1992-1993
Les McCormack 1994-1998
Leslie Howie 1999-

Flugel Horn

Willie Wood 1908-1910
Bill Beckwith 1911
Harry Smith
? Greaves
George MacDonald
Ivor Judson
Colin Casson
Sam Smith 1953-1965
John Clay 1965-1973
David Pogson 1973-1990
Gary Lord 1991
Mark Walters 1992
Ian Brownbill 1992
Steve Drury 1996-1997
Ian Shires 1998-1999
John Doyle 2000-

SELECTED BIBLIOGRAPHY

Books

Andrews, Frank (1997) *Brass Band Cylinder and Non-microgroove Disc Recordings 1903-1960*, Winchester: Piccolo Press

Bainbridge, Cyril (1980) *Brass Triumphant*, London: Frederick Muller Ltd

Barrett, F (1963) *A History of Queensbury*, Queensbury Centenary Celebration Committee

Brand, Violet and Geoffrey (1979) *Brass Bands in the 20th Century*, Letchworth: Egon

Cook, Kenneth (comp) (1950) *Oh, Listen to the Band*, London: Hinrichsen

Gammond, P. and Horricks, R. (ed) (1980) *Music on Record 1 - Brass Bands*, Cambridge: P. Stephens

Greenhalgh, Alec (1992) *Hail Smiling Morn: Whit Friday Brass Band Contests 1884 to 1991*, Oldham Leisure Services

Hailstone, Alf (1987) *The British Bandsman Centenary Book*, Baldock: Egon

Herbert, Trevor (ed) (1991) *Bands - The Brass Band Movement in the 19th and 20th Centuries*, Milton Keynes: The Open University

Herbert, Trevor (ed) (2000) *The British Brass Band - A Musical and Social History*, Oxford: OUP

Horwood, Wally (1980) *Adolphe Sax 1814-1894 - His Life and Legacy*, Bramley: Bramley Books

Howarth, Elgar and Patrick (1988) *What a Performance! - The Brass Band Plays*, London: Robson Books

Littlemore, Allan (1999) *Fodens Band: One Hundred Years of Musical Excellence*, Chapel-en-le-Frith: Caron Publications

Mortimer, Harry (1981) *Harry Mortimer on Brass, an Autobiography written with Alan Lynton*, Sherborne: Alphabooks

Mutum, Tim (1991) *Brass Band Recordings - A Complete Guide to Brass Band Recordings since 1957*, Baldock: Egon

Newsome, Roy (1998) *Brass Roots, A Hundred Years of Brass Bands and their Music, 1836-1936*, Aldershot: Ashgate

Newsome, Roy (1995) *Doctor Denis: The Life and Times of Doctor Denis Wright*, Baldock: Egon

Nicholls, Robert (1989) *Looking Back at Belle Vue Manchester*, Altrincham: Willow Publishing

Roberts, Peter (2003) *A Legend in His Own Lifetime - and Autobiography*, Stockport: Jagrins Music Publications

Russell, Dave (1987) *Popular Music in England, 1840-1914*, Manchester University Press

Russell, J. F. and Elliot, J. H. (1936) *The Brass Band Movement*, London: Dent

Taylor, Arthur R. (1979) *Brass Bands*, St Albans: Granada

Taylor, Arthur R. (1983) *Labour and Love, an Oral History of the Brass Band Movement*, London: Elm Tree

Dictionaries, directories, encyclopaedias, etc.

The Bandsman's Everything Within, (Cook, 1950) Hinrichsen

The New Grove Dictionary of Music and Musicians (Sadie, 1980) Macmillan

The Oxford Companion to Popular Music (1991 edition) Gammond: OUP

The Oxford Dictionary of Music, (Kennedy, 1986 edition) OUP
The Rakeway Brass Band Yearbook 1987, (ed Littlemore) Rakeway Music
The Rakeway Brass Band Yearbook 1988, (ed Littlemore) Rakeway Music.

Booklets

Read, David: *The British OpenBrass Band Championships - a record of results and test pieces since its commencement in 1853*
Dean, Frank (1980) *The Magic of Black Dyke*, Brighouse: Kirklees

Other Sources

Brass Band News
Brass Band Review
Brass Band World
Brass Review
British Bandsman
British Mouthpiece
The Conductor
Halifax Courier
Huddersfield Examiner
The (Manchester) Guardian
Sounding Brass
List of Prize Winners (with Selections of Music) of the Brass Band Contests from their commencement in 1853 - Belle Vue - 1973 edition
Origins and Promotion of Brass Band Contests - a series of articles by Enderby Jackson in *Musical Opinion and Musical Trade Review*: April, July, September and November 1896.

INDEX

Black Dyke Players and Conductors/Bandmasters

Some Successful Bands (except Black Dyke)

Contests

General index